rel.

D-DAY

BY THOSE WHO WERE THERE

Dedication

This book is dedicated to the development and long-term security of the Second World War Experience Centre in Horsforth, Leeds, UK, committed as it is to the rescue, public access and study of materials relating to individual experience in the 1939-45 War.

The author has particularly in mind the devoted work undertaken for the Centre by the late Keith Clifton, affectionately remembered by all his friends.

D-DAY

BY THOSE WHO WERE THERE

Peter Liddle

Pen & Sword

MILITARY

First published in Great Britain in 2004 by

PEN & SWORD MILITARY

an imprint of
Pen & Sword Books Limited
47 Church Street
Barnsley
South Yorkshire
S70 2AS

ISBN: 1 84415 079 8

A CIP catalogue record for this book
is available from the British Library

Typeset in 10pt Plantin by Pen & Sword Books Limited

Printed and bound in England by
CPI UK

For a complete list of Pen & Sword titles please contact:
PEN & SWORD BOOKS LIMITED
47 Church Street, Barnsley, South Yorkshire, S70 2AS, England
email: enquiries@pen-and-sword.co.uk
website: www.pen-and-sword.co.uk

Contents

Dedication 2

Foreword 6

Acknowledgements 8

Introduction 10

Chapter 1   Planning and Training 14

Chapter 2   Deception 35

Chapter 3   Assembling, Concentration and Eve of the
             Operation 42

Chapter 4   The Airborne Assault 55

Chapter 5   Crossing The Channel, Minesweeping
             and Naval Bombardment 82

Chapter 6   Utah 95

Chapter 7   Omaha 111

Chapter 8   Gold 135

Chapter 9   Juno 157

Chapter 10   Sword 183

Chapter 11   Air Support 204

Chapter 12   Support, Supply, Medical Provision 224

Chapter 13   Women and D-Day 237

Chapter 14   At the End of the Day 246

Recommended Reading 254

Index 255

Foreword

by

Major-General Henry Woods,
CB, MBE, MC, DL, DLitt, MA, FRSA,
(late 5th Royal Inniskilling Dragoon Guards)

Sixty years ago the D-Day assault across the beaches of Normandy and the base of the Cherbourg peninsula signalled the return of the British Army after its ejection from Europe at Dunkirk in 1940, the Canadian Army and the arrival on a large scale of the United States Army, as the prelude to allied victories and the liberation of Western Europe from Nazi tyranny. Throughout the bitter battles in Normandy the Allied Forces endured heavy casualties on a scale reminiscent of World War One; in both wars a subaltern's survival unscathed was measured in days and rarely more than three weeks. The same survival rates applied to senior and key non-commissioned officers, on whom close battle leadership depended.

On 6 June 1944, as a recently-commissioned officer, whilst on the firing point of a tank gunnery range in Northumberland with new recruits, I heard the dramatic news that the invasion of Fortress Europe had begun. My Regiment, despite adding to its high reputation during the 1940 campaign, spent the intervening years in hard training and the provision of drafts of trained men to the Middle East. We were not in the initial waves of 21 Army Group, but when we did cross in mid-July from Portsmouth the enormous allied efforts required to launch the invasion from bases throughout Southern England, ranging from Felixstowe to Falmouth were apparent. In many of the memories recorded in this book and elsewhere, we catch glimpses of the wonderment of those on both sides, at the awesome and massive invasion fleets butting their way through the short sharp Channel swell, and aircraft filling the skies with the shadows of their wings (including those of the ubiquitous gliders), and the growl of many aero-engines.

The complexity of the operations, and the implementation of the immense logistic plans, were essential to win control of the beaches, to minimise casualties during The Channel crossing and the critical phases of the initial assault, and to sustain the Allied Forces once ashore during the build-up phases, without the benefit of a major port for people, vehicles or stores. The highly personal and vivid memories and wartime accounts of those who took part in D-Day, a crucial turning point in World War Two, constitute a precious historical treasure, of immense significance, now and in the future, for scholars and descendants of those who fought there.

I am therefore most privileged to be associated, as a foundation Trustee, with Dr Peter Liddle and the Second World War Experience Centre, which is well on the way to being a great National Archive, gathering up, like the memories in this book, the personal stories of ordinary men and women, rather than the memoirs of the 'great and the good'. This meticulously researched and edited volume represents a small fraction of the archives which Peter Liddle, as Director of the Centre, has already gathered, and from which he has so brilliantly distilled the very apt memories and accounts of D-Day survivors. In this book he pays a wonderful tribute to the courage, devotion to duty and stoic heroism of countless men and women, mostly but not all in uniform, who in their different ways delivered victory. His role, and that of the Second World War Experience Centre, is to keep bright and burnished for future generations their extraordinary deeds. Though men fight best out of loyalty to their friends aboard ships, in Regiments or Corps, or in RAF Squadrons, they are aware of the precious values and freedoms, for which many made the ultimate sacrifice. This book is a lasting tribute to, and a reminder of, these 'valiant hearts', whether they lie in carefully tended Commonwealth or United States War Cemeteries, or are reaching naturally the term of their years. Their descendants can take pride in them, and keep alive the notion that our freedoms and our way of life were and are worth fighting for.

It is a great honour for me to be invited to write the Foreword for this outstanding contribution to recording not the stalwart leadership of Admirals, Generals and Air Marshals, but the experiences of those at the 'sharp end'. Not least among these are the accounts of the *coup de main* assaults on Pegasus Bridge and the Merville Battery, the American Airborne Landings, the assault on Omaha beach, or those who manned the Duplex-Drive Tanks giving close support to the gallant Beach Control parties and Infantry who secured the beaches and their exits. These are the profoundly moving recollections of the deeds of heroes. It was fitting that General Richard Gale should recite Henry the Fifth's stirring speech before Agincourt to his 6th Airborne Division staff as they emplaned in a glider en route to the Orne bridges.

The British, Canadian and United States Forces can take great pride in what their forebears did. I warmly recommend this excellent and absorbing book to all generations; to those who lived through that day, to those now serving who may well emulate the deeds recorded, to all who need to be reminded of the significance of D-Day, and to younger readers who may draw inspiration from the varied role-models found in these pages. We can all learn from the past, which is often a signpost to the future, and, hopefully, in this case towards the 'broad sunlit uplands' of a Europe at peace, to which Winston Churchill had pointed us in the darkest days of 1940. D-Day was a unique and extraordinary day, and Peter Liddle deserves the highest praise for celebrating the dramatic events of the day through so many eyes and differing experiences.

Henry Woods
January 2004

Acknowledgements

Readily I acknowledge that my greatest debt in the preparation of this book is to all the men and women whose papers and recollections I examined in the search for suitable material. The authors of that which was chosen are listed by their name and rank in 1944 in the index. I was fortunate in that evocative original material and recollections proved available in abundance or emerged following targeted enquiry. The difficulty on some occasions lay in what to choose from the riches before me. The constraints of the length of this book and the subjective nature of choice will have resulted, I fear, in regrettable but inevitable omissions. My debt is to more men and women than appear in the index.

The second massive debt, one related to the whole of the book, is to my colleague in the Second World War Experience Centre, Cathy Pugh. Cathy's knowledge, enthusiasm, research organisational capacity and sheer dedicated hard work, have ensured that this book was completed in time. Such is Cathy's approach to her work that she knows many of the men in the book through their papers and through correspondence, by 'ancient and modern' means. I have been very fortunate in having her help and in the interest and support of another colleague Tracy Craggs who also knows the riches of the Second World War Experience Centre. Another colleague, long-term helper and friend, Carolyn Mumford, was responsible for the transcription of every single Centre tape-recording from which quotation has been made. Readers will see the inestimable benefit this has been.

The work of the Second World War Experience Centre has from its foundation been enhanced by its volunteer workers; this book has benefited similarly. Robert Carrington, who has assisted me before in books on both World Wars, provided invaluable research work on wartime documentation including photographs and then recollections. Stan Hope, former Mosquito Navigator, made a preliminary search in the Centre's holdings for D-Day airmen as did Braham Myers, a former Gunner, for soldiers. Braham's command of French was also at my service. Doug Peers helped me with sailors. John Larder, our aviation expert, and young James Weatherill, gave me assistance without which I would have been under-prepared too. Some key tape-recorded interviews have been conducted by the team of volunteers and here Brian and Sheila Atkinson, Pat Clarke, Tracy Craggs, Julie Land, John Larder, Chris Nathan and David Talbot must be thanked. Vicky Britton worked extensively upon the Peter Prior D-Day papers; Trevor Mumford, by e-mail, fed me regularly with D-Day tape transcriptions and produced a data base of D-Day contacts from which the index is drawn; colleague Lesley Burke, by the same means, kept my links to assistance in Canada and the States maintained; Edie May-Bedell, Rosie Evans and Vicky Britton again, scanned photographs being chosen; Brenda Clifton and Trevor Mumford typed late-arrival pieces and kept me calm in the final stages as Trevor prepared the book electronically. Braham Myers and Robert Carrington assisted with the proof-reading. My thanks too to Ian Sayer and Ken Pugh for access to their private collections of documentation. I am truly grateful for the generous spirit in which all this help was given.

In the United States, good friends Phil Parotti in Texas and James Cooke in Mississippi in their different ways blazed trails which brought splendid returns. John McManus from Missouri gave his assistance too. The remarkable help given by Betsy Loren Plumb, Assistant Research Historian at the Eisenhower Center and the National D-Day Museum, New Orleans, went quite beyond the call of duty in assisting an external researcher. In many years of research I have never had institutional help given to match that which came from New Orleans and I am happy to record a deserved tribute to this archive and its staff.

How grateful I am to David Dilks and his long-cherished Canadian friends and their contacts concerning Juno Beach experience. In this respect my thanks are due to Professor William Rodney, W G Buchanan, Neil J Stewart, W F McCormick and John Whitton. From Canada also, Jim Lotz, from Halifax, Nova Scotia and Terry Copp of Waterloo, Ontario, despite heavy working schedules, in different ways gave me superb help. Terry's provision of the exceptional volumes of Jean Portugal's 'They were There: A Record for Canada' was of great assistance for the Juno chapter. In the same vein, Richard Campbell Begg's work in New Zealand on behalf of the Centre is evident in several chapters. It would be difficult to match his loyalty to the vision of a Second World War Experience Centre.

I am indebted to Roger Chapman of the Green Howards Regimental Museum, and Chris Dunn of the Friends of the Green Howards, for characteristically generous help and for help of the same nature from Tim Brown, Peter Francis and Tori Bennett of the Commonwealth War Graves Commission – two organisations here pre-eminently worthy of respect and of our support. David Preston gave me access to the German newspaper of 7 June 1944 and Tony Martin of the German Department in Benton Park School, Leeds, translated 1944 and 2003 German letters for me. Just in time came research assistance from France, Pierre and Francine Besson in Paris, and concerning German testimony, Gerry Kaeppner, Gotthard Liebich, Felix Wortmann and Tony Hellen all laboured to good effect.

There are still more people who played a part in the drawing together of this book, Anne Hoskot Kreutzer, John Bourne, Robert Maxwell, Dan Black, Pamela Campbell, Stan Skelacki and the design and production staff at Pen and Sword Books.

Penultimately I am so glad to record my appreciation of the fact that Major General Henry Woods has written the Foreword for this book. His keen intellect, sterling sustained support for the Centre and personal friendship are valued to the hilt.

Finally, anyone attempting a book is hugely blessed if he or she were to have a loving, supportive partner. I have one. Thank you Louise Liddle.

Peter Liddle, Leeds 2004
The Second World War Experience Centre 2004

Introduction

It is chilling to consider the consequences which hung in the balance as battle was joined on the Normandy beaches on 6 June 1944. As disturbing or as difficult fully to grasp was the sheer scale of the endeavour in men, matériel and miles. These are but two issues which immediately stimulate imagination in any reconsideration of the allied invasion of France. There are many more.

There is the complexity and potential decisiveness of planning, deception, concentration of forces, leadership at every level on that day. Still, sixty years after the event, there are publications and media presentations on inter-allied and inter-service cooperation, allied and German leadership and fighting resolve. These issues and others will continue to be subjects for debate as long as people have an interest in their past and a sense of its significance.

There is more which stimulates debate. How did the Allies perform comparatively, how did units perform comparatively? For some, considering this at the level of High Command as an assault launched became a campaign waged, the debate becomes even more relevant and more polemical. Old controversies attract new protagonists. There are those too who challenge D-Day's accolade as the turning point of the war. Surely events in the titanic struggle on the Eastern Front really determined the war in Europe? In response, those who remain convinced that D-Day deserves a special primacy in commemoration might aver that D-Day represents something different – the first mighty counterblow for 'freedom,' as the wartime democracies would have defined it. Of course fighting a long war had led Britain's National Government and the governments of Commonwealth countries and the United States to impose restrictions and controls which open the way for some to question the self-laudatory propaganda designed to play some part in uplifting the zeal of soldiers, sailors, airmen and civilians but perhaps the only legitimate growl against giving Operation Overlord this moral dimension might be from those who landed at Salerno in September 1943 – was their challenge not an earlier blow for freedom on the mainland of Europe?

Behind these controversies, the embers of which this book will not be raking over, lies the record made at the time by men who were there, in The Channel, over The Channel, on or behind the beaches, allied soldiers, sailors, airmen, German servicemen in defence of their positions, French civilians and resisters. Then there are too the memories of people who were there. Such memories may have been written soon after or very much later and, if recollections were recorded by interview, such archival garnering is likely to have been harvested recently.

What can quite reasonably be claimed is that in all probability, the experience of D-Day was an exceptionally important landmark in an individual's life story, something which left an imperishable memory, perhaps a lasting mark. In all likelihood men found themselves tested to a degree not hitherto experienced. For those who had been in action before, the combined operation nature and the vast scale of this new enterprise, ensured that this was not just 'going into action again'. The long months of training for all those involved would have built up a special degree of tension foreshadowing something significant for them as individuals and in their unit. Training for an operation, even with live ammunition under topographically similar circumstances to the real location, only goes so far in its preparing of individuals for the event itself. It is not sound of course to visualise all men fearfully imagining to a highly sensitised degree what they would face. The very lack of such imagination would be a protection for many as eve of the landing hours were passed in various forms of waiting.

Indeed, how ironic it is that we know for countless numbers of men, huddled together in bucketing landing craft transportation, that the miseries of sea sickness would anaesthetise them from imagining the perils they would face in the landing.

Be that as it may, there is no exaggeration whatsoever in linking Shakespeare's Henry V declaration of the anticipation of pride in being on the field of Agincourt, with the D-Day veteran's life-long pride in being there on 6 June 1944. A whole range of emotion is encapsulated within that pride. It may include sickening revulsion at what was seen and a sense of loss at the death of comrades, an awareness of personal good fortune even by those who were wounded but whose fate could have been worse; it may include too the sheer exhilaration of personal fulfilment in successfully carrying out a set task within a colossal operation of war. There are also likely to be sounds, smells, sights, sensations remaining vivid after sixty years and memories of the actions or fate of friends in the same platoon.

In preparing this book I have felt again that cautionary correction against trivialising real life drama by writers who have not been through related experiences. To some extent this has influenced the selection of evidence in the book. Especially from recollections, I have tried to select those which have a convincing ring but of course I was not there! Exceptionally helpful has been the privileged nature of my work in recent years and in particular since June 1999 when my main task as the Director of a newly-founded institution in Leeds, the Second World War Experience Centre, has been the rescue of evidence of the life experience of men and women living through the years of the Second World War.

In vocational satisfaction the appeal of this work never diminishes: in intellectual excitement it brings every week original letters, diaries, photographs or sections of tape-recordings encouraging a frisson which dissolves the intervening years and takes one directly into Dunkirk, Norway or the Blitz in 1940, convoy tension and action, the ordeal of Far Eastern captivity, the bomber raid, campaigning in Greece, Crete or North Africa, Italy or Burma, endurance in occupied Europe, or in European captivity and living through so many aspects of the Second World War.

Leading the team dedicated to the development of the Second World War Experience Centre has enhanced my awareness of the vulnerability of the evidence we are rescuing. This is a very rare archive in being dedicated specifically and solely to the Second World War. It has an international scope concerned to rescue Czech, Italian, Polish, German, Commonwealth and American material and certainly not just British. It is as ready to document women and children as men, civilian or servicemen, those not involved in a war effort as well as those fully involved or caught up in the circumstance of war.

The Centre is a charitable institution supported solely by successful application to fund-aiding bodies and the Centre's Association of Friends. If this book were to advance the Centre's cause, bringing in original documents or souvenirs, men or women to be tape-recorded, new Friends into the Association and funds for the Centre, a deserving, needy cause will have been aided.

The documentation in the Centre for D-Day is rich. For most of the sections into which the book is divided there is abundant material. Where the ground is less fruitful, the staff of other institutions have been helpful in offering their resources to ensure adequate coverage.

By the use of selected extracts from original letters and diaries, from photographs and from an appropriate selection of recollections from people in known locations before and during the day, the book attempts to bring the reader at least within reach of the range of personal experience on that day. To share what was seen, what was done, what happened to people, what responsibilities were filled, what was felt by individuals involved on the day; that is the aim of this book. In full understanding that all such material is subjective and, in any case, the very nature of an allied combined operation undermines the commonsense of talking about a 'general' experience of D-Day, the material is nevertheless representative in each section. The essence of the day is caught in the words of people trying to tell their own story. Embellished? I hope not, but that will be for the judgement of those who read the book. It must be added here that comprehensive coverage would require a far bigger book. Not all the military units, ships and squadrons of course, nor even some aspects related to preparation for the day like intelligence gathering by SOE operations or French resisters are represented, nor is there numerically adequate German defender and French civilian experience represented, but the design is quite emphatically that the feel of the day should be there.

When Martin Middlebrook's book on the first day of the Battle of the Somme in 1916 was published in 1976 it faced criticism from at least one distinguished historian for the inappropriateness of isolating one day from what was designed as a campaign. The same criticism can be levelled at any book which focuses exclusively on the day of the landings which launch the Normandy Campaign. However, this book on D-Day, while it has the structure of a day as it in fact developed, is not designed to be a history of that day whether or not it were appropriate to consider it separately from the ensuing weeks of fighting, but to share with readers the evidence of what it was like to be there.

The sections of the book follow a natural sequence from planning and training to the assembling of concentrations of men, the preparation and carrying out of plans of deception and then the delay on the eve of the attack, the Airborne assault, the Channel crossing and naval bombardments, the beaches – each in turn – air support, the transportation of war matériel, arrival of reinforcements and the work of medical personnel. There is also an attempt to record the response of women to this momentous day as they learned of it and finally there is evidence offering a closing summary of the day.

The perspective is that of the man in the ranks and his young officer. By the nature of a man's 'duty', on occasion, this offers us a vignette of senior command but 1944 Army 'other ranks', RAF sergeants air crew, and Naval ratings, together with their immediate officers are those who really write this book. If one were to speak for all, Ken Davenport, a Second Lieutenant in the 5th Battalion, The King's Liverpool Regiment, might be chosen for both his diary entry even though he is not in the initial assault on Sword Beach, and for his recollections.

The diary:
Tuesday 6 June.
Landed Ouistreham 13.45. Saw gliders. Beach a shambles. Bodies everywhere. Proceeded inland to Hermanville on Sherman. Sniped coming through streets. Up all night – bombing and shelling. Phil killed.

Recollections:
To be perfectly frank I was quite frightened.

The one thing I do remember on that short trip on the LCT was my batman coming from the galley with a cake. He hadn't made it but he had brought it with him. That, more than anything made me realise that although I was frightened, as everyone was of course (and you didn't admit it, of course you didn't), but the very fact that he could land with such *esprit de corps* and produce a cake on the moment of landing was quite a stimulant. And then we landed.

When I had landed and got to the top of the beach, I remember seeing a tank making its way into town. It couldn't get through a narrow passageway and it gouged the sides of two houses to get through.

We found an orchard and dug a trench, or at least my batman did. A good job we did because no sooner had we got in, than a German fighter came over and strafed us. Hit our ammunition truck and up it went, blowing to pieces two of my men who were inside it.

I also lost a friend, Philip Scarfe, a Second Lieutenant about the same age as I was. Landed on D-Day and I learnt later that there was a gun position – the Germans had positioned pillboxes (very menacing) to oncoming LC assault craft, and Philip and his men attacked it. He was shot as he ran up the beach firing his revolver. He was wounded but he carried on and was shot at again and was killed. We buried him above the high watermark. His wife sent her wedding veil to put in his grave which was rather touching. I was the Godfather to the unborn son she had later. Later he was disinterred and put in Bayeux cemetery, the military cemetery there.

It is of and from such men as Ken Davenport that this book is written and, by implication, Philip Scarfe is here too.

All textual or illustrative material in this book is from The Second World War Experience Centre in Horsforth, Leeds, UK, unless otherwise stated. Where it seems necessary to specify attribution to The Second World War Experience Centre, this is shown as SWWEC.

CHAPTER 1

Planning and Training

Serious planning for the invasion of Northern France was initiated as early as 1942, evolved into a far bigger military commitment than was ever originally put forward and while by definition concentrating on getting ashore on a fifty mile front and securing a beachhead, held to a far wider strategic vision – bringing about the defeat of Nazi Germany. The invasion of France with the liberation of Paris were stepping stones to the ultimate objective, Berlin.

With a plan two years in the making, necessarily involving large numbers of men 'in the know' to some extent, and requiring a level of detail from individual buildings on a map to estimated needs of petrol and ammunition, security against enemy knowledge was a preoccupying headache. Any German awareness of where, when, in what strength and by what means, the invasion was to be launched would have so seriously imperilled the whole venture as to threaten defeat on the first day. Success in intelligence security was to be the first victory of D-Day.

Such success was assured not least by there being so few people privy to the whole picture, but nevertheless maintaining the secrets so securely was remarkable. The Ground Forces Commander, General Bernard L Montgomery did not divulge the plans for Operation OVERLORD and its naval component, Operation NEPTUNE, to his subordinate senior commanders until 7 April 1944. It was asking a great deal that revelatory intelligence was not picked up by the Germans in the eight weeks before the landings but such was largely the case.

The intermeshing of tiny cogs in interconnected wheels driving a great design is exemplified here by the memories of men behind desks and engaged in planning for some aspect of the day and those in relatively remote areas of the United Kingdom undergoing training to fit them for their specific tasks on a great day sometime ahead, somewhere. Until very late in the day, for most of those involved, such imprecise but approaching likelihoods were all they knew.

MAJOR LOGAN SCOTT-BOWDEN RE
Special Forces, Combined Operations Pilotage (and Beach Reconnaissance).
Testing the beaches chosen for the Invasion: 31 December 1943 and 17-21 January 1944

Well, I was sent to all the Combined Operation establishments that existed to discover as much as I could about Combined Operations, including an air photographic unit and air reconnaissance – of which I was given some experience – to see what was achievable. And then, as I wasn't very fit, I went on the Commando recruits training course at the Commando Depot at Achnacarry as a Major, and that was very tough indeed, and being a Major in the squad far senior to anybody else – they were all private soldiers apart from one American Ranger Sergeant – I had to lead in every case whatever the activity, and it really was astonishingly tough.

Logan Scott-Bowden with his parents in late June 1940. He was then a Second Lieutenant on leave. His father, Colonel Jonathan, had that month only narrowly evaded capture with the BEF in France.

Back at Hayling Island with Nigel Wilmot, Head of Combined Operations Pilotage, we kept training hard there, very hard indeed, and so we remained really fit for the operations we were expecting to undertake.

We did our canoe experience in the Solent and in Chichester Harbour itself and also from a submarine up in the Firth of Clyde. We went out in a submarine and did a little night practice operation in the submarine. We got the two canoes out through the torpedo hatch and with all their kit in and then we got into them and then, well out to sea, it seemed to me – and then we had planned to row for two miles and then the submarine would pick us up. And that was the sort of training we did and later we did more with X-craft.

The normal COP method of operating involved going in in a Landing Craft Personnel – as it was called. A very small landing craft, and the idea was that we would use them for the Normandy beaches and be towed over behind a motor torpedo boat. But by that time we had actually reckoned that motor torpedo boats and messing about were an accepted fact of life by the Germans. Of course, they were fighting the E-boat war, but it wouldn't be all that secure from the secrecy point of view if they were hanging about too much opposite the beaches which were going to be used. And so Nigel Wilmot had the bright idea that these midget submarines would be just the things because they would not be detected. Having such a low profile they would not be detected by radar.

They had the added advantage in that you could go in and beach at periscope height on a rising tide close in and observe by day and we practised these techniques up in Scotland in The Mull Of Kintyre and places like that, and then we went south just before Christmas and we were waiting for the X-craft to come down. And our first operation was planned for the seventeenth of January 1944 in the X-craft. However, a crisis arose on anxiety over the beach bearing capacity of the Normandy beaches, particularly for heavy wheeled transport such as the 5.5 medium gun which only had two large wheels, and they were not twin wheels such as all the American equipment had, and so there was no satisfactory means of finding out the beach bearing capacity without going there. And Winston Churchill himself, who was Minister of Defence (as well as PM) had said no operation of any sort was to take place on the invasion beaches unless authorised by him. Well, at that time there was this anxiety about

The X craft which was used on D-Day in the British Sector. The figure on the left is Sub Lieutenant Jim Booth and on the right, the commander of the craft, Lieutenant George Honour. This particular craft was on stand-by for the January 1944 reconnaissance of Omaha.

the bearing capacity of the beaches and the American Joint Chiefs of Staff insisted on having an answer by the second or third of January, about whether beach track-way would be required on all the landing beaches, because if it was required that would only just give them time to place the contracts and get the stuff produced in enormous quantities for all the beaches. And so Churchill reckoned that it should be possible to do a reconnaissance on New Year's Eve when the German soldiers would certainly be celebrating and not perhaps so alert. And, at short notice, we were told that we would do a reconnaissance on New Year's Eve and because we couldn't do it by X-craft because they weren't there – they hadn't come down from the north – we went over in a motor torpedo boat towing the Landing Craft Personnel. There were two of them and we had two – two boats – for ourselves. We had our team – myself and Nigel Wilmot and Bruce Ogden-Smith – and then a back-up team in another one in case they would have to do the job too.

Anyhow we then were released from the motor torpedo boat and went in in a Landing Craft Personnel. The weather forecast was that it was going to be force three rising to force five, and that was exactly what it was. And so we swam in, aiming for a patch of peat three quarters of a mile west of Ver-sur-Mer, which was a good landmark so to speak and also we could take soil samples from round there and put them in our bandoliers of which we had two – ten inch or eighteen inch tubes in them which we each had to swim with in order to get samples for examination by Professor Bernal who was Chief Scientific Officer to Admiral Mountbatten.

We had our swimsuits, which were slightly positively buoyant and so that was a great help, and so we swam in aiming for this patch of peat. But what we didn't know about that was on a rising tide there was a tremendous set to the east, which is a current behind the breakers, and then you have these sets sometimes, and particularly in The Channel because of its shape and everything, which wasn't known about, and the set then stops going east and there is a period of stand for an hour or so until the tide starts coming back from high tide when the set goes the other way. So we could only swim at about two miles an hour at the best, but not in a fairly heavy sea. Anyway we swam in, but we were swept – oh, a good mile I think it was – east.

I and Bruce Ogden-Smith. Strangely to our astonishment, the lighthouse from Ver-sur-Mer was operating, and it's a low lighthouse on the right, on the west side of Ver-sur-Mer, and the beam came round every minute roughly but it didn't show up the beach at all because it was blocked by houses and the odd bit of tree and so on and Ver-sur-Mer itself. Anyhow there we were opposite Ver-sur-Mer and we got in and we could hear the German soldiers having a party and singing, and so we said, 'Well, they are not going to be very alert. That is good.' And so we then crawled round to the right to the ramp coming out on to the beach and behind it, of course, it was wired up with bits of the German type of concertina wire with tetrahedral anti-tank obstacles in amongst it and so on. But it was obviously a place where, if the Germans wanted to get onto the beach, they could easily use. And then from there we ran and dropped in accordance with the searchlight to where we really wanted to do our reconnaissance and eventually found the peat and did the sort of reconnaissance on the 'W' shaped pattern, and took the samples we wanted and shoved them in each other's bandolier of these things, because we had any amount of kit we swam with. I mean we had to have a wristwatch compass and a waterproof wristwatch. We actually had an underwater writing tablet which we could use but didn't, a Colt automatic and a Commando fighting knife and all the rest and for taking the samples an auger, an aluminium 'T' shaped auger eighteen inches long, which took a sample of about – oh, I suppose about ten inches from the bottom. The bottom bit being sort of sliced in half down to the bottom. You put it in, twisted it 180 degrees, lifted it up and you got a sample from down there. And then I took samples and shoved them in

Bruce Ogden-Smith's bandolier which he had on his back, and they were numbered, and then he did the same with me, and we each I think got about half a dozen, and we knew where we had taken them from because we had followed the 'W' design and then we had to swim out.

I should add that our swimsuits had a helmet, covered our legs and had waterproof quilting for buoyancy and retention of body warmth.

Originally COP had always used these swimsuits and separate boots, and Nigel was sure that that was the best thing because he said if you get a cut in your boot or a leak in your boot the whole suit will become useless. I mean it will no longer give you any buoyancy. I strongly objected to wearing these very tight things because I have thick bone and they made me very uncomfortable, and I said there is no earthly reason why we can't attach the boots to the suit, and Nigel was dead against this. Anyhow I and our Administrative Officer got made a couple of suits with boots attached which made all the difference in the world from the comfort point of view for me. And so we did wear suits with boots attached on operations and they were far better. Of course, you see you might be in the suit for a very long time, particularly on training, and I got varicose veins very quickly and I have them to this day and had to have treatment during training from wearing these terribly tight suits and boots.

Oh we carried a waterproof torch. There was a rule in COP that you were responsible for waterproofing your own torch because your life depended on it, and you used contraceptives to waterproof it. About three or four contraceptives, and it was a directional torch and then we swam out. We kept as close together as we reasonably could and it happened again. We had this beam of the lighthouse coming round all the time but we were sufficiently far from Ver-sur-Mer we reckoned to be clear of any sentry seeing us, we hoped, and anyway we sat in the tide looking at the breakers and studying them for a while. How the waves were formed and where they were at their lowest because the whole breaker didn't come over the full length of the beach.

We failed to get through twice. That was a bit alarming because we had orders, we knew what we had to do if we didn't get through, and we had to get out through the wired minefield and get to a rendezvous in there where the Resistance would help us. Well, that was by the way. Bruce Ogden-Smith got slightly behind and he was yelling, and so I swam back and I thought perhaps he had got a hole in his suit or got bad cramp, which was quite possible. And however, all he was yelling was 'Happy New Year' because we had been ashore when New Year came and I didn't reciprocate immediately. I told him 'Swim you bugger or we will be back on the beach.'

And then I did wish him a 'Happy New Year' and we swam out, and then we were a bit worried about recovery because it had got up to force five and so the troughs and so on were considerable, and we kept our torches going hoping that they would be spotted when they were at the top and not at the bottom of a trough. And after a bit they did spot us and we were picked up. They came in on us and all was well.

Well I went straight up to London with some of the samples and gave them to Professor Bernal. The geologists were satisfied with what we had done on New Year's Eve, but Omar Bradley, who had just taken over, said 'well look, if you have done a reconnaissance on the British beach, it's only fair that you do one on the American beach too.' And so we were allowed to do what we had been planning to do and been training to do all the time, and we did do this five day reconnaissance on Omaha beach. We went over in the X-craft on a Monday and came back on a Friday afternoon. We had been trained to do crew duties too, remember the X-craft had a crew of three.

Anyway it wasn't too difficult for Nigel because he was a Navigational Officer in The Navy anyway and so he could take charge and use the periscope and all that sort of stuff. As, of course, I had to when we got close in beached and viewing by day. And we beached at periscope height, took a fix so we knew where we were. Then we were able to look under the camouflage netting quite a lot, which you couldn't, even from an aircraft flying at fifty feet. Photographs didn't necessarily show what was underneath camouflage netting and we could see it from a – I suppose a sort of lower angle from the beach. We were able to confirm a number of suspected gun emplacements, what was in them, from the daylight reconnaissance.

We did this Omaha beach reconnaissance from the seventeenth to twenty-first of January. It was a sort of five day do. We were towed over halfway by trawler and then released in the X-craft. It was very successful. But we did have incidents. It was very calm one night and suddenly a chap put on a searchlight right on us and we were in the water luckily and we kept our heads down and we kept our bodies lined up so that he couldn't see all that well, and he kept this thing pointed at us for quite a while. They were very worried about it out in the X-craft.

We had swum in from the X-craft and so we couldn't go where we wanted to go, which was right opposite Vierville on the right hand side of Omaha beach, and so we managed to sort of ease our way back and then got into the breakers and then we were able to swim to the left quite some distance and did our reconnaissance there on what was actually the invasion area for the American 1st Division and we were then able to do an adequate reconnaissance there. Go to the back of the beach and – oh, Bruce Ogden-Smith took a sample of the size of the round stones at the back of the beach and things like that. But then a couple of sentries came along but they were chatting and they were on a track, only just a few yards behind the wire, and they were happily chatting away, and luckily we happened to be at the back of the beach at the time, but I don't think they would have noticed us anyway because they were pretty idle chaps.

We came back on the Friday and I was busy writing up our stuff on the Saturday when Admiral Creasy who was Chief of Staff for the overall Naval Commander, Admiral Ramsey, rang me up and he said, 'Are you coming up to London tonight?' I said, 'Well, not actually Sir. I am rather busy with some writing work.' And he knew we were on open line. He knew what I was talking about. 'Oh,' he said, 'I think it would be a good thing if you did and then come and see me at two o'clock on Sunday – tomorrow morning.' And I knew his office because I had been there before.

I reported to him at five minutes to two and he walked me along a corridor into a large room. Completely blacked out in every way – a completely secure room. The only furniture in it was twelve chairs. You know stacking chairs, in two rows at that end. And no sooner had we gone in and six Admirals came in. One was the Vice Chief of Naval Staff from Washington, who happened to be over, and then five Generals headed by Omar Bradley and Bedell-Smith. Then he drew the curtains back and there was a map from – well, from Le Havre on the one side and further north of Le Havre to Pas de Calais and the Cherbourg Peninsula. And he said, 'Well now, Scott-Bowden, give a description of your recent reconnaissance.' And I peered at this map and I said, 'Sir, it's going to be very difficult to describe on this very small scale map.' 'Oh,' he said, 'we have got a better one down the other end.' So we tramped down the other end and there was a perfectly good map of the American invasion beaches. And so he said, 'Come on, bring your chairs down here,' and to all these Admirals and Generals, and so that gave me a minute or two to think about what I was going to say.

So I then describe in about twenty minutes or so, exactly what had happened and then they started firing questions at me. The Navy first, but their questions I couldn't cope with because they were more interested in the slightly offshore navigation problems, pilotage problems really, and I couldn't help them. I could only help them with the close in ones, and so they then switched to the Army and they fired a lot of questions which I was able to answer. And Bradley asked me, there was a picture that was there of the beaches and it showed a transverse track going up to the ridge, and he said 'Will that take Sherman tanks?' and I said, 'Well, I would reckon that it could because it wouldn't be too steep for them, but I don't know what the width is, but I did see a two-wheeled cart taking debris from an emplacement being dug, being constructed, on the beach going up that track drawn by two cart horses.'

Then after they had shot their questions – they had asked sort of general questions – the thing broke up and the soldiers went off too, apart from Bradley, and he then took me up to the map and he then went on questioning me about this and that and the other for quite a while, and he was clearly worried and I said, 'May I say something, Sir?' and he said, 'yes,' and I said, 'this beach is a very formidable beach indeed and there are bound to be tremendous casualties,' and he put his hand on my shoulder and looked me in the eye and he said, 'I know, my boy, I know.' And he was very worried, and then I said 'well,' I said, 'our other role apart from reconnaissance is pilotage and I hoped that I would be permitted to take part in the pilotage on D-Day', and he said 'I will see to that.' And he did. *Transcript of tape-recorded recollections.*

SERGEANT JOHN GREEN
Intelligence Corps, 50th Field Security Section attached to GHQ
Home Forces in St Paul's School, Hammersmith,
being used as 21 Army Group HQ

In April 1944, to my great apprehension really, we were responsible for the security of a complete plan of the invasion area. It was laid out on the floor of the lecture room in St Paul's School for a demonstration by Monty of what his plans were to the high-ups. Two of us slept there every night and one of us was always on duty at the door, and the security was absolutely rigid there, because it was as hot information as one would find really, at that point in the war.

It was a very big model. There it was, the shores of Normandy all laid out and the lines, D plus one, D plus two, that Monty expected to reach. Very frightening, and one hoped one didn't talk in one's sleep and in the wrong place anyway. But it was rather frightening knowledge to have.

The War Cabinet came to it and, of course, even the King came as well. So it was as high level as you can get as far as an audience. Then in May we moved

John Green, a post D-Day photograph; now a captain in the Intelligence Corps.

down to Portsmouth and we had the care of Monty's Advance Headquarters at Southwick House outside Portsmouth, and we were supposed also to mix among the thousands of troops that were in that area and listen for any loose talk, really. *Transcript of tape-recorded recollections.*

LIEUTENANT COLONEL HUMPHREY PRIDEAUX
(3rd Carabineers) Staff Officer, 1/C 'Q' Maintenance Section, 21 Army Group

My brief in 1943 was to plan for the support of the Allied Army when it landed on the beaches. We were told to plan on the assumption that it would be in France and it would be sometime in the Summer of 1944 but nothing more precise than that. My concern was ammunition, oil, petrol, fresh water, spare parts, really everything. Postal services, the NAAFI, in other words supplies.

We were given planning assumptions about the size of the force, the make-up of the force, the amount of armour, the amount of infantry and the amount of artillery, the intended rate of advance and the directions of it. These were being constantly modified as the planning proceeded which didn't make our task any easier but we had to try and cater for the worst case with a bit of over-run. What worried me most was the oil, until we got that pipeline under the Channel – PLUTO. The amount of oil which an army consumed was horrendous, the sheer volume enormous.

The food was really fairly simple because we had these sort of Compo packs which they had and they were mass produced and it wasn't too difficult, given the planning assumption about numbers that you had, it wasn't too difficult to work out how much you were going to need. Ammunition was quite tricky because that depended on consumption rates in a way which was not always easy to assess, and the actual problem, of course, of getting the stuff across the beaches until Mulberry harbour was fully established was also quite a headache.

Of course we were all under the strictest security. We all had to be vetted very carefully, I remember that, and we were all under no illusion that we weren't allowed to say a word about what was happening. I never knew

Humphrey Prideaux in the winter of 1944/5.

myself, even in the sort of central position that I was in, until literally the last forty-eight hours, I didn't know when D-Day was going to be. I mean it was all hypothetical to the extent that you had a rough idea but that was all. There were certain classes of security and the actual pinpointing of D-Day was in the top class of all and I was never in that league.

We were all at St Paul's School in Hammersmith. Our officers' mess was just across the road in a big block of flats called Latymer Court and we were there at the time when the doodlebugs started. You must remember the pilotless bombs which came over London shortly after D-Day and they caused a bit of excitement there.

I remember Monty arriving, of course, because I was there just before him. I mean before he came back from overseas and took over, and I remember, I have a very vivid memory of the first time that he got us all together and addressed us when he took over. That made a great impression because, well – here was a man who was coming from his successes in Africa with the Eighth Army, and one of his outstanding characteristics, of course, was he had this great gift for inspiring confidence in people, and I remember feeling that, you know, this was a new dawn, if you like, that whereas we had been plodding along planning, it somehow brought the whole thing much more vividly alive. *Transcript of tape-recorded recollections.*

LIEUTENANT PETER PRIOR

Intelligence Officer, 5th Battalion, Royal Berkshire Regiment
(8th Beach Group with 3rd Canadian Division)

When we arrived at Creech Walk Camp near Portsmouth I was told that a very small number of people indeed would be told the real location of the landing. The vast majority of troops will have no idea where we are going until they got on the boat before they departed. However, because I was Intelligence Officer, I and the Colonel and the Second in Command and the Adjutant would all be told at a conference tomorrow at some headquarters behind Portsmouth – where Eisenhower and Montgomery were based, and we duly went there and were briefed on what was actually going to happen.

We were personally briefed by the Colonel, having been given blood-curdling threats of what would happen if we disclosed this to anybody. We were given a code which enabled us to identify whether anybody we were talking to actually did know of the location. I remember the code, and this was rather interesting. You see, if after this conference we went back to our units and some other officer of another unit came and said, 'Oh well, of course, I know where it's going to happen,' and you would say, 'Oh indeed, are you Bigoted?' And they had to reply 'yes, I am Bigot Neptune'. And if they said 'Yes, I am Bigot Neptune,' even then you wouldn't take it for certain that they were. You would go and personally check that this man had been

Peter Prior.

'Bigoted' and then that you were able to speak to him about it. And this was quite important, you see, because all the subsidiary units of the beach group - General Transport Companies, the ambulance and all the other make-up of the beach group, they all had Commanding Officers who had to be told things, and you didn't necessarily know whether you were entitled to talk to a single individual.

The 5th Royal Berks Regiment only had five people who actually were being 'Bigoted' and were 'Bigoted Neptune', and they were Colonel Taffs, the Adjutant, the Second in Command and me, the Intelligence Officer. I had to type the plans and draw up the plans for the beach group. My typist, Lance Corporal Headland, was a taciturn individual who barely spoke anyhow, but he was a very competent clerk. I got him to do all the typing, so we had five people in The 5th Royal Berkshire Regiment who knew where the landing was going to be.

When we were in discussion with General Crerar somebody had said 'we must build a model of this.' And I was instructed by Colonel Taffs, my CO, that I was to be responsible for building a model of the actual beach and it was to be, I think, thirty feet long and the whole Division would be paraded in front of it and told the night before embarkation exactly what was going to happen. So I spent some time – oh I don't know how long – building this wretched model.

I think I got permission to beg a number of other people to help build it. You know people who could make houses and churches and things like that. There was an armed guard day and night all round this building which had formerly been a farm barn I think. And we eventually built a splendid model and illuminated it and everybody did march past it and see it. We got it more or less right and this was quite a responsible job.

We had intelligence photographs and pre-war postcards and I was flown on a top secret mission in a Mosquito aircraft. I was flown along the coast to have a look at it some time before D-Day, but this sortie in the aircraft had to appear it was to do with the entire French coast. And so we set off with me lying on my stomach in the front of this aircraft with a sort of hole in the front, and we flew to the end of, I think , Holland. All down the coast and, of course, all I was looking for was a bit, and I could recognise it quite easily because you have got Fécamp and various places in the way up and the River Seine, and I knew as we passed the estuary of the Seine that we were coming up to it and I simply had to look at it to see what it looked like and so I could then have a much better idea of how the model ought to look and the model was built with my additions.

It was made from plaster of Paris, earth, wood to build buildings, all in a great barn near Creech Walk Camp. *Transcript of tape-recorded recollections.*

LIEUTENANT DOUGLAS FRANCIS RNZNVR
'J' Force Radar Officer responsible for fitting and maintaining radar
in a range of craft to be used in the planned landings

Most of the equipment, surface warning radar, IFF sets (Identification of Friend or Foe) and a navigational aid had already been fitted in dockyards. My task was to get them operational, to train the men who operated them and to maintain them over the months before the invasion.

While at Cowes it soon became evident that I would need a workshop on shore for my team of radio mechanics. We commandeered the basement of St Mark's Church Hall. I operated this workshop with three radio mechanics, including Glasgow Rangers footballer, Leading Radio Mechanic Tom McKillop.

My duties took me out to ships at anchor in the Solent accompanied by one of my team, taking meters, test equipment and spare parts. As the build-up grew we would take flotillas of landing craft to sea on training exercises loaded with Army or RAF personnel to give them and the naval crew a feel for night operational conditions and to use the beach at Studland as a gunnery range.

In Portsmouth dockyard we had an improved radar device (Type 970) fitted which gave us a presentation in plan form. The radar was fitted in the bridge area of the ship's upper works and the aerial was fitted as a perspex dome at the summit of a tripod mast.

Thirty of our landing craft were fitted with rockets held in racks. The rockets were 1200mm long and four inches in diameter, the fire power of the thirty craft being 33,000 rockets. Fired from 2,000 yards off the beach as the Captain closed the tumbler switches they would land within 30 seconds.

In late April or early May I was called to Portsmouth and taken to Supreme Headquarters for the invasion at Fort Southwick on the Portsmouth Hills, the operational control centre for the entire 'Overlord' operation. Most of the accommodation was underground in large chambers and tunnels associated with that old fortress. Here I was fully briefed on the forthcoming Normandy landing and was bound by an oath of secrecy now having to train the navigational leaders of our assault force for the quite complicated and precisely timed approach to the beaches. For this purpose special beach chartlets were prepared; because the approach would be in the very early light of the morning, great faith was placed on the use of radar now installed. *Transcript of tape-recorded recollections.*

FLIGHT LIEUTENANT HENRY ELLIOT,

Station Signals Officer, RAF Dunkeswell then Signals Liaison Officer with American
Squadrons flying Liberators on anti-submarine operations over South Western Approaches

*Henry Elliot, on the right with the pipe and two US
Navy colleagues from Fleet Air Wing 7, RAF
Dunkeswell. The man in the centre is the Wing's
Communications Officer, Lieutenant Turner USNR.*

Towards the end of May I had occasion to speak on the telephone to the Chief Signals Officer at 19 Group HQ. In the course of a very guarded conversation – we had no scrambler – I gathered that special signals instructions relating to the forthcoming D-Day Operations had been issued some time ago and he was clearly concerned that I seemed not to be aware of this. After some hectic telephoning around the base the relevant documents were eventually tracked down to the Base Commander's safe where, marked 'Top Secret', they had languished for some time and would presumably have continued to do so. Perusal of the documents revealed that in order to ensure that the enemy could not jam the aircraft communication channels at a critical time, all frequencies and call signs were to be changed at midnight on D minus One, the day before the invasion was to begin.

The US Navy aircraft were all equipped with crystal controlled transmitters and aircraft had to be dispatched immediately to various supply depots to collect the crystals for the new frequencies. Fortunately all the arrangements were completed in time. *Typescript recollections.*

LIEUTENANT ROBERT FORD

4th/7th Dragoon Guards on a training exercise
with a Duplex Drive [ie amphibious] tank.

The tanks had an inflatable skin which enabled the tank to displace its own weight in water and the skin was held up by compressed air pillars at each corner and in the middle and also struts, all this remote control operated by the commander of the tank.

We started training very simply, and in ordinary daylight. Individual tank training, getting to know the steering because it was driven by propellers at the back. But this, the Valentine, then had a single propeller whereas the Sherman tank, which was our operational equipment, had twin screws. Anyway we started our training and we worked up slowly. Daylight training – single tanks, daylight training – troop of tanks, daylight training – squadron of tanks. Then we moved to the night, and you do the same thing all over again. We had navigational, the usual green and red rear lights and so on. Doing it in a dark night and a moonlight night. Then trying to get eventually the whole Regiment in line, because the idea was that we would land at H minus five. We would then plaster the beach, and the

Robert Ford and his crew, May 1945 in Buxtehude, Germany.

Infantry and the 'funnies' and so on would go up through us – we would stay at the water's edge – through us to the top of the beach. We would be able to give support to the Infantry and therefore in theory we had sixty tanks in the Regiment. We would swim in from 5,000 yards out. Now rehearsing of course, in times like March /April, meant rehearsing in the dark.

In fact the biggest rehearsal of all that we did was in Studland Bay, which was a replica of King Red Beach where we landed. I didn't know it at the time but Churchill and Eisenhower and, I believe, the King watched it. I am not certain about that, but we were firing live ammunition but they had built a marvellous sort of totally armoured watch, a pillbox, from which the distinguished VIPs could watch it. I didn't know anything about that of course. Anyway, on the rehearsal, which I think was on April 20, 1944, we sailed from Poole Harbour in our LCTs as we had done before, and we went out into the Channel escorted by MTBs, destroyers and so on, and then part of the way across we turned round and came back towards the English coast. Pitch dark, pretty rough sea and my tank was the first- yes, the first. The five tanks on my LCT, mine was the first that had to go down. Well, at the appropriate signal the bridge went down on the LCT to the right angle, which is very necessary when you are putting a tank into the water, otherwise you will get water inside the inflatable screen. I went into the water and I struggled for a bit. Those behind me were also struggling I could see, although I couldn't see them all in the darkness and after a fairly short distance, it became obvious to my tank, and I forgot to mention that I was Second in Command of this tank, Lieutenant Gould was the Commander and I was in the operator's seat – I forgot to mention that – for this particular exercise, and it became obvious to Bob and myself that we had little hope of ever reaching the beach, which was nearly 5,000 yards away.

So he did the usual drill. We had practised all this. We had Davis escape system, of course, [a modified one, which we went through at the Portsmouth School there] and he got everyone on deck. Just the driver initially who continued pressing the old accelerators, but there was a method of still maintaining some speed without having the driver actually having his foot on the accelerator – there was an alternative method. And then he called the driver, and as he called we braced ourselves – it sounds quite stupid to say this – against the bows of our supposedly amphibious vehicle. With our backs to the bows and our feet against the turret of the tank in some vain hope of keeping the screen upright. But as we did that some of the supports started to snap, and looking over my shoulder – and I can remember this to this day – I saw an enormous wave coming over me and, of course, all the others and we were in a swirling mass of water as we sank to the bottom.

Now the extraordinary thing is that I have no memory of being actually under the water and so on. Except that when we rested on the bottom I was in an air pocket and what had happened was that the screen had fallen over us and the screen had metal edges and we were all trapped under the screen. I can't say what happened to the others at that particular moment. I had lost my Davis escape mouthpiece and all the rest of it. So I was very lucky – like the others I hoped – to have some air to breathe. But I was also lucky, the only one in that tank who was particularly lucky to be wearing flying boots, which were against Regimental regulations, and not Army boots because our feet were trapped, and with flying boots I managed to just get my feet out of them, and then with the Mae West, which we were also wearing as a back up to the Davis escape, I came to the surface.

Anyway when we landed on the bottom I fought my way out. I am afraid I have no idea what happened to the others, and I regret to say that none of them ever came to the surface. So I was the sole survivor.

I was in the water thrashing around and suddenly a searchlight hit me, caught me, and I realised that there was someone and that there was a naval ship, I think it was a frigate, trying to manoeuvre itself. My cries for help had been heard and it was trying to manoeuvre itself near me because they had thrown life belts at me and I regret to say that perhaps I wasn't strong enough, anyway I couldn't get hold of one. I realised then that I was in for a second perilous moment because this thing manoeuvring alongside me like *The Queen Mary*, really as far as I was concerned, was stirring up the water so much that I didn't think I could possibly survive it. But what happened was that the Master, or whoever it was, got some sailors to throw down a scrambling net down the side and two sailors came down the scrambling net and into the water almost with me and pulled me out and pulled me up on to the deck where I lay like a sort of gasping fish really. And I was taken down to the sick berth, stripped, pummelled with towels and filled with rum, dressed in about four sweaters and God knows what from the Naval Quartermaster, and by that time I really didn't know what was happening at all. I was totally drunk I think, to be quite frank. But they got circulation going again. *Transcript of tape-recorded recollections.*

HM Queen Mary inspects the 13/18 Royal Hussars at Marlborough, Wiltshire on 25 April 1942. She is about to shake hands with Julius Neave.

CAPTAIN JULIUS A S NEAVE
Adjutant 13/18 Royal Hussars

The set-up for organising the combined training and rehearsals was on a biggish scale. The 3rd Div under General Tom Rennie had all its troops under command in the Inverness area, and in addition to its three infantry brigades, it had ourselves, innumerable sappers, additional gunners, commandos and specialist units all involved in some particular aspect of the assault. The Navy, for their part had a force that was much the same in both size and diversity, and it was known as 'Force S'. They were distributed all round the Moray Firth, at Inverness itself, Fort Rose opposite to Fort George, and Invergordon. The two headquarters lived side by side in Cameron Barracks, Inverness, and in between them they turned out a veritable mountain of paper. They prepared and executed between them a series of combined exercises – cum – rehearsals which were in their way masterpieces, and certainly gave us a very fair idea of what we were in for.

'Smash', 'Grab', 'Crown', 'Anchor' and 'Leapyear' were all more or less full scale shows, all on much the same lines and successively more intense and more complete.

As can well be imagined, Fort George and the Moray Firth are not best suited geographically for naval and military exercises in February, especially as they involved 48 hours on virtually open landing craft followed by another 48 hours on open and windswept moorland. However by dint of wearing every garment possible, and keeping a full flask, we managed to survive; and in any case it was perhaps worse in imagination than it was in reality.

The organisation and control of these exercises was really remarkable. Considering the vast numbers of men, strangeness and novelty of the training, their success was surprising. This was all the more so because at the time it was going on, no one could be said really to know his job in the many ways he was required to.

We would embark from the hards of Fort George, usually at night on a rising tide, and steam out to sea in a big sweep, and then the following dawn, if we were lucky and not kept on board for longer, make an assault landing on Burghead Bay which is just east of the Findhorn River and Culbin Sands. Once ashore we would move almost exactly as we should have to on D-Day itself, and then motor home to Fort George after the exercise. It all sounds so simple now but in fact it was far from being so! The chaos on the beach itself was on each occasion quite unbelievable, but this strangely enough was an asset for on the day itself chaos reigned and our experience had taught us that it was the normal thing. We learned all that we had to about waterproofing vehicles, about cooking compo rations and about the bedlam of the wireless set-up, we learned the most practical clothes to wear and what 'comforts' came in really useful. We got to know the infantry with whom we would be fighting and the Navy who would take us in. Also we got an insight into the marshalling and loading problems, and the briefing and planning that would be necessary when we got south.

After each exercise a vast conference would be held in Inverness attended by all the officers and run jointly by all the officers and run jointly by the Army and the Navy. These were notable for the complete disregard of personal feelings that the Navy seemed to hold for their subordinates, who would be slated in the most outrageous manner in front of the assembled company of about 1500. The Navy certainly knew how to put these conferences over and showed up the vagueness of the Army to a remarkable degree.

One example is noteworthy to demonstrate the pettifogging attitude of the Army. A Brigadier on the Staff was detailed to watch the hygiene discipline on one of the exercises, and when it was his turn to make his comments he rose with a long face. He said he was horrified at the apparent utter disregard of the most explicitly given orders on the subject. When he went inland, he said, with a party of high-ranking spectators including the Corps Commander and the Army Chief of Staff, what should he see as he topped the first sand dune, not thirty yards away, but a soldier, obviously from some ill-disciplined unit, attending to the needs of nature. At that moment the CO of the 1st Norfolks who was sitting next to me whispered 'That was me and I had been longing for it since 5 o'clock in the morning!'

General Montgomery came to see us on February 5th on his well known tour, a particularly cold day, and he kept us waiting for about two hours. The parade which included all troops in Fort George and neighbourhood, numbering about 3000, was laid on with special care. Hence the order to break ranks as soon as he arrived and face inwards to gaze on the familiar face came as rather a cold douche. We as senior regiment in the fort had been given the job of making all the arrangements and laying on the parade. This was a monumentally impossible job since it appeared to be beyond the powers of the Brigade and Divisional Staffs to say who was supposed to be on our parade and those who were coming seemed quite unable to say how many of them there would be. Thus the problem of fitting them into ranks in the prescribed hollow square was a veritable nightmare, it nearly drove the RSM demented and we were all heartily thankful when the visit was over.' *Privately published recollections and diary.*

CORPORAL ERIC HAMMILL
East Riding of Yorkshire Yeomanry, Duplex D Tank Driver

Eric Hammill at Tidworth Barracks in 1940.

We learned about waterproofing and driving a tank on water with propellers. You also had a bilge pump. Once you were in the water you engaged your bilge pump and that pumped out any water that did get in.

The tracks stopped as soon as you drove into the water and the driver switched to dual drive, to propellers. There was also something like a plug, and this had fuses to blow all the superficial stuff off. You plugged this onto your driving panel and it would explode all these charges. They said the Germans would get a shock when they heard this. We learnt all this at Yarmouth.

The most interesting and tricky part of the training was learning to use the Davis apparatus. The training for that was in the hull of a tank in a deep pit, about 18 feet deep and you used to have to sit in there, the full crew, as if you were going into war: the crew commander, the driver, the co-driver, the wireless operator and the gunner, and they could fill these pits in two minutes. Less than two minutes. When it stopped at the top and you were sat under 18 feet of water then you would put your nose thing on. Then the crew commander would tap you on the shoulder and that would be your turn to inflate your Davis apparatus. We learned how to do this in the open-air swimming pool in Yarmouth.

There was a big lake at Fritton Park and that's where we put it into practice, this Davis apparatus. There was a tank without tracks that was a fixture there for training. All you had on was camouflage denims, denim jacket and trousers. Everything was wet through because everyone had been through it. They put you in a tank, then they filled it with water, then they drained it again and put the next lot in.

In the training, on the first day down at Fritton Park, sailing in these tanks, one went down, they don't know why, and this young lad called Lloyd got drowned, he was only nineteen. My friend, Charles, who was a crew commander, tried to save this lad. He grabbed him but his shirt came off. We all had boots on, Army boots and after that fatality they scrapped the idea of wearing boots and we had to wear running shoes to make things easy.

It was very claustrophobic in a tank. It stank. Some of the chaps didn't like water, our regiment was from Hull, with a lot of fishermen, and yet one of them was petrified of water. They couldn't get him into water. We all had our fears but I never thought of being trapped. The only thing I used to fear was the tank getting hit and being trapped on fire. That did happen.

There were escape hatches at the top and one in the bottom as well, so you could escape from underneath. There wasn't much space between the bottom of the tank and the ground, but enough to crawl out.

It was a bit fetid inside. You'd get four or five people crammed inside a little tin box and you've a big gun. When you fired it, it recoiled so you sat at the back and there wasn't a lot of room. If you were firing 75mm shells, you had to have asbestos gloves to throw the debris out. It was red hot.

After we learned DD and the Davis escape kit, we moved down to Petworth. We were there for about five or six weeks. We were kitted out with everything, all new gear, clothing, spare socks. They were dependent on the troops and the tanks to carry the gear over, even if you didn't use it yourself, your tank was fully loaded up.

We had to practise digging trenches and the 'hull down' position, which was getting behind a little hillock and you hull down so that your gun is just over the top of the land in front of it, so you are protected. *Transcript of tape-recorded recollections.*

BRIGADIER S J L HILL
in command of 3rd Parachute Brigade

I had in my brigade about 2,200 fighting men. Two battalions were English County Battalions. Now they were asked, would they convert to a parachute role and being good county chaps, the last thing they wanted to do was to convert to the parachute role but they all said to a man, of course we will. After, we put them through two sorts of training course, first of all through physical training to get themselves up to standard and then we put them through the parachute training. At the end of the training they each produced 156 parachute soldiers (they had started off about 650 strong or thereabouts). Quite extraordinary in both cases it was 156 and they were good men. Now those people had joined the Parachute

James (S J L) Hill, second from the left.

Regiment because they were asked to do so and they thought it was their duty. No *joie de vivre* or anything like that. They felt it was their duty. Now the other battalion was a Canadian battalion and they were far more like my 1st Parachute Battalion which I had taken to North Africa and that battalion held a great number of soldiers of fortune. They had people who fought in the Spanish Civil War and so on.

They wanted to fight and fight for freedom and this, that and the other. They were keen to get in on the battle and they were far more like my first battalion than the other two so you got two entirely different types of parachute soldier, those who really wanted to fight and then the other a quieter chap altogether who went in because it was his duty to do so. So your training had to embrace both and the point really was that the soldiers of fortune, if you gave them absolute discipline and kept them just there they were absolutely magnificent but if you let them off the hook they became slightly untidy. They would become rather unmanageable. Now the other chaps of course were good solid people. They did exactly what they were told and they did it immaculately and I wouldn't like to choose between the two. Provided always that the soldiers of fortune were disciplined.

I also had a Field Ambulance and this was of great interest. Before D-Day came they came to me and said would you mind if we took conscientious objectors in to your field ambulance and I said no, certainly not. I would be delighted to have them and we took, I think it was 46 conscientious objectors into 224 Parachute Field Ambulance. I knew these would be good men because they were prepared to face danger. They were prepared to give up their lives but they were not prepared to shoot or kill anybody else. They were prepared to act as stretcher bearers, act in the field, look after people whether they were Brits, Germans or anybody else. They were splendid chaps and also I understand that they were all volunteers for bomb disposal, so what better chaps could you have?

So I had a wonderful band and then last but by no means least I had the 3rd Parachute Squadron, Royal Engineers, who were quite outstanding. They were engineers in civil life, they all ended up engineers in civil life after the war. They were of a very high category. Very intelligent and you couldn't have wished for better. So here was I, three splendid battalions, one Canadian, two British, a remarkable Field Ambulance and top class engineers and they were fighting men. So what better could you have to go into battle with?

The training of them was very interesting. I used to have three things, if I can remember them now, one was speed, the next was control, the third fire effect. Speed, control and fire effect. *Transcript of tape-recorded recollections.*

SIGNALMAN ALAN WHITING RN
undergoing three weeks of Commando training at Spean Bridge
preparatory to being a 'Beach Party Signalman'

I was instructed in how to kill swiftly and silently in different ways, to use anything as a weapon, swing on ropes with full kit, ammunition pouches and a rifle over water and pits full of barbed wire, to run across tree trunks and jump over trenches also full of barbed wire and to learn how to fall across a barricade comprised of barbed wire and make a bridge in order that others following you could run across and over your back, cross an obstacle course and still be able to bayonet somebody at the end of it, all under sporadic fire from rifle and automatic weapons, accompanied by smoke bombs. Then we commenced our amphibious assault landing training in earnest.

The crews of the landing craft were affectionately dubbed 'saltwater cowboys' because in any sort of swell, the LCAs behaved like bucking broncos and you had to be some kind of cowboy to 'ride-em' and stay on.

Through experience in training I came to wear naval bell-bottoms and boots with naval green-blancoed gaiters, plus navy blue woollen jersey, but an army khaki battledress tunic with navy red-on-blue badges and insignia, 'Naval Commando' shoulder flashes, crossed flags, crossed rifles and the Combined Ops badge, a navy blue Royal Marine beret with the Royal Marines crest.

I had green-blancoed ammunition pouches and webbing belt, a service .45 revolver and holster, the low power battery in its case strapped to my back, a 4″ Aldis signalling lamp in its carrying box and my tin hat with 'Sig' and crossed flag insignia on it.

I also acquired two Royal Marine Commandos as body guards to cover me when I was signalling seawards. *Typescript recollections.*

Alan Whiting in Melbourne, Victoria, on the first anniversary of D-Day, 6 June 1945.

MAJOR T S BIGLAND RA
one of General Montgomery's Liaison Officers
with General Bradley's US 12th Army Group

On 15 May, three weeks before D-Day, I took up what was to be my most fascinating appointment of the war as Monty's Liaison Officer with General Bradley and reported next day to HQ First US Army at Bristol. Meeting the many officers with whom I was to work, I thought my position was going to be most difficult, but the following day my mind was put at rest, when General Bradley interviewed me together with Colonel "Red" Akers, Head of Operations, and told us both that I was to have all the information I required and that, if I thought it necessary, I could always go direct to him – a privilege which I did not use any more than about three times apart from reporting on important occasions. I took a great liking to both men and was to consider Akers one of the best Staff Officers in either Army.

Monty's use of Liaison Officers, young men trained to bring back up-to-date verbal reports on the battle situation, was unique and had been developed since Alamein. American officers were at first somewhat reluctant to entrust us young men with secret information for direct transmission to Monty and his small Staff at Tac HQ. Their Liaison Officers were senior officers carrying out-of-date reports in sealed envelopes between higher HQs.

On 19 May I had to pack my jeep, which my driver was to take to France to meet me on D + 2. With it I packed a 'utility' bike which Dad had bought me for use in London and which I thought would be useful in the chaos of battle, but I never saw it again. I kept only what I could carry – my bed roll and my pack. There was nothing more to do at that point, so I went back to Southwick Park and on for a weekend in London.

Lieutenant General Omar N Bradley's signed photograph given to Major Bigland 'in appreciation of your fine work.'

...At Bristol on Monday 29 May, Bradley suggested that I should meet General George Patton, commanding the US Army near Chester. Part of the cover plan for the invasion was that the Germans should be persuaded that the main attack would be in the Pas de Calais, commanded by Patton, who was senior to Bradley.

Next day, I drove to Chester and met this extraordinary commander and his staff, who would do anything for him. He was obviously a great leader of men, a most flamboyant character, but to me he seemed unbalanced. He gave me a manuscript copy of a pamphlet he was writing. In the middle of describing features he expected in attack, he had broken off and written: 'Officers of the US Army will shave once a day, preferably before 1200 hrs!'

Typescript recollections.

US MERCHANT MARINE
PETTY OFFICER HILTON M FLOYD
selected for a classified mission

We were stationed aboard an old Panamanian registered ship crewed mostly by foreigners – Chinese, Portuguese, Jamaican. We had intensive training and classroom instructions including chemical warfare, clothing use, enemy aircraft recognition, some commando tactics, small arms use, target practice and so forth. Our instructors were both American and British.

In addition to the special training we received in London we had to see to the upkeep of our armor and equipment (40 mm anti-aircraft gun and an old 3 inch 23 forward; we also had six or eight small caliber anti-aircraft guns.) My battle station was gun captain of the 40 mm.

Late in May, having taken on coal at Methil and undergone lifeboat work in Loch Ewe we learned what our upcoming mission was. We were on one of the ships to be scuttled parallel to the beach off the coast of France to create a breakwater so our troops could have a smoother landing site during the Normandy invasion. These ships were called block ships. While anchored at Loch Ewe, a detail of men came aboard and placed two charges of explosives in each of our five cargo holds which were partially filled with small pebbles. The explosives were placed just below the water line on the port and starboard sides in each hold. I am not certain but I think we were told that each charge contained 5 lbs of TNT. The 10 charges could be simultaneously set off electrically from one of two positions, amidships or aft. This was done with batteries equipped with switches. *Typescript recollections.*

Two American sailors in the winter of 1943/44, insist on being 'snapped' with two British Land Army girls in Honiton, Devon. The Americans serviced aircraft at Dunkeswell in Devon. Sadie Greaves, SWWEC

CHAPTER 2

Deception

Parallel activity in attempting to conceal from the Germans the Normandy coast focus of allied planning was to encourage them to believe that the troops' real threat would be mounted elsewhere – Norway, the Pas de Calais, Brittany, the Mediterranean, the Aegean or the Balkans. The date by which a strong enough force could be built up for such an assault, particularly from England across The Channel, was itself something to be shrouded in secrecy or falsely presented.

Attracting German attention to Norway and the Pas de Calais was imaginatively and persistently attempted with agents and double agents planting false intelligence. Phantom armies in Scotland and in East Anglia, built very largely from carefully constructed wireless traffic dealing with routine and build-up preparations, were part of a very serious 'game'. The creation of a phantom force in Scotland lay at the heart of the Norwegian lure, and a largely unreal American force in East Anglia was designed to threaten the Pas de Calais.

Cleverly conceived air operations bombed targets cutting communications throughout Northern France not just in Normandy and also hit other targets outside the designated area for seaborne assault. On the eve of the landing, RAF squadrons and a skeleton Naval force too, laid bait in the Pas de Calais, with 'chaff' from the air alerting operators of a deliberately undestroyed radar installation and magnified noise from the sea also was designed to put the coastal defences on high alert. Deception work continued of course up to and beyond the actual landings, the 'Ruperts' might be mentioned here, the dummy paratroopers, some with sound effects and some with explosives, dropped in the Pas de Calais area and east of the real landings.

Complete success in deception was not achieved: the Allies were to a considerable extent expected by those watching from the coastal defences above the beaches, but for valuable long hours, then days and even over two weeks, the landings posed for the Germans a critical question. Was this but a diversion for the main assault still to come across the Narrows from Dover?

COLONEL RORY MACLEOD, RA
ordered on 4 March 1944 to GHQ Home Forces (Hounslow)
where he was directed to the Signal Officer in Chief, Brigadier Barker

He told me I was to operate a deception plan to cover the invasion of Normandy which would take place about the end of May. I was to go to Scotland and represent an Army about to invade Norway with the object of pinning down the 9 German divisions there and prevent them interfering with the landings. This would be done by means of wireless traffic which the Germans in Norway and France would pick up. The Army would consist of Army HQ and three Corps each of 3 divisions. One Corps would be actual, the XV Corps in Northern Ireland, and in each of the two Corps in Scotland there would be one actual

eis 20 Pfg.

Münchner Neu... Nachrichten

Wirtschaftsblatt, Alpine und Sport-Ze...g, Theater- und Kunst-Chronik

Nr. 157

Die Schlacht um Europ...at begonnen

...gen des Feindes von der Normandie bis Dünkirchen / Hauptstöße geg... Carentan und Cherbourg / Hohe Feindverluste

Angriff und Abwehr am ersten Tag

Stunde der Entscheidung

A Munich Newspaper, the day after D-Day, announces that the enemy has landed in Northern France in Normandy from Dunkirk to Cherbourg. David Preston

division, the 52nd near Dundee and the 58th in SW Scotland. All the rest, Army and Corps HQ's and two divisions in each Corps, would be represented by wireless. I would have the reserve signallers of the Army to do it, also 2nd Corps HQ was being disbanded and I would have some of their officers and staff to run it; there would also be an American Signal detachment to communicate with the XV Corps and with SHAEF at Norfolk House in St James Square in London. The Germans would be able to plot our various HQ within an accuracy of 5 miles and could tell the type of HQ by the signals from the sets being used. The dispositions of the troops was left to me, and I could ask Scottish Command for anything I wanted.

I was given a paper showing periods, with dates, of normal wireless activity, intense activity, and of silence. Operators were to be seldom changed because the Germans would note the 'characteristics' of each. Some time after 'D' day the Army would want its reserve signallers back.

I was to open on 17 March. As it was now 4 March it did not give me much time to make plans and have everything organised and arranged.

I was told that the 'bluff' was not likely to last more than 3 months because by then the Germans were bound to suspect there was something phoney about it, and that would be long enough to cover the landings. I was to take the utmost care that no mistake or indiscretion was made which would give the game away and wreck the deception. Only the very minimum of people were to know about the operation.

Knowing Scotland well I then made a provisional plan, and next day went to SHAEF at Norfolk House and discussed it. They told me that the picture would be strengthened by the use of agents, and I might get the Navy and the RAF to co-operate with me. While I was active in Scotland, 21st Army Group and the Americans in England would be comparatively silent.

I travelled to Scotland that night and reported to HQ Scottish Command next morning. Only the GOC, Gen. Thorne, and the BGGS were in the know. I asked for the old Command HQ, Riccarton House, 5 miles SW of Edinburgh, to be allotted me for Army HQ Signals. I was given a house in Edinburgh to work in, and houses and quarters in the country for Corps and Divisional HQs.

About 20 officers now arrived from the disbanded 2nd Corps HQ, including three 'G' Majors and an 'A & Q' Major. The remainder were in about the same proportion, and Capt. Ingersoll, liaison officer from the XV American Corps, came over. Gen. Thorne also gave me Lieut-Col Horn as 2nd in Command.

All officers were to act as if they were actually the people they represented; Major Rumsey as Commander of 2nd Corps and Major Bowles as Commander of 7th Corps.

52nd Division was training in mountain warfare and had some Mountain Artillery and two companies of pack mules with Indian drivers, which would help in putting the deception over.

Three types of messages were to go out:

(i) Operational (ii) Training (iii) Routine and administrative

All messages, whether operational, training or routine and administrative, would be within the framework of an outline plan for the invasion of Norway. Fortunately I had been Military Assistant to General Ironside, the CIGS, when he was making plans for the invasion of Norway in 1940, so I knew something of what was involved. My appreciation was as follows:

Object of Fourth Army

To seize and occupy Southern Norway with ultimate objective the capture of Oslo which is the German port of entry and from which railways and roads diverge to all parts of Southern Norway.

Considerations:

Our strength and that of the Germans are equal – 9 Divisions each. In order to gain success in Southern Norway it will be necessary to divert forces from there to protect a vital locality in the North. Fortunately there is such a place – the Gallivare iron-ore fields in North Sweden which are essential to the German war economy.

I then had a meeting of everybody at Riccarton House and explained that we were on a very secret operation which was to cover a landing in France. They were not to breathe a word about it for the success of the landing would depend on complete secrecy. They were bound to be asked what they were doing, and were to reply that they were training the reserve signallers of the British Army.

Scottish Command put their security police to check on this especially in pubs and restaurants, and there was not a word of leakage which I think is rather wonderful.

Our date of opening was now postponed to 22 March for which I was thankful because there was still a tremendous lot to be done.

Everybody now dispersed to their stations and stacked up messages to open with on our opening date.

In due course we were much encouraged when SHAEF Intelligence told us that the Germans were commenting on some of the exercises, such as 'This seems to be a brigade exercise.'

I asked SHAEF for aeroplanes to make reconnaissances of the Norwegian coast as if we intended invading there and this was done.

I also inserted one or two calculated indiscretions into messages to give the Germans the impression that Norway was the place we were bound for. In one message a reference was made to a mountain battery, and in another to a demand for a return of skiers.

Another move to fox the Germans was declaring the Firth of Forth a Protected Area, that is to say that within 10 miles of it nobody could come into it or leave it without a special pass, and everybody in it was checked for security. Apparently we were going to use it to embark troops, and their obvious destination was Norway.

There are good sandy beaches about Troon so with Combined Operations again we practised landing exercises. We had an HQ ship and sent parties from 52nd, 58th and the wireless divisions ashore to establish beachheads and beach parties with wireless communications and calls for naval bombardments on enemy resistance, and then an advance inland. I was given a DUKW to run about in from the ship to the shore and then across land.

We now had two very encouraging bits of news. SHAEF Intelligence told us that the Germans had sent three more divisions to Norway making a total of 12. These all remained there over D-Day and until the end of the war. And General Eisenhower sent a letter to Gen. Thorne in which he said that our party was worth two army corps to him.

On May 20 during a silent period Fourth Army HQ moved to a large house south of Ayr race course. We were now told to cease threatening Norway and with the other Army of First United States Army Group (FUSAG) to switch our threat over to the Pas de Calais. The Normandy landings were to appear as a feint, and ours, some time later, as the main invasion.

I made out a new plan to land on beaches about Etaples and between Calais and Dunkirk... *Typescript recollections.*

R S PEASE
Government Research Scientist appointed to RAF Bomber Command,
High Wycombe, in relation to navigational issues – 'Operation GLIMMER'

The idea of using aluminium foil dropped from aircraft to simulate ships, I think came from Robert Cockburn. Certainly my first introduction to this was to go along to the boss's office with locked doors, where Cockburn explained his ideas and the operation which they were going to carry out, and why we and me in particular, got involved. The idea was that aircraft would fly in racetrack orbits, and each racetrack would be a bit further forward than the last one, dropping aluminium foil so that a radar station looking at it would suppose that there was a target moving towards them at some five or ten knots, or whatever was the requirement. I think it was eight knots actually, and hopefully would think it was ships. And the reason that I got involved was that invasion forces generally speaking invade at right angles to the coast, so what was needed was a

R S Pease, 1947.

A section from the Top Secret map showing the coordinates, plotted by Pease, along which Bomber Command aircraft were to fly, releasing 'Window' in Operation Glimmer to convince Germans in a radar installation kept free from allied air attack that an allied landing operation was taking place in the Pas de Calais. The coordinate lines cross the French Coast at Boulogne at right angles as an invasion would have done. R S Pease navigational system which made it easy to fly in these eliptical orbits, racetrack orbits, and advance at right angles to the coast in the Pas de Calais. And this could be done with 'G-H' but less easily with 'Gee'. The easy thing to do is to fly on one fixed co-ordinate and make your circles at intervals where you cross the other co-ordinate which can be calculated, and so we were involved, or the thought was that using the 'G-H' Station at a place called High Street, north of Ipswich, and if you drew circles about that it intercepts the Pas de Calais coastline at right angles at Boulogne.

So the aircraft were asked to fly in racetrack orbits. Round a racetrack the wrong side. It was always part of a circle about High Street near Ipswich, and where the points of termination were determined by another co-ordinate, which I think came from Truleighhill in Brighton. And so these lumbering Stirlings of 218 Squadron were selected, their crews having been trained in the use of 'G-H' on mine-laying operations. They were the obvious choice for this operation, and that was what I was asked to do was to calculate the various co-ordinates of which they had to encircle and discuss these with the Navigational Officers at 3 Group and at the squadrons. And we had to have training flights and, to my shame, I can't recall where the training flights took place. There weren't a great many of them because we didn't want anybody to see aircraft flying in racetrack co-ordinates advancing at eight knots in a particular direction, because the pennies might have dropped as to what was going on, but we must have had a training area, and certainly the crew was sent on training, practised this, and my job was to help the crew do this and calculate the co-ordinates for them and I generally did my best to make the operation a success, which meant all sorts of things like flying at a constant speed had to be fairly accurate. Knowing when to turn. We had to know what to do if the navigational equipment broke down, so we had aircraft in reserve that had to be called in if the apparatus broke down. We had actually radar mechanics on the planes to replace equipment if it broke down. In the end the operation, I think, had about a dozen crew on each Stirling, and there were chaps shoving out 'Window' at the right speed and these chaps standing there making sure the navigation was right and it was a very tedious business flying like this for, I suppose, the best part of four and five hours in these elongated racetracks. We were told, or I was told, that underneath these circling aircraft were naval auxiliary boats carrying balloons and playing gramophone records over loud speakers of anchor chains going down, and bosuns cursing and so forth. I remember we had to be careful about the timing, because the Navy's dawn I think was half an hour before sunrise, the RAF dawn is an hour before sunrise.

218 Squadron was at Woolfox Lodge which is an aerodrome, rather an obscure aerodrome, on the Great North Road north of Peterborough. The airfield was on one side of the road and the mess was on the other, and it was a utility airfield. We were all in Nissen huts. I remember standing by watching the chaps take off for this operation while the Flight Commander was cursing the fact that the Americans were also flying that day fouling up his training operation. But yes, my recollection and it is only a recollection, is clearly that on the next morning at the eight o'clock news, the BBC reported that the German radio stations had reported that we had landed in the Pas de Calais, or forces had landed in the Pas de Calais.* So we felt that perhaps the operation had been a success. *Transcript of tape-recorded recollections.*

* *Broadly confirmed by BBC archives; Peter Liddle.*

SIGNALMAN HARRY H PARKER

Royal Corps of Signals, Special High Speed Wireless Section

We were a completely mobile unit. I was one of twelve operators. We had technicians, drivers, even a cook. We had two articulated wireless trucks, a transmitter in one, a receiver in the other which also had perforator machines to punch out the tape for sending messages and an undulator to receive incoming messages. We had an automatic transmitter, which operated at about 100/120 words per minute. We had to erect 72 feet transmitter masts and 48 feet receiver masts for the aerials.

The day before D-Day we were sent to Horsforth on the outskirts of Leeds in Yorkshire from Putney in London. Our task was to transmit 'red herring' wireless traffic to put the Germans off what was about to happen. We set up our transmitter masts in a field opposite a row of houses, the occupants making us welcome with cups of tea. On D-Day morning we pulled down our station and returned to Putney. *Typescript recollections.*

Signalman Harry Parker operating from the wireless transmitter lorry. In fact this was taken in September 1944 with the unit operating from Versailles, transmitting to Bletchley Park, call sign BRAD.

CHAPTER 3

Assembling, Concentration and Eve of the Operation

O ne should not think exclusively of the New Forest and the Hampshire coast and its ports as one envisages the progressive concentration of soldiers and Royal Navy and Merchant Navy shipping ready for the landings in Normandy. Coastal areas and ports in South Devon, Dorset, Sussex, Kent, around the Thames, North into Essex and East Anglia were involved in the holding of troops, guns, tanks and various military vehicles, ammunition, petrol, stores and supplies, marine transportation and warships destined for France.

Such were the numbers involved that dispersal was a necessary element in advance of the concentration required later.

Concealing these forces behind their ports of embarkation was a massive undertaking and in the case of those whose outlet would be the Solent, then the New Forest certainly did offer helpful camouflage.

As the men made their last preparations, enduring the attempt to seal them for security hermetically from the world outside their encampments, weather conditions in the Channel increased their waiting by a day. Some were already embarked, their testing as soldiers postponed but not their capacity as 'sailors in khaki!'

CAPTAIN JULIUS A S NEAVE
Adjutant 13/18 Royal Hussars

On the 1st of June we got our orders to move off to the marshalling area and in perfect weather rumbled down to Portsmouth and moved to our appointed camp.

I very clearly remember this journey on minor roads through the heavily wooded Sussex countryside in early June. I suppose it was only natural in view of what was ahead of us to wonder whether one would ever see England again, and to make the most of it under such rare and quite beautiful conditions. Portsmouth was an incredible sight. All along roads to it and every little suburban street were tanks and assault vehicles, bulldozers and infantry carriers and vehicles of every sort. Every few yards there was a camp and the place was a display of military signs, while loud-speakers blared continuously.

After being in the marshalling camps for two days, we moved down to the hards, to load onto the LCTs. Each craft load was called forward by its serial number, and after an early start we were on board by about 10 o'clock. All this time we had been surprised and quite pleasantly so, that the German Air Force (at this time) paid Portsmouth so little attention. It is true that they did come over the place in twos and drop an occasional bomb but the damage was negligible in spite of a bomb on movement control HQ.

'A' and 'B' Squadrons meanwhile were still living in their own billets, but they were still feverishly working to get their tanks ready: and right up to the moment of loading onto their craft they were still hard at it. The Signal Officer Stuart Watson was also involved in the hectic last-minute rush in organising the 101 sets and nets that were required for the assault. The communications were immensely complicated and for security reasons all netting had to be done by wavemeter. This meant a personal visit, since there was only the one to each set and these were distributed between Tilbury, London and Aldershot, Portsmouth and Gosport, and indeed some of the sets were already at sea. The Technical Adjutant, Tony Lyon Clark, was also dashing at increasing speed between Ordnance depots and manufacturers in frenzied attempts to collect the spares and parts that we should otherwise have had to go without.

At last we were all on board and then there was nothing that we could do till the order to 'Go' was given. This would be the signal to undo the top-secret packages containing operation orders and maps and then we should really be able to see where we were going and what it was all about.

Briefing – which had been done with bogus maps and bogus names – did no more than give the details and information as to the lie of the land. Only those on the 'X' list knew our real destination. *Privately published recollections.*

LIEUTENANT ARTHUR H OATES
2nd Battalion, East Yorks Regiment

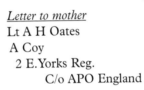

Letter to mother
Lt A H Oates
A Coy
2 E.Yorks Reg.
    C/o APO England

5.6.44

    Dear Mater,
      Just to let you know that I'm fit and well although up to my ears in work – it's not intended to be a proper reply to your last letter – I'll need more time for that, but don't worry I'll manage it some time soon.
    Lots of love
      to you all,
    Arthur

Arthur H Oates.

1ST LIEUTENANT HAROLD AKRIDGE
Anti-Tank Platoon of HQ Company,
1st Battalion, 8th Regiment, 4th Infantry Division, US Army

Just prior to D-Day General Eisenhower wanted to see and talk to the men who were to lead the attack on France. Our unit was assembled on a parade ground early to wait. The rumor was out that some high brass was coming. Finally a jeep drove up and we saw a passenger, who was Ike. Driving up to the center of our group, Ike got out, climbed up on the hood, yelled, 'Break ranks and gather round.' I was pressed up against the jeep and Ike gave a typical speech, short and peppy. As he drove off he yelled, 'Remember, when we get to Berlin, I'm buying the champagne!'

Typescript recollections, The Eisenhower Center for American Studies at the University of New Orleans and The National D-Day Museum, New Orleans, USA.

Officers from the U.S. 101st Airborne Division HQ at Greenham Common, Berkshire, 5 June 1944.
Lieutenant-Colonel N R Hoskot is on the extreme left.

PTE CLIFFORD R SORENSON

L Company, 3rd Battalion, 12th Regiment, 4th Motorized Division, US Army

About five days before D-Day they sent us to an embarking area. You couldn't get out of it and it's all hush hush, near Plymouth. They tried to entertain us for the time we were there. The Glen Miller Band came in and played for us, and the Artie Shaw Band but Artie Shaw wasn't with them. It was under the direction of Sam or Al Donahue.

Typescript recollections, The Eisenhower Center for American Studies at the University of New Orleans and The National D-Day Museum, New Orleans USA.

MAJOR T S BIGLAND RA

General Montgomery's Liaison Officer with General Bradley's US Army Group

Another Liaison Officer, Bill Bradford, and I had discussed with our own HQs and with General Bradley whether we should cross the Channel with him in the cruiser *Augusta* or on the 1st Army HQ ship and we all decided on the latter, as Bradley would also be there for much of the time and there were better communications. I was ordered to report next day, 1 June, at 3pm at Pier No 4 in Plymouth to board *MS Ashenower*. After a final conference

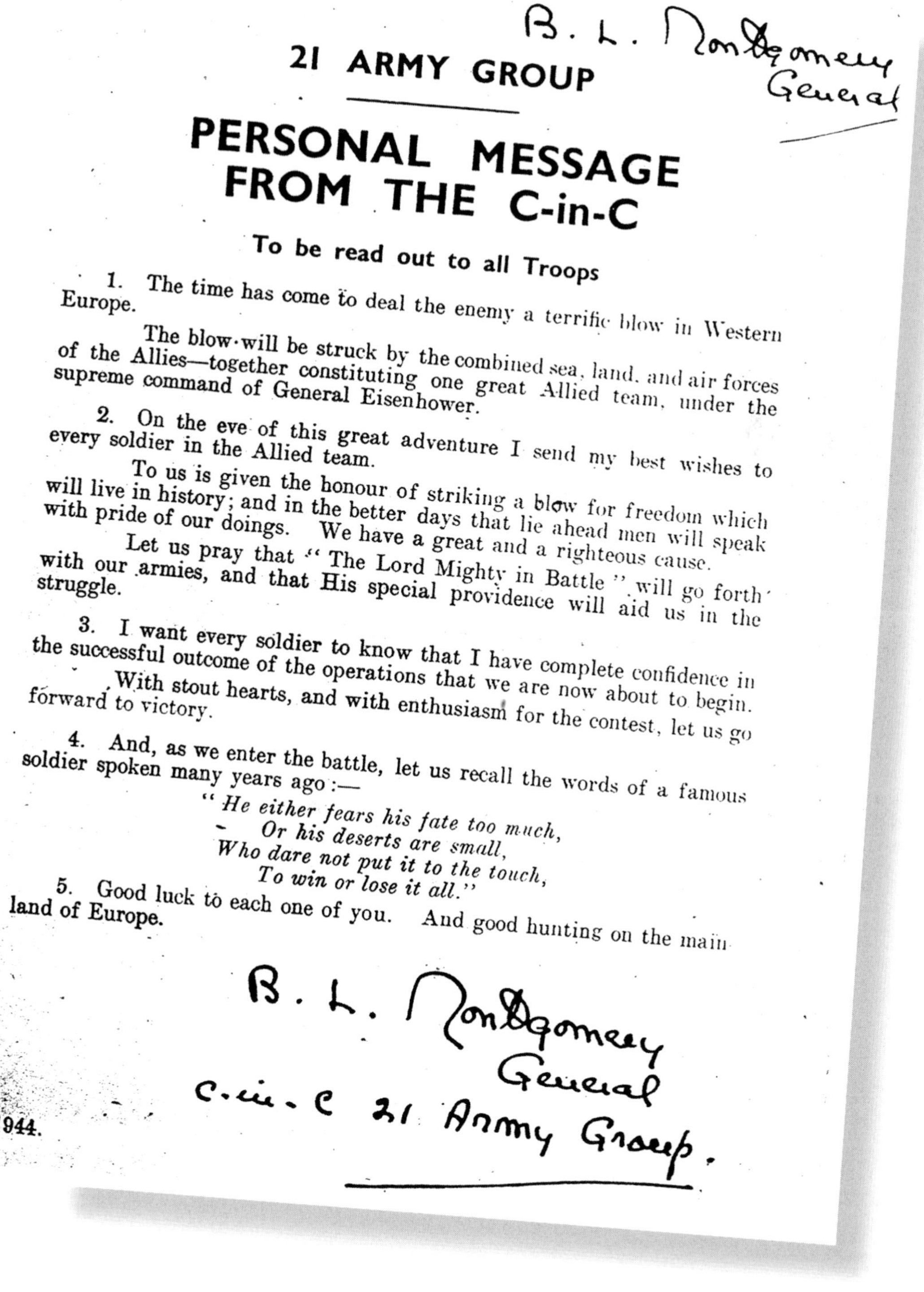

21 ARMY GROUP

B. L. Montgomery
General

PERSONAL MESSAGE
FROM THE C-in-C

To be read out to all Troops

1. The time has come to deal the enemy a terrific blow in Western Europe.

The blow will be struck by the combined sea, land, and air forces of the Allies—together constituting one great Allied team, under the supreme command of General Eisenhower.

2. On the eve of this great adventure I send my best wishes to every soldier in the Allied team.

To us is given the honour of striking a blow for freedom which will live in history; and in the better days that lie ahead men will speak with pride of our doings. We have a great and a righteous cause.

Let us pray that " The Lord Mighty in Battle " will go forth with our armies, and that His special providence will aid us in the struggle.

3. I want every soldier to know that I have complete confidence in the successful outcome of the operations that we are now about to begin.

With stout hearts, and with enthusiasm for the contest, let us go forward to victory.

4. And, as we enter the battle, let us recall the words of a famous soldier spoken many years ago :—

" He either fears his fate too much,
Or his deserts are small,
Who dare not put it to the touch,
To win or lose it all."

5. Good luck to each one of you. And good hunting on the main land of Europe.

B. L. Montgomery
General
C.-in-C 21 Army Group.

1944.

General Bernard L Montgomery's message to the troops.

45

Officers of No 2 Field Dressing Unit, RAMC, in their New Forest, Hampshire, tented camp at Chandlers Ford during exercises, 25/5/44, not long before this unit embarked. From left to right, Lieutenant J Dixon, Captain W Cormack, Captain I D Campbell, Major D F Hutchinson, Captain A L Blair, Captain R Droop, Lieutenant E Horton. I D Campbell

7th Heavy Recovery Unit moves out of the New Forest to embark on 'Landing Craft Tanks'. A H Barnes

The 7th Heavy Recovery Unit's cooks prepare to serve up. A H Barnes

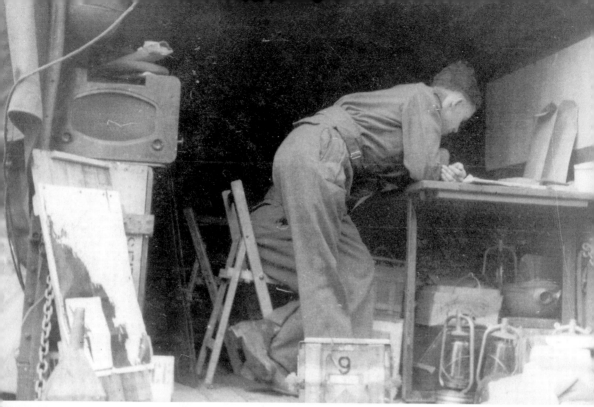

Office work for a HeavyVehicle Recovery Unit in the New Forest getting ready for D-Day. A H Barnes

at Army Group Tac HQ, I had a last night out in London before a very early start for Plymouth.

I had not allowed for the very heavy traffic of troops moving to the Channel ports to embark and reached Pier No 4 with only five minutes to spare. There was no sign of 1st Army or of any Americans and security was so tight that I had to go to the Port Commander, an Admiral out of retirement, before I dared ask about General Bradley. He said no one ever told him anything, but gave me the use of his barge to look for *MS Ashenower* which was the first ship we went to. I had foreseen being courtmartialled and was most relieved. To keep the embarkation as secret as possible, they had decided to have an alarm call at 3 am and all had embarked by 8 am. I had been forgotten. Neither Bill Bradford or I had been catered for. We had no seat in the Ops Room and we shared a 4-berth cabin with two full Colonels and a Lt-Colonel, I sleeping on a camp bed.

Typescript recollections.

Captain Alan H Barnes, in command, 7th Heavy Recovery Unit, REME.

CAPTAIN PETER L de C MARTIN

'A' Company Commander,
2nd Battalion Cheshire Regiment, 151 Brigade

About the third of June we marched down to Southampton Docks. We had practices on marching down to Southampton Docks from our concentration area before the Hayling Island exercise, and we had been subject to a lot of ribald shouting from the natives of Southampton. 'Come on lads, get cracking', and things like that, and all with very good natured banter, but it was odd that on this occasion when we were going down for real there were a lot of people about but they were absolutely silent. They must have realised this must be it, or perhaps they saw it in our faces.

So we arrived down at Southampton docks on the third and we went aboard our little LCI, which was very cramped of course, and we were due to sail on the night of the fourth for D-Day on June 5 and I wrote a letter to my sister, elder sister Peggy, on June fourth saying 'I have absolutely nothing, no news to report of any sort whatsoever'. I intended that letter would be posted that day because they were coming round collecting the mail a number of times, and she, hopefully, would have got it on the 5th June at the same time as hearing the news that we had landed. And I admit that it was just a sort of childish idea to give me a sort of little kick, but, the weather stopped us leaving and, in fact, I took that letter to my sister with me across the Channel rather than posting it and spoiling the effect. I posted it to her later, from Normandy. *Transcript of tape-recorded recollections.*

MAJOR ROBIN DUNN

in command 16th Field Battery,
7th Field Regiment RA

The invasion was postponed for twenty-four hours, and so we sat in our landing craft in Portsmouth harbour for the whole day watching the WRNS boatmen. They had these boats running about in the harbour and they were manned by WRNS and there were two WRNS, one on the tiller and one standing up in the front – in the bow – with a boat hook like that, held horizontally above her head showing off her figure, and, of course, the soldiers were absolutely entranced by this, and you can imagine the kind of remarks and wolf whistles which went over the water. So we were able to keep them more or less interested during that day. And we set off in the evening and we went down to Spithead. The whole Regiment was embarked in six landing craft. There was a troop in each landing craft.
Transcript of tape-recorded recollections.

D C HOLDSWORTH

a young boy in Gosport

The Hardway at Gosport was a big embarkation point where large landing craft pulled up to load on lorries and tanks. Convoys of lorries and tanks converged on the Hardway in their hundreds via all the roads in our area and this caused a major disaster for me. Tanks travelled down my road, Bramble Road, two abreast, the outer track of each tank ran along the pavement and cracked every paving stone and sank them into the ground. It completely messed up our roller skate runs.

My second disaster was more serious: I was following a convoy of American lorries, picked up a thrown-away American petrol can with its star and US Army on it. It was a

1944, Derek Holdsworth with his mother at home in Gosport, Hampshire.

treasure trove in our hobby of collecting war souvenirs. It was left near a gas boiler (for clothes washing). When I opened the lid of the jerry can the petrol fumes caught on fire like a flame thrower straight into my face. Prompt action by a neighbouring nurse wrapped a wet towel round my face and head. An ambulance took me to hospital where I spent a week but I only suffered singed hair, eyebrows and eye lashes. *Manuscript recollectons.*

ROYAL MARINE CORPORAL JACK BEST
Gunner's Mate aboard a Block Ship

Twenty-five of us were taken by truck to a restricted area near Cardiff and put aboard a large merchant ship, on its side was painted a large number '1'. It had four anti-aircraft guns mounted forward and four aft. We were taken to a mess deck where a Naval Lieutenant was waiting to address us. He explained that we were now aboard a 'Block Ship' and that no-one would be allowed off the ship under any circumstances. All water-tight doors had been removed and the ship was rigged to explode when a plunger was operated on the bridge. At this point, the explosion would blow out the bottom of the ship, which would then sink to the ocean floor in a predetermined position to start an artificial harbour. There was a Merchant Navy Captain plus a Chief Engineer and a skeleton Merchant Navy crew. The ship was more or less a sailing hulk but two ship's boats had been left for our use when the time came for us to leave the ship just before she was blown. A Naval officer would be put aboard later and he would be in charge, until then we were under the orders of the Captain.

We would sail the following day around England and Scotland and our arrival at the embarkation point for the invasion had to be spot on. Our job was to protect the ship from aircraft; one near miss we were told would be enough to fire the charges. When we got to Methil in Scotland the Captain had to go ashore to check our orders had not changed and so the bloke in charge of the Merchant Navy men decided we would have a dummy run at leaving the ship. The correct procedure should have been that we all took our places in our respective boats, which would then be lowered by people on deck. The drawback to this, of course, was that there would be no one left on deck to perform this vital operation. After struggling with the lowering gear for about 3/4 of an hour, the crew managed to get the boats lowered and down went a rope ladder. It was a hell of a drop but we had no choice, we all took our places in our respective boats and did our imitation of Captain Bligh being cast adrift and that was when the trouble started. We hooked onto the falls and climbed up our rope ladder to the deck, the other lot were up before us and were trying to get their boat back on board, eventually they succeeded and started to retrieve ours, but no such luck. The crew couldn't get the lifting gear to work and in the end took an axe and cut the ropes.

[Our already strained relationship with the Merchant seamen was worsened.]

The Captain came to see us regarding the lost boat and said we would all have to manage with the one boat and that we could get forty men in at a pinch. He added that the boat would have to lay off away from the ship and pick the Naval Officer up after he'd blown the charges, also that other block ships were following us round the coast but had to be kept apart for safety's sake. We dawdled along. Relations aboard were slowly improving as the crew realised our job was to try and keep us all safe. *Typescript recollections.*

CORPORAL GEOFF STEER

'B' Company 1/4 King's Own Yorkshire Light Infantry

[After hard training on the Isle of Bute and then Lowestoft] where we did the river crossing, fast route marches, digging in and sleeping in trenches, on the 5th of June 1944 we signed for 200 francs, then we knew where we were going. This we received in transit camp. We said our goodbyes to our friends in Lowestoft, they turned out to see us off and we knew in our hearts this would be the last journey some of us would make in our native land. But we had our own silent thoughts and the spirit of comradeship was first class. We were about to embark on what is now history and I am proud to have been part of it and to have served with gallant men who did not return home.

The marshalling area was behind a Polish fighter aerodrome in a wood, under canvas. We passed the time away playing cards or listening to the wireless. Some of the lads had their hair shaved off to ward off lice. Shaving the head was a good idea but after we had been in action a few weeks some of them got wounded and were flown home, so the first thing they had to buy was a flat cap.

Orders came to move out and we made our way to Newhaven Dock where we boarded our LCT. We spent four or five hours on board waiting for the tide, then we were away at about 11pm. *Typescript recollections.*

GEFREITER FRANZ GOCKEL

3rd Company, 726 Regiment, 716 Division, *Wehrmacht*, at a machine-gun post in defence of emplacement WN 62, Colleville sur Mer, Omaha Beach

Letter: Sunday 21 May 1944.

Dear Parents, Brothers and Sisters

Your son and brother Franz wishes you a most happy Whitsun. I hope you're spending it in better health and undisturbed by 'Tommy'.

Today we were christened here by the bombs. Exactly at twelve the first planes came over. 'Tommy' obviously wanted to salt our lunch. First there were five low flying aircraft, but they left us undisturbed.

I was first in the kitchen, which is downstairs in the house, sharing out the milk I'd fetched that morning. We had a low-lying layer of cloud and then it was very stormy, so that we could hardly hear the planes. We were never aware until the window panes blew in on us that two bombs had fallen some fifty metres from the house. Immediately we ran out , wanting to get to the cover of the tanks, but we were hardly out of the door when there was another explosion. The blast blew the cook, the Frenchwoman and me back into the kitchen. Several sizeable lumps of earth flew through the door and window into the kitchen. Then it was just a question of going all out to get to the tank trenches and then it was over. Altogether ten bombs fell about fifty metres from the house. It's a good job we already live in the bunker otherwise by now we'd be sleeping in a house with no windows. We'd all been really lucky – and you do need luck here. It was the first visit we'd had from 'Tommy' in a long time and this time 'Tommy' had paid us a really good one. How are you anyway? Still lots of air raid alerts?

What are Heinrich and Hubertus doing all day long – still going to Kindergarten or staying at home because of so many alerts?

By now I expect that Tom is certainly on holiday. Where is dad now?

As ever John (name used with parents) and brother Franz.

SUPREME HEADQUARTERS
ALLIED EXPEDITIONARY FORCE

Soldiers, Sailors and Airmen of the Allied Expeditionary Force!

You are about to embark upon the Great Crusade, toward which we have striven these many months. The eyes of the world are upon you. The hopes and prayers of liberty-loving people everywhere march with you. In company with our brave Allies and brothers-in-arms on other Fronts, you will bring about the destruction of the German war machine, the elimination of Nazi tyranny over the oppressed peoples of Europe, and security for ourselves in a free world.

Your task will not be an easy one. Your enemy is well trained, well equipped and battle-hardened. He will fight savagely.

But this is the year 1944! Much has happened since the Nazi triumphs of 1940-41. The United Nations have inflicted upon the Germans great defeats, in open battle, man-to-man. Our air offensive has seriously reduced their strength in the air and their capacity to wage war on the ground. Our Home Fronts have given us an overwhelming superiority in weapons and munitions of war, and placed at our disposal great reserves of trained fighting men. The tide has turned! The free men of the world are marching together to Victory!

I have full confidence in your courage, devotion to duty and skill in battle. We will accept nothing less than full Victory!

Good Luck! And let us all beseech the blessing of Almighty God upon this great and noble undertaking.

Dwight D Eisenhower

'nothing less than full Victory!' The Supreme Commander's eve of operation exhortation. J M Parker

53

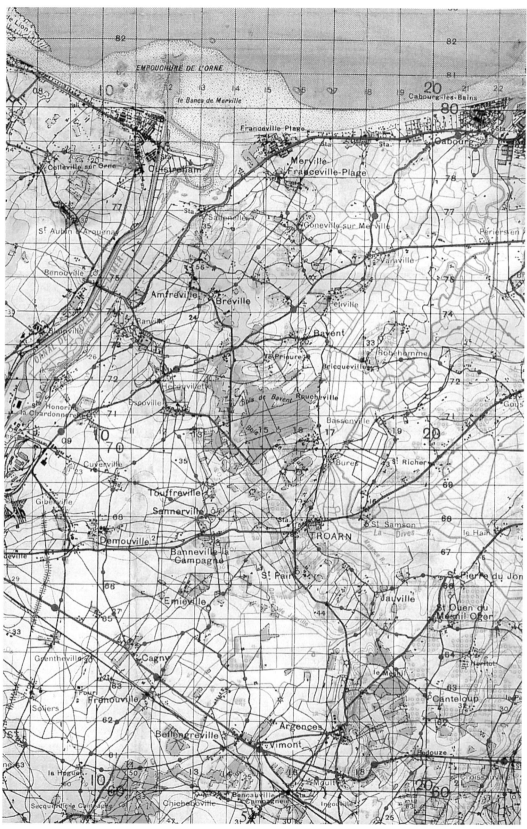

Map issued to officers of the British 6th Airborne Division.

CHAPTER 4

The Airborne Assault

The airborne element in the Normandy landings was recognised as being of critical importance in preventing German concentration on sweeping the invaders from the beaches and in helping isolate coastal defence from counter-attack routes from the rear. The interdiction of reinforcement from the eastern and western limits of the intended landings and then, if fortune favoured the Allies, the hampering of German retirement before the invaders, were potentially the prize. There were however poor precedents in the use of this method of attack. Over Crete in May 1941 many German paratroopers had been killed or disabled by ground-fire as they descended and, in the sea off Sicily in July 1943, many American glider-borne troops had been drowned because of precipitate release of gliders from their towing aircraft. Would the grander scale of the Normandy drop lead to a relatedly large scale of casualties?

There were obvious problems of possible wide dispersal of the paratroopers and the gliders from their rendezvous points close to their objectives. Wind, weather, darkness, would affect navigational accuracy. Flak and, just possibly, air to air opposition also needed to be taken into consideration with the photographed evidence too of systematically erected poles on potential landing areas and the deliberate flooding of low-lying ground further impediments to success.

Troops would need immediately to hand, glider-carried vehicles including light tanks, mobile artillery and other weapons with necessary petrol and ammunition supplies. The biggest glider employed, the British Hamilcar with a wingspan of 110 feet, could carry forty fully-equipped troops, or two scout cars, or a 25-pounder gun and a tractor or a Tetrach Mark IV tank and crew. The Hamilcar had two pilots; the smaller Horsa (also British), with a pilot and co-pilot, could also carry vehicles, two jeeps or a jeep and a 75mm howitzer with ammunition and crew. For its troop-carrying role it took twenty-eight fully-armed men. The American Waco gliders were smaller with a capacity to carry thirteen soldiers or a jeep and its driver or the howitzer mentioned above.

The American 82nd and 101st Airborne Divisions were to be dropped behind Utah Beach at the South Eastern base of the Cotentin Peninsula. They would be up against serious difficulty, the deliberate flooding of the rivers Draves and Merderet, the prolific 'sowing' of anti-invasion poles against gliders and the fact that the flight avoiding the anti-aircraft defences of Cherbourg allowed but four minutes for the dropping of gliders and men on a restricted zone. Wide dispersal as the melancholy possibility was matched by another, drowning in the sea or in the flooded areas. The 82nd, to drop over Ste. Mère Eglise capturing the town and its crossroads, had suffered from dispersal severely over Sicily in July 1943.

The 101st, to land around Carentan, capturing together with securing the landward exits from causeways connecting Utah Beach with dry land inland, and the bridges over the River Douvres, was comprised of troops seeing action for the first time. In all, thirteen and a half thousand men were to drop or be glider-landed from 0100 hrs on 6 June. In the event there was wide dispersal in the dropping, with poor visibility, high winds and anti-aircraft fire contributing to the confusion. In this confusion individuals and small groups rather than units, fought with determination to reach the rendezvous points and take objectives. Important objectives were to lie uncaptured, Carentan and its bridges in particular, but confusion reigned among the defenders too and distracted as the defenders were, Americans got ashore at Utah more economically than upon any of the beaches on 6 June.

The British 6th Airborne Division (which included Canadian troops) had a glider unit, the 6th Airlanding Brigade. It was from this unit that six gliders left their Salisbury Plain base before midnight on 5/6 June with the *coup de main* role of securing a bridge over the Caen Canal and one over the River Orne at Bénouville. This first action of D-Day was carried out faultlessly. There were two other objectives to be carried; taking Ranville and the destruction of bridges over the River Dives from which counter-attack could be expected and, second, to knock out the guns of the Merville Battery at Franceville Plage as they commanded the beachhead to the West and potentially could bring devastating fire upon the landings. As with the Americans, high winds, the difficulty of night orientation, the deliberate flooding and the anti-invasion poles, made for great difficulty. The dispersal was severe, for example the six feet of concrete-encased Merville Battery had to be tackled by far fewer men, far less well-equipped than had been planned. Reinforcements and equipment in the late afternoon helped to secure what had been won and held with the support of units which had forced their way inland from Sword Beach to establish a link from shore to Airborne objectives. The 6th Airborne Division had suffered in taking its objectives but all had been taken.

RIFLEMAN AND FIRST SCOUT IRWIN 'TURK' SEELYE

E Company, 505 Parachute Infantry Regiment, 82nd Airborne Division, US Army

We spent a couple of days and nights living in barracks close to the landing strip at Cottesmore, near Grantham. We spent the time here getting our equipment ready for the next mission, playing cards, trying to figure out where the mission would take us, sharpening knives and bayonets and, in general, having feelings of apprehension of what was to happen next. On the 3rd or 4th June, we were billeted in the airport hanger. We took our meals at an Air Force mess hall. Our beds were blankets spread on the concrete floor. We were issued with grenades, ammunition and other supplies that we would carry with us when we jumped into combat. The weather at this time was unsettled, cloudy, with some rain showers.

Briefing consisted of studying maps and using sand tables as well as showing each unit the scope of their particular mission. It was at this time we learned the invasion would take place in Normandy.

My squad, the second squad of the third platoon, Company E, 505th Parachute Infantry, after assembling and getting the equipment from the equipment bundles that were dropped at the time my squad left the aircraft was to move off the drop zone and set up a road block near the village of Ste. Mère Eglise. Other activities at the airport included shooting craps and playing poker, using the French invasion currency issued each soldier, watching a movie in the evening and attending religious services. Chaplains George Wood and Father Matt Connelly reported that attendance at these services was greater than usual.

Due to bad weather, the Supreme Commander, General Eisenhower cancelled the 5

June invasion. On the evening of 5 June, the invasion was on. The paratroopers were ready. We walked to the aircraft loaded with the equipment and supplies we would carry on our person into battle. The C-47 Aircraft were decorated with three bands of white paint. These were bands of white paint around the fuselage and each wing. This was the distinctive marking of allied planes. At each plane were the equipment bundles that would carry the materials that would be dropped at the time the paratroopers exited the aircraft.

Included in the bundles were 30 caliber machine guns, spare parts, 60mm mortars, rifle and machine gun ammunition, plastic water bags filled with water, type K and type C rations, hand grenades, etc. Also with each plane were the parachutes. A main parachute and a reserve chute for each trooper. Before putting on our parachutes, we attached the equipment bundles to the underside of the C-47 Aircraft. The order to chute up came just as darkness was settling on the airfield. This was about 10 p.m. British double summer time. Each man selected a chute that had been carefully packed by the riggers and began the task of getting into the parachutes and buckling the chutes and equipment in place. Squad members helped one another with this task, as it is almost impossible to do this alone. The many pockets in the uniform, the jump suit, which was gas impregnated, were filled, as was the canvas pack called a musette bag that each man carried on his back once he hit the ground. Materials carried by each trooper amounted to about 150 pounds. These included the following items:

These are the items that I carried on my person: an M-1 rifle and carrying case, four K-rations, 150 rounds of 30 caliber ammunition, four hand grenades, one anti-tank grenade called a jammon grenade, a gas mask, a handkerchief, two pairs of socks, one pair of undershorts, a canteen filled with water, two first aid kits, tooth brush and tooth powder, safety razor with five blades, one bar of soap, a wristwatch, identification – dog tags taped together, ten packs of Camel cigarettes, a billfold with invasion currency, an entrenching tool – a pick mattock, musette bag with cartridge belt, steel helmet, a switch blade pocket knife, one trench knife, twenty four sheets of toilet paper, pencil and paper, a French phrase book, Halazone tablets used to purify water, matches, and cigarette lighter and bayonet.

At about twenty two fifty hours, I climbed up the boarding ladder into the C-47 aircraft. The name carried on the nose of this plane was 'Miss Carriage'. No sooner had I sat on the aluminium bucket seated benches than I had to urinate. There were no latrines on these flying boxcars as they were often called. This meant getting up and being helped down the boarding ladder and under the wing of the plane to relieve myself. This is not an easy task when one is all bundled up in parachute straps and equipment. This 'nervous pee' syndrome was shared by almost all of the members of the squad. There was a steady stream of troopers going up and down the boarding ladder.

There was little to no talking as the noise of the motors was deafening. I was trying to visualise what it would be like once we hit the coast. Would it be like the night jump into Sicily? Would I make it out of the door okay? Would I be shot down as I floated to earth? Would my chute open?

As we neared the Normandy coast the jump master, seeing the red warning light, issued the order to stand up and hook up. At this point each trooper attached his own parachute static line to the steel cable that ran the length of the plane. When one jumped out the door of the aircraft, the static line would pull the parachute from the backpack causing it to be exposed to the propeller blast of the aircraft and open properly. The next order was shouted by the jump master. 'Sound off for equipment check'. Each trooper in line would sound out his number indicating that he had manually checked, that is, felt with his hands, the static line and other equipment of the man standing directly in front of him. I shouted 'Number 6, okay'.

At this point the jumpmaster was standing in the door of the aircraft, with his eyes glued to the red light that would soon turn green. At that point, he would shout 'Go!' and leave the aircraft. The other fifteen men would follow him as fast as possible. The speed of the aircraft was the cruising speed of about 150 mph. I could see little standing in the aisle of the plane, but trying to look out the very small windows. I did see some tracer bullets pass by and also saw what appeared to be a burning plane on the ground.

As the plane neared the drop zone, the pilot flashed the green light and the stick with 16 troopers made a speedy exit. Everyone had left the plane in less than 30 seconds. The pilot of the plane, no doubt anxious to return to the safety and comfort of his home base in England failed to reduce the speed of the aircraft as the green light 'go' signal was given. The normal exit is 90 mph. Just as I left the door, the plane nosed downward. Prior to my chute's opening, I watched the tail of the plane pass a few feet over my head. Then, as the prop blast forced air into my chute, I got the strongest opening shock ever. The high speed caused the chute to open with a violent jerk. The sudden jolt caused a 765 mm Biretta pistol taken from an Italian Naval Officer in Sicily to be torn loose from my body, as well as a new Gillette safety razor that was shaken from one of the pockets in my jump suit. The time of my exit was about 0145 hours. 1:45a.m. This is D minus five hours on D-Day, 6 June, 1944. Since it took a very short time to reach the ground, certainly no more than 30 seconds, I would estimate the altitude of the plane at the time of the jump was no more than 325 feet. Very low.

As I hit the ground, I was shaken up a bit, but even though nervous and scared, I immediately did the following. I rolled up the parachute and put it under some bushes along with the reserve chute. Then I put together the three pieces of my Garand M-1 rifle. The trigger assembly, the barrel and the stock. Next I put into the chamber of the rifle a clip of ammunition. And I fixed the bayonet. This was done in total darkness. In the darkness I could hear automatic weapons being fired and saw some tracer and some anti-aircraft bullets heading skyward.

The first human sound I heard upon reaching the ground was a cry for help from a squad member. Two others from the squad also heard the voice and found our friend Maryland J Golden, of Tallahassee, Alabama lying on the ground unable to move. His left leg was broken. He was given a shot of morphine and carried to the protection of a hedgerow to await the arrival of the battalion medics.

I now walked about in darkness seeking other Americans. I had landed on a French farm and now I was walking in the farmyard. Somehow I got separated from the two members of my squad that had helped the injured man. Now I was alone. I used my 'cricket'. This device was given to all members of the invasion force so that when used it would identify one as a Yank, an American soldier.

I happened to run across three Yanks from another airborne unit. We moved about the area in the darkness looking for other Americans and trying to avoid contact with the enemy. We saw none of either. In the distance we could hear sounds of war. We encountered no contact with the enemy, and none of us fired our weapons. At dawn, we came across several Americans who seemed to know what was going on. We joined with them and walked the two or three miles southward to the village of Ste. Mère Eglise. The company area was an open field about the size of a football field, located at the north edge of the village. At the south and east edge was a deep trench. This trench was like those dug in France in the First World War. It apparently had been dug and used by the Germans. A hedgerow bordered the north edge of the field.

The day was spent setting up a perimeter defense around the field. Outposts were set up beyond the perimeter. Two light machine guns were placed with fields of fire to the east and west. I spent the time with members of my rifle squad waiting for something to happen. During this day, there was no enemy activity at this spot. We dined on K-rations and I attempted to get some sleep on the ground very close to the deep trench. A Frenchman, obviously very sympathetic to the Allied cause, brought us several bottles of an alcoholic drink called Calvados. I drank a cup of this rather tasty beverage and after draining my canteen of water, filled it with the fluid. Moments later, the platoon leader, Lt. Ted Peterson, having seen me fill the canteen ordered me to pour it out. Reluctantly, I did this, although I did not share the officer's belief that the wine could be poisoned or that it could be hazardous to my health.

During this day there was much air activity. Fighter planes, P-51s and bombers were visible all day long. In the afternoon I watched three C-47 aircraft, loaded with supplies, fly over our position to drop parachutes carrying supplies into the hands of waiting Germans. The pilot got the wrong drop zones.

Later in the afternoon, I assisted in placing anti tank mines on the road alongside the western boundary of the company area. These mines were set on the road in a random fashion as a deterrent to enemy vehicles.

As darkness approached, I rolled up in a parachute and went to sleep. *Typescript recollections, The Eisenhower Center for American Studies at The University of New Orleans and The National D-Day Museum, New Orleans, USA.*

PRIVATE 1ST CLASS, JOSEPH A DAHLIA
'E' Company, 2nd Battalion 507th Parachute Regiment,
82nd Airborne Division, US Army

We jumped. We were scattered all over the countryside. Our full platoon did not assemble. My jump was good. I landed in a cow pasture in a pile of manure. As I was coming down I could see some movement on the ground. For one moment I thought they were all Germans, but to my surprise, no Germans. Just cows.

The first buddy I came across was Sergeant Johnson. He almost shot me as I didn't respond fast enough. We assembled about eight men. Sergeant Carlquist, Sergeant Johnson, Dupuy Pauxtis, Hassel Jones, Demidio and myself. Late that afternoon I was wounded by a sniper's bullet. The bullet ricocheted off my rifle into my left hand, shooting the bayonet and the gas chamber off the rifle. I was moving up fast from hedgerow to hedgerow. My buddies all froze. But Private First Class Demidio from New Jersey administered first aid as the blood was all over. I think it severed an artery.

My weapon was out of commission. I was no help to them. So they left me. All I had was a knife and four grenades. After they were gone I managed to get to a French farmhouse where the people took care of me. But it wasn't long when two Germans came to the farmhouse looking for food. They found me and took me prisoner. They transported me by horse and buggy to a town about 11km from the farmhouse and then to a German aid station that was set up in a Catholic monastery where I was operated on by a German doctor who amputated my left index finger and sewed my thumb back on and removed the metacarpal bone. The French doctor spoke English. He said 'Are you an American?' I turned my right shoulder and showed him the American flag that was sewn on my sleeve. The doctor told me he received part of his medical training at the University of Chicago and he was a guest of the late Cardinal Mundelion.

After the operation I found myself in a room with six other wounded Americans. *Typescript recollections, The Eisenhower Center for American Studies at The University of New Orleans and the National D-Day Museum, New Orleans, USA*

LIEUTENANT JACK ISAACS

Platoon Leader, G Coy 3rd Battalion. 505 Parachute Infantry,
82nd Airborne Division, US Army, trying to reach Ste. Mère Eglise.

Unfortunately as we approached the coast, we hit a rather dense fog bank forcing some evasive action on the part of the pilots in order that they didn't run into other planes. I knew that my flight of three planes was veering to the left or the north, and that I would probably be off target. This was to be my 3rd combat jump, and it was my 28th parachute jump. Breaking free of the fog, some maybe 3 or 4 miles inland, I saw no other planes. There were a few floating clouds. There was a goodly amount of German anti-aircraft fire both light machine gun, 20 millimetre, some 88 I'm sure, high explosive stuff. Whether you looked north or south or east or west, you could see plenty of anti-aircraft fire. I didn't feel that my own plane was being fired upon directly, and I know that we weren't hit. The red light came on at approximately the right time for the drop, and when the green light came on, seeing that I was over land and it made no difference where I was over land, it was my duty to take that stick of 18 jumpers out, and this I did upon receiving the green light from the pilot.

I could see as I approached the ground in the dark that I was coming into a fairly good size field for Normandy, approximately 150 x 250 yards. All of the sides had hedgerows. I could see that there were cows in the field as I came down, and that was reassuring because if there were cows in the fields, certainly there would be no mines in that field.

I landed without event, and getting out of my equipment, of course set out to roll up the stick and find my men, any men that I could, and take command of them and move to our objective. I found one man immediately. I didn't know him, which indicated there were probably other planes in the area but I just had not seen them. Shortly after finding this man, we heard the sound of an approaching motor vehicle, and I didn't know at the time that that field was bounded on the east by a blacktop road, but we immediately set out for the sound of that vehicle, knowing that it in all probability would be German and we should ambush it and do whatever we could. The vehicle was speedier than we were and it had passed us on that blacktop road before we could get there, but we did take up a position just in case another vehicle might come along, and it was then that we determined that it was a blacktop road, and would carry quite a little bit of traffic if it came that way.

We didn't spend more than 5 or 10 minutes in this position, and nothing else came along, so then I set about again gathering up what men I could. It was then that I began to hear one of those cricket sounds we were prepared to give or hear, and following the sound of that cricket, I came upon a man who was badly injured. The Germans had staked out the large fields in Normandy to prevent glider landings. They had set poles in the ground, about the size of one of our own telephone poles. Not that high, but maybe 10-12 feet off the ground and in their delight, I'm sure, they sharpened those, and they looked like large pencils sticking in the ground. Unfortunately, this man had landed right on one of those poles and had broken his leg about midway between the knee and the hip, and he had a severe fracture of the thigh there, was in great pain, was effectively out of the fighting, could do nothing at all. There was no way that I could take him with me. Each man carried a first aid kit which contained morphine in the parachute units. I took his morphine, gave him a shot of morphine, took his rifle, put his bayonet on it, stuck it in the ground, put his helmet on top of the butt of the rifle. This was somewhat of a universal symbol that a man was out of action and certainly did not intend to fight. Then I went on about trying to find additional men.

Moving to the north side of the field, and this is about an hour after we've dropped, I came

60

across some other American parachutists, none of whom I knew at that time, and moving along the hedgerow on the north side of the field, I eventually came upon Lieutenant Pat Ward of the Battalion, the Plans and Training officer, and he had gathered up a few men, and we combined forces, of course, the idea being to gather up what we could and immediately make our way to Ste. Mère Eglise. We had learned in Sicily and Italy that if you missed your drop zone, you took command of whomever you could find and move to your objective, fighting if you had to get there, and just doing whatever you could to help carry out the mission.

We did find 2 or 3 equipment bundles, and gathered those things up and then discovered along about daylight that there was a small house in the northwest corner of this field and we gravitated to that house and kind of used it as an assembly point, and we were sending out 1 and 2 man details to see if we could find additional jumpers in the area, and ultimately we had about 35 men, the bulk of whom I did not know. I did have from my own company, from my own platoon, I had Corporal Quentin Echols from Tulsa, Oklahoma. Corporal Echols had a broken ankle, and well, he had great determination. He was unable to do anything except hobble along. There was Private Whistler from my company. I found my own runner, Private Robert Treet. One man that I found that was to stay with me for a long time was an artillery man from the 101st Division. Finding this man told me that the drop had been badly scattered because I knew that the 101st was supposed to be in the vicinity of Carentan in Normandy, quite a number of miles to the south of where we were.

At about dawn, while we were around this small French house, the Frenchman himself came out of the house, and was quite surprised to find his farmyard occupied by Americans who certainly hadn't been there the night before. There was a great deal of consternation on his face, and I'm sure alarm as to what our intentions were and for his own personal safety. We subsequently learned that his wife was in the house and his early teenage daughter, a girl 10 or 12 years of age. It was at this point that the French phrases we had been studying would have come in handy, except neither Lieutenant Ward or myself could remember a single one of the phrases, so with sign language and a great deal of pointing and looking at the maps and so forth, with the help of the Frenchman, found out we were somewhere about 6 miles north of Ste. Mère Eglise.

Also about this time, the gliders started coming in, and one of them chose this field that I had landed in to make his landing. He with unerring accuracy managed to hit one of those anti-glider poles, demolishing the glider, of course, and demolishing his load which was a jeep and some other equipment and injuring in varying degrees every member of the crew of that glider. So these people, rather than serving as reinforcements to us, in effect became a liability to us.

We managed to get these wounded glider men to our little French house, and shortly thereafter, we noticed a German soldier step out into the field over on the east side and approach the injured man that we had left there. He came over to him, looked him over, and then shot him. Of course, this infuriated all our jumpers, and he didn't survive his trip back to the hedgerow for having shot this man.

By now it is probably 0700, the Frenchman made by sign language to go down to a large French house which we had observed but which I had not noticed on my landing. The farm house, the large farm house, was actually only a few yards from where I had landed although I had not seen it in the dark coming down, and it was approximately 40 or 50 yards south of us and approximately the same distance or maybe a little more to the east of us. The Frenchman indicated that that was where he was going and he did go. I wasn't particularly alarmed about it because he left with us, in his own farmhouse, he left his wife and child, so I was reasonably sure he would come back and not bring the enemy down upon us or anything of that sort. I suppose I grew apprehensive about that Frenchman going to that large house, and since he hadn't returned, I decided to go there myself. I picked Private Henry Voges, and one other man, and decided to take just the three of us down there on reconnaissance and see what there was to be found.

We were moving on a gravel road. I was in the lead on the north side of the road, Private Voges was about 5 yards behind me on the south side of the road, and the other man was about 10 yards behind me on the same side of the road I was.

We were nearing the French house when Private Voges threw a pebble at me to get my attention, and turning towards him, he was motioning frantically for me to come over to that side of the road and to be quiet about doing it, and he was pointing at the French farmhouse. I got on that side of the road, and looking through the hedgerow there, I could see that we indeed had stumbled upon something. The Frenchman was standing there talking to some German officers, and there were approximately 35 or 40 ranks of one sort of another, standing around in this farm yard. I recognised from my experience in Sicily and Italy that I was looking at some rank in the German army and concluded that we were looking at a battalion headquarters in all probability. It was my immediate intention to get back to Lieutenant Ward and with our group of 35, we would attack this group. We had the means to do it. We had recovered two light machine guns, we had one Browning automatic rifle, we had one 60 millimetre mortar and each of us had his personal weapon, and the element of surprise would be with us and we could attack that group and do great harm.

Unfortunately, at just about this time, a guard, a German guard stepped out of the gateway of this farmhouse and discovered us. Fortunately I fired first and he went down, but the fat was in the fire. There would be no surprise in this thing now. We decided to beat a hasty retreat back to the lane which would give us cover, and somehow or another we made that without anybody being hurt, and got back to Lieutenant Ward, it still being my intention to fight.

Lieutenant Ward agreed with me that the thing to do would be to attack immediately, and we set about making our plans which would not have taken and did not take more than 4 or 5 minutes, and we were ready to set out. I was going to set up the mortar and have it fire from where we were, and the 2 machine guns to deliver fire on the French farmhouse and the infantry to move down the lane and then attack along that road. We didn't have time to implement this plan because all of a sudden from the north down this lane we were fired on by a rather large group of Germans down there. Looking down there I could see that there were probably as many as 25, and they had at least 2 German light machine guns, and they were aggressively approaching and firing and had covering fire and in effect all but had us pinned down in just 2 or 3 minutes. Simultaneously, we were getting fire from the east side of the field near the black top road, and we knew from what we had seen there was a large German force to the south of us. Except to the west we were surrounded. We returned fire as best we could since we were in a position of getting ready to launch the attack that we were going to but were unable to. I personally was on the east side of that lane, and the German attack we could see was coming from the north and was only 50-60 yards away, and the covering of the 2 machine guns covering fire was bearing down on us rather intensely. With me was my runner, Private Robert Treet, and we were returning fire, firing left handed which we were trained to do. I am naturally right handed and it was an awkward position to be firing from. Also, the ditch we were in was so shallow that it was hardly giving us protection from anything. I said to Private Treet, 'We will have to get on the other side of the road or we will be killed or captured here.' He agreed without any hesitation. I crawled across the road and he started to crawl across the road immediately behind me, and he was hit and killed in this position.

We took several other casualties. I'm not sure how many. It became apparent that we were in a bad spot, and in talking with Lieutenant Ward, he agreed that we should evacuate immediately to the west because the Germans were obviously trying to pin us down with that automatic fire. Then they would either move in on us easily or they would bring mortar fire to bear on us which was a standard tactic. We, not having had foxholes dug or anything or not being in a defensive position, were vulnerable.

We immediately set out after returning fire and slowing up the German attack, we set out to consolidate our group and to evacuate to the west. I was senior to Lieutenant Ward and I directed him to take the point guard, move to the west slightly veering to the south, and to get us through there, and that I would stay with the rear guard and offer him what protection I could. I had 5 or 6 men with the rear guard. We set out to do this immediately and carried it out rather successfully. Not being pursued by the Germans when the column stopped, I went forward to see what the hold up was, and I came to a man lying in a hedgerow by a field, and I asked him where Lieutenant Ward was, and he said, 'He's been captured.' And I said, 'What do you mean he's been captured?' He said he went through that gate over there and that hedgerow there and there was a German on either side of the gate, covered by the hedgerow, and they had him dead to rights. He would either surrender or die right there, so he was taken prisoner. I also lost Private Henry Voges in this action and I assumed that he had also been captured. Subsequently I was to learn that he had not been captured, had managed to evade the Germans, and just became separated and ultimately made his way back to the unit.

This action had lasted the better part of perhaps 3 or 4 hours. Not being pressed by the Germans at this time from any direction, I decided to set up a perimeter defence in this field where we were and allow the men to get some rest, to take food and water. They had been up and going for something like probably 20 hours now, and fatigue was a matter to be concerned with, and we did set up just a perimeter defence in this field from which we could defend ourselves from any direction. [Fortunate in being missed by a column of Germans] and making a personal reconnaissance, I found another field that I thought was better suited for defence than what we had, so I moved the group to that field, and I deployed men around the perimeter of the field and took up defensive positions. By this time, it was approaching dark and it was our intention to get some rest and defend ourselves and see what would come on tomorrow with the idea of getting to Ste. Mère Eglise if we could.

Tape-recorded recollections, The Eisenhower Center for American Studies at the University of New Orleans and the National D-Day Museum, New Orleans, USA

THOMAS J BLAKEY

82nd Airborne Division, 505 Parachute Infantry Regiment, US Army

We were ready, honed sharply, ready to go. The morale was wonderful. They wanted to go and they wanted to go now so when we got on that plane the first time, everybody was thrilled to death. But you can imagine what the feeling was when we turned around and came back and landed in that same damned old aerodrome that we were in and back in that same old bunk. The next night we got ready to go again but there was not the outward elation of the first night because we were still afraid that it would be stood down. We were going to wait and see, (and then when we were really off) the men were very serious and you could tell, they were praying, (lost in) their own thoughts and some were doing their beads. If there was any conversation there wasn't much.

I was Number One – I could see the ground vaguely. I could see spots where fire was coming from too. I went out, the chute opened, I swung underneath it, I swung back, I went one more time and I was on the ground. It was pretty soft – pasture.

I was six or seven miles from my drop zone, west of it. I got my rifle (put together) and went to get into a hedgerow to take cover. I got my compass out and tried to see which direction was which.

I had to find some sort of road junction. I'd hear fire over there but when I got to where I thought it was it had gone. I decided I'd get some place and let somebody find me. I saw this guy and I clicked him and he came over and he was from the 504th but he was somewhat out of sorts because he had been told he wouldn't have to go back to the continent!

After a while he got mad and left. About daylight I began to move around and found some other guys and we found a road junction and went down one of the roads (and two of us were hit and killed). We went back and found another road and it lead to La Fière. There was a big fire (fight) going on there, five miles from Ste. Mère Eglise and we were four days in this area and it was nip and tuck during a German counter attack.

Transcript of tape-recorded recollections, The National D-Day Museum, New Orleans, USA.

LIEUTENANT COLONEL NATHANIEL R HOSKOT
Communications 101st Airborne Regiment US Army

We jumped when our plane was hit and I was able to reconnect with four or five from the plane. We headed North trying to evade Germans, cutting communications when we found some but we were surrounded. I shouted that we would surrender and the reply came, 'Well bud, if you've had enough, then come on out.' It turned out that this German soldier had lived in Brooklyn, New York for fourteen years.

On the following day our column of trucks of Germans and their POWs was strafed three times by allied planes. The truck had no POW or Red Cross markings and as the senior officer in our group of prisoners I had protested about this and when some of the trucks were

Lieutenant Colonel Nathaniel R Hoskot's identification card as a German prisoner. He was captured on D-Day.

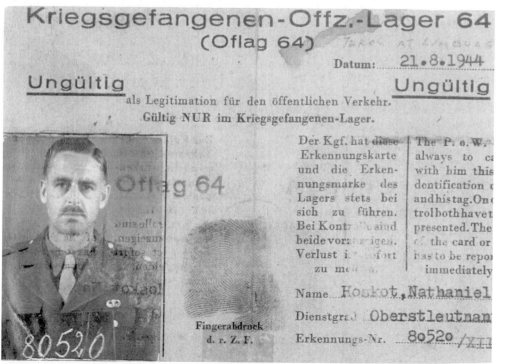

„Alle müssen sich damit abfinden, daß die Welt in drei Teile aufgeteilt wird: in einen amerikanischen, einen britischen und einen sowjetrussischen", glaubt der US - amerikanische Oberstleutnant Hoskot. Danach ist klar, warum alle, die von USA „Befreiung" erhoffen, sich selbst täuschen

A German Army official newspaper, Unser Heer, *prints a photograph taken at the time of Nathaniel Hoskot's interrogation later in June. The article reported the American as 'arrogant, self confident and declaring that the US, Britain and Russia will win the war and divide the world into three spheres of influence'.*

hit and on fire, a German guard shot and killed a POW trying to get out of one of the burning trucks. (This was later the subject of a war crimes trial.) I was in a car following the trucks and helped injured POWs get into the fields by the side of the road. No one fired at me but nineteen POWs died and were buried in a mass grave. I have their names, some serial numbers and some unit affiliations.

The Germans marched the unwounded POWs off South and I and two more were left under guard with the dead and about forty five wounded who were taken to a nearby farmhouse and placed on the dirt floor of the barn. The locals were fabulous doing their best to bring sheets, draperies, clothing for bandages and whatever food they could gather. The German guards were no help nor would they summon medical assistance. *Typescript recollections.*

RIFLEMAN H W CLARK
D Company, 2nd Battalion Ox and Bucks Light Infantry – 'Pegasus Bridge'

The morning of the 5th was much brighter and we were informed that it was 'on' for that night. The company had a day of rest. Sleep, however was out of the question, we were all too keyed up. A service was held in the afternoon and very well attended it was. All the Company sinners, including myself, were present. That evening about 8pm we donned our equipment, loaded our personal weapons and boarded the vehicles which were to transport us to the airfield. When we arrived at Tarrant Rushton dusk was just falling. I was amazed at the large number of people around the drome. We drove direct to the Horsa and sat on the grass beside them chatting to the glider pilots. The pilots appeared somewhat dismayed at the weight we were carrying. Some kind soul appeared with a large dixie of tea, on tasting it we were highly delighted to detect a good measure of rum in it. We entered the Horsa at 10.30pm amid cries of 'Good luck!' from various bodies. The atmosphere in the glider was somewhat like a London tube train in the rush hour. We were in good heart. John Howard came along and wished us well, we could all feel the emotion in his voice. The glider doors were closed. We now sat in a world of our own. The first Horsa was airborne at 2259 hrs. the second, of which I was a passenger was up at approximately 2300 hrs. the remaining Horsas followed at one minute intervals. The tug planes were Halifax Bombers of 298/644 Squadrons. The success of our mission was now in the hands of our tug crews and of the six pairs of glider pilots.

Harry Clark in 1943 aged 20.

The flight across the Channel took just over an hour. We encountered very light turbulence. The platoon were in great spirits, singing their heads off until we crossed the French coast. Suddenly we cast off from our Halifax tug. We were now on our own and there was no going back. The time was approximately 0019 hrs. on the 5/6 June 1944. We knew that our glider path would take us a further three and a half minutes. Lt. David Wood, the Platoon Commander stood up and opened the glider front entrance. The rear door was also flung open. With about sixty seconds to touchdown, Lt Wood shouted 'Brace for impact!' We linked arms and prepared for the inevitable. After what seemed like an eternity we hit Mother Earth with a splintering crash. The very violence of hitting the ground threw us forward, breaking our safety harnesses. I was propelled through the wrecked side of the Horsa to land flat on my back, several other members of the platoon were in a mass of bodies alongside me, including Lt David Wood, still clutching his canvas bucket of grenades. Within seconds we had formed up and moved off towards the bridge. We heard small arms fire. A grenade exploded and a

German flare went up. 25 Platoon, commanded by Lt Den Brotheridge had crash landed a short time before and had gone hell for leather across the bridge and were now attacking the outer defences on the Bénouville side. We, being the second platoon to land, had the task of taking out the inner defences. As we neared the bridge we passed the shattered wreck of the 25 Platoon glider, Major John Howard, the Company Commander, had been a passenger in this one. He had set up Company HQ at a pillbox on the eastern bank. By the time we reached the road that crossed the bridge the sound of heavy firing and grenade explosions were heard from the Bénouville side. My platoon, 24, were given the order to attack our objective. We moved forward across the road shouting 'Baker, Baker,' which was the platoon identification signal. In the darkness one relied on this call-sign to identify friend from foe.

As we crossed over the road we came immediately under fire from automatic weapons in the trenches to our left front. Myself and Cpl 'Claude' Godbold threw our stun grenades and two figures were seen running towards the canal. Further firing was heard from our right front. We took up a defensive position in the captured trench. Shortly afterwards we heard a burst of LMG fire to the right of our position and prepared ourselves for the inevitable counter-attack. A few moments later I heard Cpl Godbold calling for me, it appeared that the last burst of fire had wounded Lt Wood, Sgt Leather and Pte Chatfield who was the radio operator. 'Claude' Godbold was now our Platoon Commander. I was to take over the 38 set radio and act as his runner. The heavy firing had now ceased, just a sporadic shot or two could be heard. We had our bridge and word soon arrived that the Orne Bridge was captured. One glider had gone astray which left us short of thirty men. This left us with about 135 men to defend the two bridges until our relief came from the 7th Parachute Battalion who were to drop with the 5th Para Brigade at 0050hrs. Their drop-zone was to the north of Ranville and we did not expect to see them until at least 0200 hrs. Several probing attacks were made by the enemy and the sound of the vehicles was heard from the Ranville area. We stayed in a tight defensive position and waited. The company had been ordered to capture the bridges intact and to hold them until relieved. We had achieved the first part, now we were into the second act. Soon the sound of heavy formations of aircraft was heard. The 3rd and 5th Para Brigades began their drop to the east of our position. We were no longer alone in France.

By now the Germans had their counter-attack well under way on the west side of the canal, the tempo of firing was stepped up and tracked vehicles were heard in the vicinity of the Le Port road junction. An anti-tank weapon was carried forward by Sgt 'Wagger' Thornton and with his first shot he put a tank out of action. The ammunition in this tank began to explode and catch fire. This, coupled with the cries and screams of the trapped tank commander did little good for our nerves. The battle was well and truly engaged. We had little or no idea of what to expect from the enemy. If he had armour in the area we were in for a very rough battle indeed. At about 0200 hrs Cpl Godbold asked me to accompany him over to the west side of the bridge. The situation was looking tough. The enemy were pressing in greater numbers. We were to move one of 24 Platoon's sections across to the west bank to cover the area looking toward Le Port. By this time (0245 hrs) the leading elements of a much depleted 7th Para Battalion were taking up position in and around Bénouville. The time was now about 0300 hrs, and the situation was getting more desperate by the minute, Lieutenant-Colonel Pine-Coffin of the 7th Para was now in command of the bridge area. Shortly after 0300hrs the section returned to the east bank of the canal and resumed their position in the captured enemy trenches. I settled down behind a pill box and started to get a brew going. It was like nectar and filled me with hope. The battle was raging all around us now but with six Parachute Battalions within a few miles of us we felt more secure. The first sign of dawn was now in evidence, with it came heavy renewed attacks on the 7th Para positions just over the canal. As dawn broke we stood to, in expectation of heavy counter-attacks from infantry and tanks. This situation never happened. The sound of Naval bombardment on the beaches reminded us that the sea-borne troops were coming ashore. It was now a question of holding out until relief came. With dawn came another serious problem. Intense sniper fire came down with great accuracy causing a number of casualties among our troops. The bridge was well covered by one very accurate sniper. One ran like hell when crossing to the west side, to dawdle was to invite death. Later in the morning the Division got some support from the navy, 16 inch shells passed over our heads making a noise like an express train. We had a visit from General Gale and Brigadier Poett during the morning, we even got a shout of 'Good Morning, chaps' from them.

During this period the 7th Para. were taking an increasing number of casualties in Bénouville and Le Port. A German patrol boat was spotted coming from the direction of the coast. When it was some 200 yards away Cpl Godbold, myself and Pte Cheesely ran with a PIAT to some cover on the canal bank. We kept a close eye on it. There was no sign of life. The engine was ticking over and someone appeared to be steering it. A wicked looking gun was mounted on the forward deck. At about 50 yards range Cpl Godbold fired a PIAT grenade. It struck the boat just behind the wheelhouse and exploded internally. The boat drifted in to the canal bank. Two very scared Germans appeared from below deck. They were lucky to have survived the blast. We ordered them ashore. The NCO, a blond Germanic type started to argue and shout, so I thumped him on the shoulder with the butt of my rifle and he immediately became meek and caused no further problems. John Howard ordered me to march them down to the 5th Para Brigade Headquarters. This entailed a walk of some 1000 yards or so along a stretch of road which was exposed to enemy snipers. All went well until we came to the Orne Bridge where we came under fire. Like myself, the prisoners were reluctant to cross, but it had to be done so we set off at a gallop and arrived safely on the other bank. From there on it was safe going to Brigade HQ. I handed the two prisoners over to an MP Sgt, scrounged a mug of tea and started the return journey back to my Company. I managed it without incident. It was now nearing midday and I was very hungry. I decided to open the 24 hour ration pack, it contained a load of rubbish in the form of soup and oatmeal cubes plus some very hard biscuits. The only items of any use were several cubes of tea, sugar and milk. The remainder was consigned to the Caen canal. It was fortunate that I had hoarded my chocolate ration for 6 weeks. The sounds of battle from the beaches was now more pronounced. Word came through that the Commando Brigades leading elements were in the vicinity. Within a few minutes the wail of bagpipes was heard and Lord Lovat and his piper crossed the canal bridge. It was shortly after 1300 hrs. our spirits rose, relief at last.

We sat in our trenches and watched the whole Brigade come across the bridge. A number were killed and wounded by very accurate snipers. They had a tough time fighting their way from the beaches and now were on their way to join our Para boys to the north of Ranville. We stayed in a position of defence around the bridges and had a wonderful grandstand view of the 6th Air Landing Brigade's gliders coming over during the evening. We were relieved by troops of the 3rd Division just before midnight on the 6 June. *Typescript recollections.*

RIFLEMAN D V ALLEN

2nd Battalion, Ox and Bucks Light Infantry – 'Pegasus Bridge'

In the glider there was an eerie silence and all we could hear was the wind rushing by. After what seemed an eternity we hit the ground hard and rushed along on our skids having lost our wheels on impact and in coming to a sudden stop we were all thrown about but in moments we had gathered our kits together and it was all out. The time of landing, about 0020 hr. D-Day 6 June, 1944.

With Sweeney in the lead we charged across the bridge calling out our 'call signs'. We had taken them completely by surprise and in no time at all, the Company had taken both bridges intact and the call signs 'HAM' and 'JAM' rang out and this was the signal to let everyone know that we had successfully accomplished our mission and I, for one, was glad to be alive – not like poor Lt. Den Brotheridge who was the first to be killed on D-Day – shot through the neck.

Things were soon to change and we knew it wouldn't be long before the Germans counter-attacked and it was a great relief when some 7th PARA started to arrive to help defend the bridges. We had to hold on at all costs until relief arrived from the beaches. There was a lot of firing coming from both Le Port and Bénouville and some tank movement had been heard, later one of the tanks was knocked out by Sgt. 'Wagger' Thornton with a PIAT. This seemed to stop the others moving forward – Thank God. At one time a dispatch rider and Mercedes Staff Car came over the bridge and were brought to a sudden stop with bursts of fire wounding the driver, an officer, and sending the Dispatch Rider into the river.

After being reinforced by the 7th and 5th Para, John Howard pulled us back between the two bridges, in reserve.

One thing that sticks in my mind was when the Navy, using their 16 inch guns fired a creeping barrage, and as the shells came over like the roar of an express train and got nearer and nearer, one of the lads said, 'I hope the sods stop before they get to us'.

Later that day we heard the sound of bagpipes in the distance. Coming towards us was Lord Lovat and his scouts. What a great sight – we all cheered for we knew that they had fought all the way from the beaches to get to us.

After being in Reserve for a time, we moved round Ranville and Escoville where we came under heavy fire and some of the lads were killed and wounded. We were told to withdraw to Hérouvillette. By this time we were down to about half our strength. We waited for them to attack which we knew would come and when it did we opened up with all we had and mowed them down as they came in. *Transcript of tape-recorded recollections.*

LIEUTENANT DAVID J WOOD

2nd Ox and Bucks Light Infantry – 'Pegasus Bridge'

Diary written four months later

5 June 1944. After a day of quiet and final preparation the trucks arrived and we were taken to the Airfield. After a cup of tea and a couple of air sickness tablets we got in our gliders and took off about eleven. There were six gliders in all and the trip was to take about 1 hour and twenty minutes. The moon was obscured by cloud and the weather was not good. We were all a bit quiet and the time passed quickly.

6 June 1944. At about 12.30 we landed in France. The landing was decidedly rough and I was thrown out of the glider. After releasing myself I found we were about 100 yards from

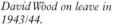

David Wood on leave in 1943/44.

Some of the officers and men of D Company, 2nd Ox and Bucks Light Infantry. D J Wood

the bridge. I collected the platoon and we assaulted after collecting John. The enemy had mostly fled and I found a perfect MG34 with a belt of ammo. I was hit in the leg on my way back to John who had sent for me over the wireless. Sgts. Leather and Chatfield were hit at the same time. I think an NCO with a Schmeisser M. Pistol fired from short range. I went down and was in some pain and bleeding. Soon afterwards Cheeseley came up followed by Radford and gave me morphia and put a rifle splint on my leg. Cpl. Godbold had to take over the platoon. The bridges were not mined and there were no poles in the ground. Later I was moved to the CCP on a stretcher. On the way I saw a tank blazing and a 'shot up' German staff car. Den was in CCP but died very shortly afterwards having been shot in the neck. Next we were sniped in the CCP and Lawson nearly shot me with his pistol. The Naval barrage was terrific and scared us a lot. I was moved to a Parachute Field Ambulance on an old French lorry. Was very sick all the time. Arrived at the F Amb. and felt rotten. Saw Sandy Smith there. Spent the day in F. Amb and the night. Could not eat at all.

MAJOR R J HOWARD

Officer Commanding, D Company, 2nd Ox and Bucks Light Infantry

Letter written to his wounded Lieutenant, David J Wood, 25 June 1944

Dear David

Was good to hear from you and I hasten to reply. I believe Tod wrote to you yesterday via your home, so excuse us if our news is duplicated.

We're still in the thick of it but doing fine. I've had to re-group, 22-25 together under Chalky White from Recce and 23-24 under Tod – it's an odd organisation, but quite workable for our present job. Chalky's turned out fine, almost up to D Coy standard ! We've done exceptionally well as a Coy. and are the envy of the Regt. The bges [bridges] of course gave us a flying start, and since then we've had a glorious finger into everything. Our nicknames are various, the Commando Coy, Robin Hood's Outfit (I'm Robin Hood!), The boys etc. Our captured German equipment is wonderful. We have an Armoured Car (semi-tracked) which we're permitted to take with us whenever we move. Everyone has a German pistol, watch & binoculars. Every section has an MG. 42 or 34 in addition to its Bren. Gosh, you

Aerial reconnaissance photograph of the gliders at 'Pegasus Bridge'. D J Wood

Andrew Huxley's photograph taken shortly after D-Day of the Bridge over the Orne (left) and gliders to the right. A proprietorial sign has swiftly been erected!

have to see it to believe it ! You'd simply revel in being with us now.

I was terribly disappointed to lose you so early on, David. Your cheery self has been missed lots. I can assure you, there's many a job I'd have definitely sent you on had you been here. Still, it was meant to be and moaning won't alter it. Claude has done exceptionally well, as all your remaining lads. I mention L/Cpl Roberts for special praise, he has an MG.34 which he fairly nurses and has given the hun hell with it on many occasions. Cpl. Ilsley is another good egg under fire. Yes David, your lads have done their share in your absence. Remember what I've always firmly believed about a command reflecting its commander – its been done in 24.

Lts. Fulford and Sunray returned to us yesterday, the former gave news of your wounds. I was terribly sorry to hear about the smashed femur.

Everyone this side was satisfied with the way we did our job. I only hope your side know of it. The paratps [paratroopers] seem to have had all the praise. I've written a full report on the capture of the bges [bridges] which I hope will get beyond Regt.History, in fact into the Press! Mark did fairly well after Sunray went.

A glider, east of the Orne, photographed by Andrew Huxley.

[?] got it badly and Teddy Favell was killed 2 hours after taking over B. Brian has it now and seems fairly happy. Chesty was killed next to me in a trench, a very sad loss. Gosh I've had some narrow escapes; may be Tony told you a sniper seared my head, hole front and back of my helmet! and also got shrapnel in the back when Chesty Fearon(?) copped it – But never say die!

No news of going, though I still cherish hopes of being home for Terry's 2nd birthday.

The loss of Den upset me, was an awful job writing to his wife. I recommended him for a big decoration which I hope his wife will get. Confidentially, I put you and Sandy up too, but don't think about it too much, a recommendation is only part of the way. The Brig backed it up.

Chin-chin David, hope this helps to satisfy your natural lust for news. Yours John Joys's very well – write if you've time.

LIEUTENANT COLONEL T. OTWAY
9th Parachute Battalion – The Merville Battery

Half past eleven we took off. We had thirty six aircraft, I think. I know I walked down the whole line of aircraft and I spoke to the Captain, every Captain, of each aircraft and all the troops before we took off. I put a flask of whisky in my own hip pocket and took a bottle of whisky, which I passed round the aircraft, and we took off dead on time. We didn't have any excitement until we got over the coast. Some people said there was no anti-aircraft fire. There was – because there was a very loud explosion by the tail of our aircraft and luckily we weren't damaged, and there was another one as we were jumping. Myself, I got the blast of it standing in the door. The man in front of me got even more. He shot out like a bullet, but he wasn't hurt. We were fired at by small arms fire and you could see the tracers. I could actually see the tracer bullets going through my chute, and it had never occurred to me that my chute might catch on fire while I was in it, but I thought of it then going down – but it didn't. We were widely dispersed due to all this small arms fire coming up, and due to various factors we were scattered.

The Germans had flooded the area. I, myself, waded through water somewhere between my waist and my chest. I met several people, our Staff Captain, John Woodgate and he and I tried to pull some of these men out of these flooded marshes, but some of them were carrying sixty pound kit bags. The suction was unbelievable. We just couldn't get them out. I lost a lot of men in there. They just went in and were drowned. When I arrived at the Battalion rendezvous I found my batman, who had jumped behind me, just behind me, ahead of me. He was waiting for me and he said, 'I believe Sir, you have only got fifty men'. (However) without telling anybody, I had kept a spare fifteen minutes in my timetable and by the time I was due to move off to attack the battery the total had got up to 150 and eventually I got up to somewhere just under 300. When I came out of the battery I had sixty-five men, including myself, on their feet.

Terence Otway, 9th Battalion, The Parachute Regiment, here in August 1943, second in command of the battalion he was to command on D-Day.

(At the rendezvous) I waited to the fifteen minutes beyond the time we should have moved off, when I had 150. En route to the battery we found that the RAF, which had bombed the battery several times and had also missed it several times, had, quite by accident, put a lot of their bombs along our route, so we were clambering in and out of bomb holes anything up to eight to nine feet deep. That wasn't funny in this pitch darkness... we were near bomb holes when we heard some troops marching and we got into them, and the Germans went straight past us. I could have reached out and touched one by the ankles. They never saw us. When I got to the rendezvous, the second rendezvous, which is to say outside the battery, I had to re-plan because I only had this small amount of men. So, instead of going for four gaps in the wire with Bangalore torpedoes, I only blew two, because it was essential that I had a lot of men going through two gaps rather than a few men going through four gaps. I had sent an officer called Paul Greenway and a Company Sergeant Major, up to the wire ahead and their job was to sit down outside and listen to the German conversation, watch their cigarette butts and so on. And they crawled through the minefield and defused the mines in the dark with their fingers. It was a very, very brave thing to do. They had to do it. Luckily there was enough moon, but they weren't spotted. Then they crawled back and turned round on their backsides and went through backwards dragging a path, making it with their heels, for us to follow. They both got decorated, needless to say.

So that when I arrived at the wire I was told about this, and that is when I re-organised and we went in on time. I put two battery attacking assault parties through each gap one after the other so that they fanned out and went in. They went round at the front of the casemates, you can't get through the steel doors at the back, although I did have in my Battalion two anti-tank guns which came by glider, but again they were dispersed and they weren't there. So the only way of getting in was where the guns pointed out. Once the Germans saw that we were parachutists they put their hands up. They shouted, I could hear them, 'paratrooper', and we killed or wounded the whole garrison except for twenty-three. We took twenty-three prisoners and took them out. The problem was as I said to one of my officers, 'how the hell do we get out of this place? The bloody mines are still there'. And so I said to the Germans, and luckily then my German was fluent, I said to them 'show me the way' and they refused. (But when I ordered them out they had no option).

The assault troops had put grenades down the barrels of the battery's guns, but they don't have any effect on very shiny, polished, hard metal, but there was a whole lot of splintered grenade that had to be cleaned out. But we also took all the breech blocks out and threw them away, so they couldn't fire those guns without getting new breech blocks. (Though they managed this later in the day with not being able to leave an occupying force before moving to our next objective).

I went in with 150 and came out with 65 only on their feet including myself. Of the casualties not all were dead, some of them were wounded, but we did have to leave the wounded with the doctor there. We captured a German doctor to whom full marks, he went back inside the battery to get the medical supplies to help our people, but we had German wounded as well. We had about the same number of German wounded.

Our padre, who was with us but at the back, he went off to a local village with some local men and he got a couple of German trucks and a car, a couple of German staff cars. Brought them back, put all the wounded on and drove them back into 6th Airborne Division. Stuck a Red Cross out the front and the Germans let them through. *Transcript of tape-recorded recollections. [Otway was to be awarded a DSO as a result of this action]*

75

BRIGADIER S J L HILL

in command 3rd Parachute Brigade – making for the Merville Battery

I had a football painted in phosphorus with the head of Hitler on it and I had hung this up and over my tent and the Canadians were delighted with this and I said I was going to drop this on the coastal defences as we went through and so they gave me some bricks to put out as well and I found myself standing in the doorway of this aeroplane. Crossing The Channel looking out, it was quite windy. There were a lot of sea horses all over the place and I remember thinking to myself that I had a good friend called Earl Prior Palmer who was commanding a swimming tank battalion and I thought God, how lucky I am to be in this aeroplane and not going in to battle on D-Day in a swimming tank.

Anyhow we got to the thing. There was flak all round. I don't think undue flak attending to our particular aircraft but plenty of it. So the red light was on and I was all ready. I picked up the bricks and the football of Hitler and the green went. So I had to go. You orientate yourself and I remember it was a cloudy night but the moon was just coming through enough for me to do some orientating. To my horror I found myself dropping in to the flooded valley of the Dives. I was about 2 or 3 miles from where I ought to have been. So in I went into 4½ feet of water. So you sort of re-organise yourself to the circumstances and I remember the first firing that I heard. I heard an exchange of shots and I was in the water. Then I found it was one member of my bodyguard shooting the other bodyguard in the leg by mistake. So that was an additional problem and, being a professional soldier, I had about 60 tea bags sewn in to the top of my battle dress trousers and of course, these tea bags did nothing but make tea and it took me 4 hours to get out of that water and I made cold tea all the time.

However there were a lot of other people in the flooded valley and water meadows and they had deep ditches 10 or 15 feet and a lot of chaps were drowned that night. However we established a drill. We all carried toggle ropes and everybody that I was able to pick up and collect, we all tied ourselves together with toggle ropes and that helped us.

April 1945 and Brigadier James Hill is decorated yet again for Conspicuous Bravery. This time it is presented by US Major-General Ridgeway following upon the crossing of the Rhine at the end of the previous month. There is top level British scrutiny of the proceedings!

The other thing was the valley had been wired before it was flooded, so you would come up under water against wire barriers and on your own you couldn't get past them but if you walked out together with toggle ropes you could help each other. One way and another, to hell with wire barriers. You got through them but the long and short of it was, 4 hours later we turned up on the edge of the flooded valley. On the edge of our DZ where we were supposed to have been. Four hours later and I had with me, collected and tied together, forty two chaps. So the first thing I did was to send the Canadians who were supposed to capture the dropping zone and capture the enemy principal headquarters on the edge of it and I sent for an officer and got hold of one to find out what the position was. The Canadians had captured the dropping zone. They had liquidated the enemy headquarters but were having trouble with the nearby pillboxes.

So I thought, well now, the important thing is to get to this battery we are supposed to have destroyed, the Merville Battery. So I set off with my string of stragglers and I will always remember that there were two naval bombardment officers who I had attached who were supposed to fire the guns of an 8 inch gun cruiser which was in support of my Brigade for the first 48 hours of the battle. They were there. There was one of my parachuting dogs of course, who was delighted with me and his handler and so on. So we set off and it was dark, just turning light and we went on a track across very boggy land. Only a very small track found by rather careful map reading. To get up to where the 9th Battalion should be. Then the naval bombardment started and you have never seen such a splendid firework display in all your life. It was heartening but then there was something which was less heartening. I heard a horrible noise and having been in battle before, I knew exactly what that noise was and we were caught in the middle of an anti-personnel bombing by low flying aircraft and we were on a very narrow path. Water on both sides.

So I shouted to everybody to get down and next to me was the mortar platoon officer of the 9th Battalion, he threw himself down. I threw myself down on top of him and this horrible noise and everything went over. A 200-pound bomb and it's no pleasant thing and one realised one was being bombed. I realised I had been hit and then one was left with the smell of dust and dirt and cordite and death. Very much death and so I looked and I saw a leg in the path and I thought, my God, that is my leg and then I looked again and it had a brown boot on it and I didn't allow brown American jump boots in my Brigade and I knew the only chap who had one was Peters whom I was lying on. So it was his leg and not mine and I was lucky. Only two of us in the area where I was were able to get to our feet. One was myself and one was my defence platoon commander and Peters on whom I was lying was dead, and so I thought, how lucky you are.

So what does a Commander do when he is surrounded by dying chaps and badly wounded ones. Does he stay and look after them or does he push on and, of course, the answer was as Brigade Commander you had to push on but what we did do before we pushed on, we injected all the wounded with morphia which they carried and we collected what morphia we could off the dead and gave it to the living.

Anyhow we pushed on. I got to the Regimental Aid Post of the 9th Battalion and I found that they had taken the battery successfully, eliminated the German threat and had pushed on and there were 70 of them left. I knew the vital thing was that the battery had been dealt with, liquidated and then I was seen by the doctor, a very experienced doctor, a fellow in the 9th Battalion called Watts, a chap aged about 40. He was the only one who was older than I was I think in the Brigade and he looked at me and he said to me, 'you look bad for morale.' And I said to him, 'You bloody fellow. If you had been wading in water for 4½ hours and then had your left backside removed by a mortar bomb, you wouldn't look good for morale.' So he thought that this was an impossible discussion and he put me out for a couple of hours and patched me up and at 11 o'clock I came to. They had a ladies bicycle there. A parachute pusher and I set off from there to see the Divisional Commander at his headquarters. To tell him what I knew about the Canadians and the 9th Battalion and to get any information he had to give me. So I bicycled down the hill. It was a distance of about two miles. But I had a pusher. So I was pushed and we went downhill and it was interesting because across the road that the British sometimes ran across, Germans used to run across.

I arrived at Divisional headquarters if you could call it such and who should come out to greet me but the Divisional Commander, Richard Gale, and he said 'James, I have splendid news for you. Your Brigade has achieved all its objectives.' So I felt very happy indeed and he and I then exchanged information. Well, the next thing that happened was the ADMS who was the head doctor in the Division seized me and said, 'You have got to go off and have a major operation.' So I said to him, 'No.' and he said, 'Yes. I am going to take you now.' So I said, 'Well, I will go on one condition. After the operation is over you will promise to take me to where my Brigade headquarters are and the surgeon said, 'Yes. I will.'

Transcript of tape-recorded recollections. (Hill was to be awarded a DSO as a result of this action)

SGT A B FRIEND

RAF 512 Squadron 'A' Flight, Broadwell, Dakota III aircrew

From his logbook

June 5 2325 (hrs) F Sgt Perry (pilot) Jump Master. Op 'D' Day minus One: Drop paratroops six miles NE of Caen whose objective was coastal battery. Drop further supplies nearer Caen. LAA opposition. 3 (hrs) 40 (mins).

June 6 2230 (hrs) F Sgt Perry (pilot) Op re-supply with panniers and containers: 'D' Day Navy prevent sortie from being carried out. Our aircraft damaged, others in 'vic' destroyed. 3 (hrs) 25 (mins).

CAPTAIN RICHARD TODD

7th Battalion Parachute Regiment, 6th Airborne Division

The men had been so scattered that when the Commanding Officer said we must go (from our rendezvous point) we only had about 150 men out of 600.

We had to get down to those bridges because he knew damn well that if there was a counter-attack and there would be a counter-attack from the Germans, John Howard's chaps weren't strong enough on the ground to cope with it. So we set off down to the bridges and (when we got there) we were beginning to trot from the river bridge across to the canal bridge. There was a quarter of a mile causeway joining the two. There was marshy ground on each side. As I looked ahead, just beyond Pegasus Bridge was a huge explosion and I thought, oh God, a real battle has started here because there was rifle fire and there were tracer bullets going up and there were explosions and bombs going off and all of a sudden it died down and I still hadn't quite got to the other end and it was an old German tank which had been probing the bridge and had been hit by a Piat fired by one of John Howard's chaps. A lucky hit which got it and blew it up. That was wonderful and then we, 7th Para, took up our positions around, on the west side of Pegasus Bridge. We had formed a little bridgehead separate from the main 6th Airborne one. Our task was mainly to hold , well, entirely to hold the bridges and to rebuff any attacks coming from Caen, armoured attacks in particular because we knew that 21 *Panzer* Division was down there. Within a very short period of time we did have to cope with tank attacks. It was quite a noisy and difficult sort of day. *Transcript of tape-recorded recollections.*

On the right, Richard Todd, a future actor and film star, indeed, starring in the 1960's movie about D-Day, 'The Longest Day', here with Lieutenant T Bowles the officer in command of the Machine-Gun platoon of the 7th Battalion, The Parachute Regiment. This photograph was taken on a field firing exercise in the Brecon Beacons shortly before D-Day.

PRIVATE SIDNEY M PECK

C Company 7th Battalion Parachute Regiment, 6th Airborne Division

My job, as soon as we landed on the ground, was to make a dash for Pegasus Bridge as it is known today. I made one dash over the bridge and while all the fighting was going on, I must admit the adrenaline was flowing, and I just went straight through with my rifle. I had a rifle and hand grenades. That was all I had, and I got with the other people who had dropped before, the gliders, and I remember coming to this particular wall and we stayed there and snipers were firing at us [perhaps from the trees or the church]. Suddenly this young lad by me went on the floor. I looked at him on the floor and I said, 'What are you doing down there?' He was dead, and then I thought, 'I wonder if I am next,' and I stayed by that wall and I heard these tanks going on the road just not far from us and as I say, we were just firing at Germans if we saw or heard them and when the tanks rolled past we kept our heads down.

I was near the bridge, not far from the bridge. I was with other lads around me and suddenly from out of the distance came these bagpipes. We couldn't believe it, and we knew it was Lord Lovat. Lord Lovat came across this canal where we were, and I am almost certain there were tears in the eyes of some of our lads to hear the Pipes. We cheered when they got there but,

A field of gliders, east of the Orne. A Huxley

of course, there was fighting going on all the while. I think with my officer, Lieutenant Atkinson, we were detailed to go to the chateau behind what is now Madame Gondrée's café. I was sent up to the chateau and we were firing up there and I got separated from my small party. After I had done my job I went down to the river, the River Orne. I jumped over this wire fence and then there were two canal barges coming along and they fired from the bridge at these two canal barges and they turned and ran. I myself turned back too. I turned into a ditch which was right at the back behind where I had jumped over this wall, and I ran straight back to the bridge, which was a matter of some 400 or 500 yards. I raced along this towpath. There was the river on one side, a path and then this ditch, and I ran right back until I came back to this bridge and then I was with the other people and I was okay then. *Transcript of tape-recorded recollections.*

SIGNALLER HARRY READ

J Section, 6th Airborne Divisional Signals, 3rd Parachute Brigade

A few weeks before D-Day we did a couple of jumps with two days in between. On the first I injured a knee and on the second I made it worse. The extent of the injury I concealed because I really wanted to be on the D-Day landings.

The briefing for D-Day for the 3rd Parachute Brigade was simple and clear. We were to overfly the famed Atlantic Wall and land by parachute some three or four miles inland. One battalion would attack a well-fortified gun position overlooking, and therefore threatening, the invasion beaches. The two remaining battalions would blow up certain bridges over the River Dives to prevent the movement of German reinforcements in the area. With tasks completed, we would then consolidate a defensive line to protect the eastern flank of the allied bridgehead. Nothing in those orders was beyond the capacity of a well-trained parachute brigade.

On the afternoon of June 5 we assembled at the airfield, much later settling ourselves in the Dakotas which were to take us into battle. Shortly before midnight we took off.

In the aircraft there was the usual banter, but this time there was the occasional lull as the seriousness of the occasion swept over

Harry Read.

us. An announcement from the pilot informed us that we were over Bournemouth and flying directly to Normandy. In the spasmodic moonlight the English Channel looked cold and uninviting but soon, all too soon, the prepare to jump order was given. We stood in a line facing aft, hooked up our static lines and checked each other's lines in the approved manner. The red light came on, helping us to concentrate on the need for a good exit and what we should do on landing. Suddenly, anti-aircraft fire exploded all around us; we gasped as the aircraft lurched violently upwards and were reassured when the pilot told us that this movement was caused by the release of anti-personnel bombs 'to keep the enemy's heads down'. The green light came on. I was number twelve in line. A quick shuffle down the plane, right turn at the door, a grab at the door-frame to assist with the jump, a steadying and energetic hand from the dispatcher and I was out. The slipstream seemed to batter harder than usual but the chute opened quickly and I was suspended over Normandy. My war had begun.

The anti-aircraft fire was impressive; tracer bullets climbed gracefully upwards; in the distance an aircraft plunged in a ball of fire. The darkness seemed to intensify as I neared the ground and in seconds I had landed. It was a splash landing! It was also 0120 hours. I had landed in a flooded area but fortunately the water I had splashed down in was only a foot or so deep. Off with the chute, sten gun at the ready, I looked for our markers but the water landing was convincing evidence that I was way off course. The expected solitary, dominant, large green light marking our assembly point was missing, instead I was surrounded by many little lights from equipment containers dotted all around.

Walking towards a cluster of lights I stumbled into a trench. Before flooding the area the Germans had excavated long, deep trenches at frequent intervals. In the dark they were impossible to see and I proved that falling in was much easier than climbing out. After my third submersion I met another of my Signal Section and we decided to make our way out together. Frequently in water up to our shoulders, it took hours of wading to reach dry land. Sadly, in some deeper areas we could see where parachute canopies had collapsed in silken circles on the water. We concluded that the soldiers had plunged to the bottom and had been unable to free themselves from their heavy equipment. A number of men died that way.

In the distance, between where we were and where we should have been, battles were being fought with rapidly increasing intensity. Obviously, lines were being drawn and we were substantially on the wrong side. In the late afternoon of D-Day we approached a farmhouse. After keeping it under observation for a little while we knocked at the door to receive a generous welcome from the family, and other paras who had found this same refuge.

In spite of moments of fear and excessive fatigue, I had a comforting, mysterious and unexpected feeling that God was with me. *Typescript recollections.*

CHAPTER 5

Crossing The Channel, Minesweeping and Naval Bombardment

T he scale of allied naval commitment to the Normandy landings is exemplified by the warship total of over 1,200, a number including seven battleships, two monitors and twenty three cruisers. Over three quarters of the total of warships was British and Canadian, 16.5 per cent American and there were contributions from the Free French and other allies which from their exile took part, the Netherlands, Norway, Poland and Greece. Mindful of this there is another statistic to grasp: over four thousand vessels, transports, landing ships and craft fulfilling specialised roles, had to cross The Channel and in the case of the transports had to hove to well off-shore for an open sea embarkation of the troops into landing craft to head for the beaches.

From as far west as Lyme Bay and as far east as the Thames Estuary and north even to Felixstowe but in greater numbers from ports between Poole and Portsmouth, sections of the great armada sailed for rendezvous in most cases south east of the Isle of Wight and then set course along mine-swept corridors for their designated Normandy beach.

It was recognised, of course, that the landed force would be at its most vulnerable in securing the beaches and while troops pressed forward for inland objectives and the beaches were cleared and organised for further troops, armoured vehicles, ammunition, petrol and essential supplies. Concerning the hours while these endeavours were proceeding, it is worth noting that a major naval unit in shelling its designated targets had seen action just over twenty eight years earlier at Jutland. This was HMS *Warspite* with her 15 inch guns. Kindred to such an evocative historical image was an American battleship in support off Omaha, *USS Texas* with its fourteen inch guns and of a similar vintage. *Texas* was launched in 1912, and reinforced the British Grand Fleet in Scapa Flow in 1918. [Today it is still afloat, splendidly preserved at Houston, Texas.]

Important as was this battleship and monitor shelling of German coastal emplacements it was necessarily supplemented by nearer shore shelling from cruisers, destroyers and actually by some of the rocket and mobile artillery-carrying landing craft as they made their way to the beaches.

Two more essential roles remained for the warships; one was the constant minesweeping activity and the other, destroyer protection of the naval flanks of the landing against any potential E-boat strike by these German warships faster and superior in several respects to anything possessed by the Allies. The role of the allied navies can be oversimplified into transportation and helping the troops ashore but the many aspects of this responsibility and the potential penalty of failure emphatically re-emphasize that a review of D-Day demands a blue just as much as a khaki perspective.

LIEUTENANT ALASTAIR BANNERMAN
2nd Battalion, Royal Warwickshire Regiment

A notebook in the form of a diary/letter written during and immediately after the events.
Privately published by Alastair Bannerman who was captured, escaped and re-captured, 7 June 1944.

Alastair Bannerman in 1942.

Alastair Bannerman's wife, Elisabeth.

Operation Overlord begins tomorrow or the following day providing nothing unforeseen happens. Another message from an MTB: 'Departure 12.30'. So tomorrow must be D-Day. If that is so H Hour is 7.25 and we land at 11.35, DV James is mad with joy. We have made up a list of the things which we now have to pack. I am not allowed to open anything yet, not before we are actually sailing. We have to arrange measures dealing with fire, the use of life-saving apparatus, the arrangement of air-raid precautions and for sleeping and eating for tonight. I have caused the men's room to be cleared, so we can spread out our maps there when our secrecy pledge has been removed. The sea is still terribly rough but there it is, my darling, it seems now that we're off.

Good news from Rome. Our boys there must have a splendid time. The Italian girls will throw roses at them and they will make all the troops very happy! They must have had a very difficult time there and I hope that your David is well. He will be very interested in this great city and centre of Christendom. I must now stop writing because I have some organising work to do. I love you, I love you, I love you.

We sailed at 12.45. I called all the men on the boat together and told them that we are now on our way. It was very difficult for me to speak to them for I had to cling to the railing to hold my papers and to prevent the megaphone from being blown out of my hand by the wind whilst I was speaking into it. I had to talk very loudly for I had to overcome the wind, the sea and the noise of the engines. I told the men, with a strong feeling for the drama of the moment, that tomorrow would be D-Day and that the first boats would land at 7.25. Our goal is the town of Caen, so I was mistaken before. Normandy and Brittany are to harbour our invasion forces, the Allied Expeditionary Force, and so all guess work is now at an end. I announced to them all the orders about ARP, rescue rafts and all the rest and then I read them Monty's message and two messages from Eisenhower. Most of my lads stood under the camouflage net which went over the whole of the deck so that I could not see their faces. The megaphone also prevented me from seeing. But I am sure that they all felt that this was one of the moments for which we have waited and for which we have practised. Then James and I unpacked our papers and put them in order. Now we are going at full speed and the sea became very rough having left behind the friendly coast. I said 'Au revoir' to England and you, my dear family, and I felt extremely excited about this gigantic adventure. As I felt a little seasick I took a pill which worked miracles! It is the first which I have taken but it is rougher than we have ever experienced in Scotland. Still, it must be a good reason for which we sail in this weather. We are thrown to and fro and the waves break with a tremendous roar and a cloud of foam, and the deck is swamped with water. I depicted to all my men all the details showing them the maps which were now French ones and not practice maps any more. Then I went through the whole marching route of the enterprise with my NCO's and despatch rider Toon Poynton, naming the real names of Beuville, Bieville, Periers, Lion-sur-Mer. I felt a kind of homesickness reading the names on the map when I remembered I spent a painting holiday there in the vicinity of Concarneau. Then I had driven through Deauville and Trouville which are quite near. It is lovely country with quiet old villages and women in black clothes and big wide lace collars and head-gear. If I have to fight at all, then I think I shall prefer it here. I can help to liberate a country that I love and this is more than poor old David can say of Burma. I spoke to the men again about the greatness of the enterprise and told them that Rome had fallen. I had supposed that they knew it already but it was a pleasure to see their faces lighting up and their eyes shining and to feel how the blood pulsed with a new rhythm through their veins when they heard this news. I have slept for two hours in the navigation room but then I heard James swearing because he got wet and big breakers shook the boat. I thought it better to find out how we were getting along. I ate a sandwich and stumbled up to the bridge. In long rows the craft came over the waves, the barrage balloons flew bravely overhead and the spray gushed over the sides of the ship. A destroyer wired that we would soon take course to the south, then the boats would not roll so vilely. At the moment we seem to sail south west and I guess that it is our intention to confuse the enemy. Just now two Lightnings were flying across and a new group of ships can be seen to starboard. Without doubt, they are joining up with us and also the accompanying ships of the Navy will join our group. There are five fleets, I believe, each with approximately two hundred groups, so 'some navigation' some might say.

I am writing still in the navigation room. The navigator at the steering wheel follows the orders and steers after the ship in front. The engines roar regularly and alter their rhythm only according to the orders of the Captain. James wears a rain cape and looks like a fanatical monk with his dark, brilliant eyes. I have been below deck to see what the men are doing. Most of them lie on their boards which protect them against the wetness of the deck. What a painful discipline of body and mind this all is but it is certainly worth the trouble to bring peace and goodwill to this earth.

6 June, D-Day

I believe that from time to time we have the strange feeling that we are dreaming. James expressed it to me like this: 'I have the feeling like when my wife gives me a slap on the behind and tells me that I am half an hour late for breakfast.' It is now 0300 hours in the morning and I have just been up to the bridge. It is rather light because the moon is shining, though heavy clouds cover her. One can see the row of small ships and of darker balloons silhouetted in front and behind us against the grey sea. We are still rolling a little but the wind has subsided somewhat, thank Heaven. The Captain and his first officer are on the bridge. They make sure where we are and look for the coloured lights which should guide us through one of our own minefields. There seem to be a great many lights about but a green one ahead seems to be the one which we need, and so we sail on towards Caen.

You, my angel, sleep gently in the nursery, I hope. Your thoughts have helped me so much. They have given me real strength. I can imagine how you listen to the news at 9 o'clock and think of me with love. I hope that Andrew's golden head rests gently and quietly upon his small pillow and that Richard is nice and comfortable lying in his narrow little carrycot. The engine of our boat rocks and rattles, the Officers' Mess particularly, because suddenly the speed is increased. With me sleep three officers; James, Raf and a special Navy officer who is really only a travelling observer. How childlike and natural we all look when we are asleep. I slept almost from 10-12 o'clock and must now go back to the bridge if I am not going to fall asleep again in this stifling and sticky atmosphere. The landing craft in front of us has steered an extraordinarily irregular course about which our Captain was swearing. I gave him a tin of self-heating cocoa to warm him. James relieves me at 4 o'clock and then I have a few hours to myself before dawn breaks. I have wakened James. A long line of flares hangs over Cherbourg and a few anti-aircraft tracer shots go up in the air above the immediate front line. Funny to imagine that there Germans run around their guns. I would like to know what they are thinking. The whole Channel between us and Cherbourg is filled with little ships which all quietly and efficiently sail towards France. The British, Canadian and American fighting forces on the war-path.

It is now approximately 10.30 which means that we have another hour on the sea. We can now see everywhere warships that stand watch, especially on our left flank. Up to now there hasn't been much to be seen or heard. Occasionally a battleship or a cruiser fires at an invisible target. The sea is still very rough and while we are rolling I feel sea-sick just as a few others do. But my pills seem to help though they leave a dry, disagreeable taste in the mouth. The air is free of aeroplanes. The best we can do now is listen to the wireless which reports freely and openly about the invasion and now already mentions the Cherbourg Peninsula. I would like to know whether you have already heard it, my beloved. My eyes become wet when I think of you listening to the news. We have just learned that the Eighth Brigade has landed. Resistance was slight, only occasional mortar fire. Very curious, but I suppose that the coast is under the fire of our heavy guns. Would that it be so! I heard that our CO has also landed, therefore our infantry must be there by now. God bless them and good luck to them. I do not believe that I can now write for very long. We can now see the French coast and very soon we will have to play our part. I must go now and look for the landing markings with my binoculars to ascertain our landing points. So, my darling, on we go! I know that you are with me. Come on the Bannermans! Let us be happy, Au revoir, God bless, I love you!

LIEUTENANT R FREEMAN RN
Second in Command of a Minesweeper, ML 450

We went down the Solent, past The Needles and out into The Channel where all the landing craft, which were very slow, had already set off. We then came up with the fleet sweepers, our flotilla that we were attached to, and we sailed in front of them. The channels had already been swept approximately halfway across The English Channel and buoyed. So we then dropped our sweeps and we swept on towards France for about two hours. But the speed that we were going we were quicker than the landing craft. So after two hours we hauled sweeps, turned around and went back.

We never turned up a mine at all in our channel. Then when we came up with the landing craft again, we then turned round and went back and swept all the way to France. I was there about five o'clock in the morning just at dawn. We hauled our sweep and the fleet sweepers went in and swept an anchorage parallel to the shore. They did that. Then the cruisers came in and one of them, I think it was *Belfast* opened up on the shore. On the chart which we had of Arromanches we had the details of the six inch gun emplacements waiting for us, and one of them was right at the end of our channel. But when we got there, there was nothing came from there and it was when I went ashore some days later, we found the gun emplacement had been hit and broken the barrels.

One thing I might mention is that at the end of the sweep there was a float so we could see where the sweep was in relation to the ship. On the float we had fixed a red light and when it was suggested that sea water might put out the light, I had the idea of putting a condom on the top of this light and I can say that I wish I had done something about this in later life. We swept half The Channel with a Durex at the end of our sweep, and when we got off at the end it was still pure and not damaged. I think I could have made some money from the Dunlop Rubber Company for that.

During the morning when the Skipper got his head down and I was on the bridge we got a signal to go and pick up a DUKW which had got Americans in who had been going to land on Omaha Beach. A DUKW was a universal machine which floated and could be used on water or land. It had a propeller on it which propelled it to the shore and then you engaged the driving wheels that took it up to the land, and it was used for carrying supplies. Well, these Americans had been supposed to land on Omaha Beach, but the weather was so rough that their engine had got swamped and they had been afloat for about six hours in this rough sea. There were eight of them on the DUKW and I had heard the expression 'pea-green', and all of their faces were pea-green. They were violently ill with seasickness and we picked them up, took them on board, towed the DUKW to a main transport where we put the Americans onto their own ship again and left it there. And then we just stooged around waiting for any other thing which we had to do. During the day they brought in some old merchant ships which they sank in semi-circles, and were called – the name was 'gooseberries' – so that they gave some protection to anchor at night in the gale. And we stayed anchored there and just before dark, a plane flew right over which was a Focke Wulf and the whole of the anchorage opened up and this Focke Wulf flew right through it and nobody ever hit it. *Transcript of tape-recorded recollections.*

LIEUTENANT COLIN KITCHING RN
Aboard an LCP

I was First Lieutenant of a flotilla of twelve tiny boats known as LCPs – Landing Craft Personnel, but in fact these wooden unarmoured craft were no longer used for carrying troops, they were to be used for smoke-laying – chloro-sulphuric acid pumped under pressure through a jet at the stern. As soon as the droplets of acid hit the air, a huge cloud of white smoke was formed. We sailed from Calshot on the Solent, part of assault group 321 and our task was to provide smoke screen cover for amphibious tanks in the Juno landing area and for some of the bombarding warships.

The mood of the flotilla's officers and ratings was remarkable, high-spirited bordering on ebullience. On our previous operations the mood had been determined, but quiet and low key. The difference was that this was the day we had been waiting for, training for – and we knew that if things went well it was the beginning of the end of the long war in Europe.

The journey eastwards along the Solent was almost like a carnival. As one of the first assault groups to get on the move we passed scores of big ships, of every kind, waiting their turn to sail. Soldiers crowded the rails of their troop transports and gave us, in our tiny craft, volleys of cheers. All these years later I am still touched when I think of it.

The speed of group 321 was set by the unwieldy tank landing craft a mere six knots.

About 5pm on the day before D-Day, 702 LCP(L) Flotilla leaves Nab Tower and the Solent astern on its way to the Normandy Beaches 'Note the World War One twin Lewis guns in the stern of my boat (192) and the bracket supporting the nozzle for the emission of the smoke screen'. Colin Kitching

The journey seemed endless and the force five wind made life extremely uncomfortable for us; incidentally, of the 6000 vessels which took part in the invasion, the smoke-laying LCPs were the smallest to cross The Channel under their own power. At 11.15 pm we sighted the first of the light buoys which sweepers had put down earlier to mark the safe passage through The Channel mine-field. Daylight came at 5.15 am, remember we were on double summer time, and at 5.40 am the Normandy coast came in sight.

About 9am on D-Day off Normandy. Colin Kitching (on the right) with the Flotilla Commander, Lieutenant Dennis Stephens who appears less than pleased to be photographed. He has just exclaimed: "For God's sake Kitch we're supposed to be invading France, not taking bloody pictures." Note the goggles Stephens has in readiness against smokescreen blowback.

At 6.05 am six of our LCPs went in with the tank landing craft for their approach to Juno 2 beach. The rest of the flotilla took up smoke laying positions to cover bombarding warships. LCAs (landing craft assault) were going in, crammed with troops. These initial landings met severe resistance.

Three miles or so off the beach the situation was surprisingly peaceful. The RAF and the USAAF had virtually overwhelmed the Luftwaffe, whose response seemed to be limited to hit and run attacks. British and American battleships and cruisers kept up an awesome bombardment of German positions ashore. At 9.30 am John Snagge announced, on BBC radio, that the invasion had begun; it was nice to know that it was official.

The day moved on, full of excitement and interest. Above all I had to admire the brilliant planning of this colossal undertaking; at sea, certainly, everything seemed to click into place as intended. The flotilla made smoke to cover warship bombardment; we were very much on a high. At 8.00 pm we gaped at the sight of hundreds of gliders being towed over the anchorage to launch further attacks inland. At 11.00 pm a lone Messerschmitt 110 was shot down close to us and we picked up a deeply shocked German pilot. *Typescript recollections.*

LIEUTENANT WILLIAM O'BRIEN, RN
in command of a Hunt Class Destroyer, HMS *Cottesmore*

We were allocated to Gold Beach and *Cottesmore* and *Pytchley* and *Cattistock* were detailed as escorts for the minesweepers to go over to the beachhead. The minesweepers were ahead of us. We sat in the swept water below them and followed them across, overnight, to the Normandy beaches. We had an absolute grandstand view of all the bombing going on and all the RAF and American aircraft crossing over the top of us on their way to all their missions. But it was so quiet off the beachhead – unbelievably so – that in due course we both decided to anchor. So we, at I suppose about three in the morning, something like that, we dropped

HMS Cottesmore, *Lieutenant William O'Brien in command, seen from* HMS Glenroy *off Gold Beach just after the initial bombardment.*

D Company, 1st Canadian Scottish (from Victoria, Vancouver Island) transferring from their troopship, *Prince Henry* to LCA's at 6am, D-Day. The Canadians have bicycles for what was hoped would be a quick exit from the beach towards inland objectives. I D Campbell

Personnel aboard *Prince Henry* wave farewell to the Canadians and men of No 2 Field Dressing Unit, RAMC.I D Campbell

Prince Henry, *taken from an LCA. The choppiness of the sea is evident.* I D Campbell

anchor about six miles off the beach and stayed there until the actual invasion time and all the rest of the ships came across. This was unexpected. I had thought we would get there and people would be firing at us and knew that we were there. But that wasn't the case – we were all fitted with lots of jammers. I had three round my bridge jamming various, no doubt, frequencies, radar and wireless frequencies. I have no idea what the jammers were for. Nobody had told us. I knew what particular frequency they were on, but clearly it was extraordinarily effective and the German radar must have been totally jammed by all this blasting that was taking place from every ship that was facing them.

(As for an E-Boat attack) Well, that was also something we were expecting but it didn't happen. Nothing, absolutely nothing. It was totally quiet and minesweepers went on, having done the channel up to the beach, they then swept the anchorage areas where the ships were going to come in and bombard or anchor and discharge their soldiers.

Then at H-Hour, an absolutely amazing sight of ships coming. Ships and landing craft coming down the channels that we had swept. As the minesweepers swept the channel, of course they buoyed it, and there were the lighted buoys for these people to steam in between. And we took up positions between two columns of landing craft, Tank Landing Craft, the Rocket Landing Craft, the LCIs – which had personnel in them. None of the really big stuff, but masses and masses of landing craft, and we had one column on one side of us and one on the other, and we went slowly in with them at whatever speed. They weren't very fast. And then at a given time we started the bombardment. We started first of all, if I remember, on the beach trying to destroy beach obstacles or explode beach mines and then inland where we had some specific targets.

We were being fired at by the Germans, they had a number of mobile 88 millimetre guns which seemed to change their position rather cleverly and caused either trouble to us or to enfilade the beach. We spent a long time trying to get one 88 millimetre gun and finally I went right inshore and went just aground, or almost aground, in order to be able to get it because it was hidden behind some obstruction or other and we couldn't get at it.

The rocket ships were the things that really stuck in my mind, the Landing Craft Rocket, I don't know what they were called, because the noise those things made as they went. They seemed to be always going off just as they passed us or we passed them as we went in, and this looked tremendous and didn't look as though anybody could be able to survive at the other end of that. We now know lots of people survived the other end of those things for a long time. Very surprising. Those were impressive. I had never seen them before. They stuck in my mind as something pretty formidable. *Transcript of tape-recorded recollections.*

PIPER BILL MILLIN

Piper to Lord Lovat, in command of 1st British Special Service Commando Brigade

...went along to the Hamble River, aboard the landing craft with twenty-one others, and we went in the leading one and I had the Pipes in the box. I had been playing to the troops waiting to go aboard the craft and then I put them back in the box and Lord Lovat said 'you better get them out of the box again because once we set sail by nine thirty or nine o'clock, you can play us out of the Solent. We will be in line astern. You will be in the leading craft with me', so that was the start of it then. He never mentioned what to do. He realised that I knew what to do. I had to pipe ashore in the water up onto the beach and then later he would tell me when to play.

Well, the music I played sailing up the Hamble River towards The Solent was *The Road To The Isles*. That was the main tune I played. I was standing in the bowsprit, as you would call it, and this music was on the loudhailer. Someone put it on a loudhailer and, of course, you could hear it over, I could hear it even above the bagpipes. And in the Solent just off the Isle of Wight were thousands, thousands of transports. Large ones, small ones and troops aboard and, of course, they heard the Pipes and they were throwing their hats in the air and cheering. I could even hear the cheers above the sound of the Pipes. And then a destroyer came in close. It was a destroyer with a name like Montrose, and Lovat looked round and smiled and waved because his family was associated with the name Montrose, and they came in close and then swerved away again and we continued towards The Isle of Wight, and then the sea began to become choppy so I was beginning to lose my balance a bit. I didn't want to take a header into The Solent so I stopped playing the Pipes and that was it. We were right into the Channel by this time.

After we had left The Solent and were out into sea – into The Channel, the hatches were put down and we were downstairs in a very cramped situation. There were some people playing cards, but most of the people were sick – some violently sick – including myself. Then I slept fitfully throughout the night. Then next morning the noise of the engines – instead of the thump, regular thump and it was calmer. So I went along to the hatch and pushed it open and looked out at a grey dawn and the wind was blowing and freezing cold so I shut it very quickly and got back down where the heat was. Then after about another half an hour people were starting getting gear together, their rucksacks on, picking their rifles up and making towards the hatch, and then we all got up on deck. The rails were down ready for action. Instead of being line astern the fleet were spread out and we could see in the mist the French shoreline. Bungalows along the seafront.

Everyone was behaving normally, I mean checking their kit, putting their kit on... I didn't think of being shot, how many Germans there, what was there, whether the smell or feeling of seasickness was still on me. We all got up on deck and we stood in the freezing wind watching the shoreline. *Typescript of tape-recorded recollections.*

The flowered fields of youth no more
Beguiled with life fresh joy the way
I long since left behind the shore
Where joyous insight lit the way
Through secret glades where spirits soar
And life seems one enduring May

Peter Prior's unfinished poem written soon after 4am on D-Day.

LIEUTENANT PETER PRIOR
Intelligence Officer, 5th Battalion, The Royal Berkshire
Regiment, 8th Beach Group

On board our big ship, the *Monowai*, I was sharing a cabin with a Canadian officer named Tomlinson and at 4 in the morning I crept out of the cabin and left him asleep. To my surprise there seemed to be no one on deck. I found the boat was going quickly through a line of lights – I think green on the left and red on the right, the lines separated by perhaps two hundred yards and the whole convoy was passing through this mineswept channel. I found this immensely impressive and moving. In the distance you could see a slight blur – the coast. I fancied myself as a bit of a poet and, deeply stirred, began to write a poem. I've kept it still but it was never finished because Tomlinson and others came up on deck and that made it impossible to continue.

In due time we slid down canvas chutes into the waiting craft, in my case Landing Craft Tank (LCT) 1542, and we set off at a leisurely pace for the French coast.

*Peter Prior in Bernières
shortly after the landing.*

We were a mixed bag, Canadian and British, infantry, sappers, signallers, gunners and stretcher bearers. The sea was rough. Many of us were beginning to feel sick. Getting killed is one of the things which never happens to you, but being sick is one of the things that often does.

SERGEANT H E G WALLACE, HAC

From Tilbury on board an American Navy Landing Ship Tank, down the Thames and through the Straits of Dover we arrived in The Solent off Portsmouth during the evening of 4 June alongside Horsesands Fort in Spithead off which I had used to fish for bass. As we entered the area of The Solent so we passed the entrance to Longstone Harbour where my family lived almost alongside Fort Cumberland.

I could see the Royal Beach Hotel alongside South Parade Pier, a hotel which had been taken over by the Portsmouth City Council after the Portsmouth City Guildhall had been firebombed on 10 January, 1941 and where my father was stationed as a police guard on the main door. I saw him a couple of times when he came to look out the front door – of course he could not see me but with my binoculars I could see him and several other Portsmouth police officers whom I knew. The pier itself was being used to embark troops on to small landing craft, LCAs.

Because of very bad weather the assault day was postponed twenty-four hours and so we, together with eleven other landing craft and an escort of a destroyer and a corvette chugged towards our destiny on the coast of Normandy during the late afternoon of 5 June. Except for the other eleven ships and escort there was not another craft in sight except an occasional nosey MTB. It seemed to us that we were to carry out the invasion all by ourselves. However, our anxieties on that score were quickly replaced by another more serious misgiving which developed into a certainty. Our tablets, hyoscine bromide, issued to all ranks certainly did not prevent sea-sickness! In fact our superiors could hardly have thought so either, as we were also issued with strong brown paper bags labelled, 'Bag – vomit'.

It was on this LST that we British first came across American style breakfast. Very early on the morning of the 6 June we were called up over the ship tannoy system with the call 'Now hear this, now hear this, line up at the galley for chow!' Lining up with our billy cans at the ready, we had ladled into them very generous helpings of rice mixed with honey or strawberry jam and coffee so thick that a spoon could almost stand upright in it. At dawn on the 6 June I saw the beaches ahead and it became very obvious we were not the only participants. As far as the eye could see the coast was fringed with hundreds of craft of all shapes and sizes. *Typescript recollections.*

MAJOR ROBIN DUNN
in command of 16th Field Battery, 7th Field Regiment RA

The run-in shoot was a unique method of fire. We had practised it in Scotland and in the Clyde Estuary, firing on deserted parts of Argyll. The gunners were in fact the first soldiers apart from the 6th Airborne Division, to fire their weapons on D-Day. The 'Priests', the guns, were loaded four to a landing craft, or LCT. They were loaded in pairs so that there were 18 LCTs carrying the 72 guns of the 3 regiments of the 3rd Division Artillery and the LCTs sailed in arrowhead formation with 7th Field Regiment leading and the other two regiments on each side dropped back slightly. There was a motor launch with us equipped with radar for calculating the range. The fire was observed by one FOO from each regiment in a personnel landing craft or LCP. The 7th Field Regiment FOO was Captain Hendry Bruce who was awarded the MC for his work that day. The LCPs each had a crew of four Royal Marines. They were equipped with three wireless sets and they had a powerful engine giving them a considerable turn of speed. They were taken in tow across The Channel attached by hawsers to the LCTs carrying the amphibious tanks which were to land just in front of the Infantry, just before H Hour. A skeleton crew of two was left on each LCT. Due to the rough weather all the hawsers snapped during the crossing. Captain Bruce's hawsers snapped three times. Each time the craft was recovered and it was eventually secured by a wire hawser.
Tape-recorded recollections, Royal Artillery Archives, Woolwich and SWWEC.

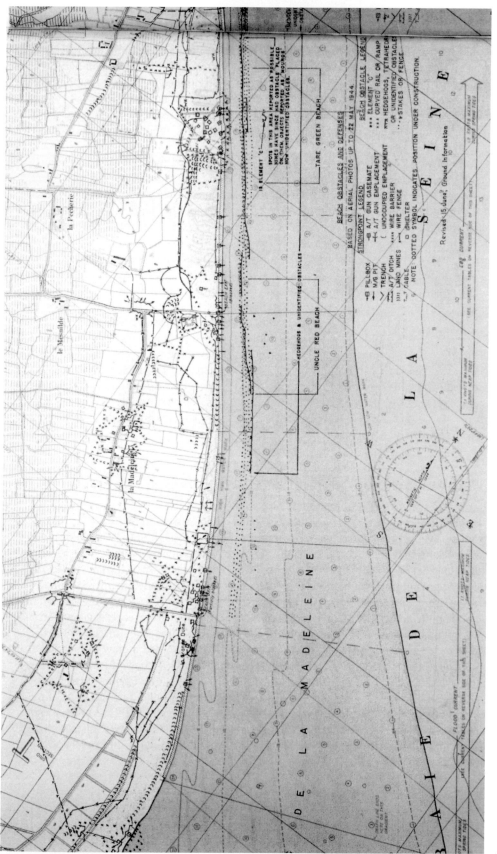

Map of Utah Beach obstacles and defences issued for the landing.

CHAPTER 6

Utah

On the extreme western flank of the allied landings lay Utah Beach forming a sector of the eastern coast of the Cotentin Peninsula at its base. There were no cliffs here dominating the beach but the gently shelving shore and extensive tidal shallows were defended by many man-made obstacles, a proportion of them mined. In the absence of higher ground with commanding positions, a sea wall offered cover from which the beach was defended.

Inland, the low-lying terrain and two rivers, Merderet and the Douvres, created swampy conditions rendering movement off causeways potentially difficult when flood conditions obtained as they did in June.

The naval bombardment and the aerial bombing were relatively effective at Utah in contrast to what was achieved in these respects at Omaha, and when the initial landings were made a little further south than intended, the assault force was fortunate in facing opposition not entirely but largely limited to small arms fire from behind the sea-wall.

There were further reasons for success at Utah despite the loss of three of the four key landing craft to offshore mines and a subsequent degree of confusion in that some of the amphibious tanks made for the wrong beach: those reasons included the US Airborne troops having secured some tactical objectives in the early hours of D-Day, the maintenance of naval bombardment on inland targets during the landing and the work of Army engineers in demolition of obstacles with the US Navy 'Seabees' similarly engaged and then seeing to the early installation of artificial harbour facilities. The demolitions and the harbour construction were noteworthy achievements here.

Rough sea conditions and the mines were challenging to the men and, as has been made clear, for landing craft on the run-in to the beach but casualties were relatively light and twenty-three thousand troops and large numbers of vehicles were landed during the day. By the evening Utah beach had been cleared of obstacles, declared secure and, apart from a failure to make swift progress towards Cherbourg – perhaps an optimistic objective like Caen from Sword – the western flank of Operation OVERLORD, was quite clearly the success it needed to be.

1ST LIEUTENANT HAROLD AKRIDGE
Anti-Tank Platoon of HQ Company, 1st Battalion, 8th Regiment
4th Infantry Division, US Army

The water was very, very rough. I carried two sealed envelopes. They were to be opened and read to the men at a certain time. One was from Gen. Omar Bradley and the other from Gen. Eisenhower. I read the two letters as loud as I could to the men. The only thing I can remember was one had the phrase, 'The eyes of the world are upon you.'

We were due to go in as the 5th wave, about 9.30 am but it was about an hour and a half later due to the choppy seas and being on the water so long I had become very seasick.

I laid on some mattress covers that were stacked in the two and a half ton trucks. Just prior to going in, the men were yelling that it was the greatest show in the world. They tried to get me to get up and watch all the fireworks but I was just too sick.

When the ramp was lowered, my seasickness was cured and I leaped in the water giving the command, 'Follow me.' At 6′3″ the water came just under my nose. Some of the shorter men were floating in the water as they had activated their lifebelts. We had to pull them in so they could get footing. And one jeep which was floating had to be pulled in before it had any traction. I had a cracker-jack of a platoon sergeant, Mike Kastracheck, who immediately ordered all the men up on vehicles and we all got to shore without losing any men or equipment.

When the ramp first went down there were four enemy artillery rounds that landed directly in front of our boat, about one half the distance to the shore. The units assigned to knock out the enemy's long range artillery had done a wonderful job, but one battery had not been knocked out and it was raking the beach. It was probably this battery that had sunk a few boats that we had noticed as we came in.

We drove through a causeway where the dunes were high on each side. It was a terrific jam. It reminded me of New York City. It was slow going. I kept thinking all the time, if that battery of guns would swing over and start shelling us, we would be in trouble, but this did not happen. It apparently was blind firing and I guess their last orders were to fire on the beach and that is what they did. *Typescript recollections, The Eisenhower Center for American Studies at the University of New Orleans and The National D-Day Museum, New Orleans, USA*

PRIVATE CLIFFORD R SORENSON
L Company, 3rd Battalion, 12th Regiment, 4th Motorised Division, US Army

The uniform of the day for this landing business was long underwear, OD shirt and trousers, the woolen ones, and we had impregnated overalls. They were impregnated against gas, in case we were attacked by gas, and they had an experimental jacket that they gave to some of us. It was a jacket that was sleeveless and it came down just below your buttocks, and when it got wet it rubbed against the backs of your legs. It had many pockets in it, it was made to carry a lot of junk. But mostly it was made to carry your K-rations, because we were issued K-rations to last us three days along with our other equipment and hand grenades, ammunition, and I was a 60mm gunner but they had put me in the mortar section.

I had two life preservers on the mortar, and one on me. They told us that the mortar was not expendable but we were. That was a nice thing to say. That sure cheered us up for that day. Anyway, that's how we were dressed along with our helmet, liner and our own personal gear, our gas mask and stuff like that.

Well, when we got close enough to the beach, we transferred from the LCI into an LCM for the ride to the beach, and it was so rough that you could almost break a leg jumping from the deck of the LCI into the LCM. If you didn't time it right, you could hurt yourself. But we all managed to get down without hurting ourselves badly, and we sailed for the shore.

But as we were approaching the shore, there were shells dropping on the beach right in front of us. Our pilot kept going right toward it. Another shell would drop, and another shell would drop, and we were still heading right toward it, and I began to get kind of apprehensive.

When we got fairly close in shore, we got hung up on some of the underwater obstacles, we couldn't go any further, so the guy running the boat dropped the ramp and said, 'Ok, everybody off.' An LCM has a grill work on the top of the ramp, and if you step in that, you

American Troops at Utah. US Signal Corps/Ken Pugh Collection

could break your leg very easily, and when it drops about 200 to 150 yards off shore, it's underwater and you can't see it. I was in front of the landing craft, so I had to get out there first. And I'm gingerly feeling my way out toward the end of that ramp, hoping I ain't going to step in one of those grills and break my leg, when I felt I got to the end of the ramp, I made one giant step and I went down over my head. The undertow took my feet right out from under me and I got soaking wet from the first step, and when I got my feet under me, I was about chest deep in the water.

There was a wall along the beach, the back of the beach rather. They had blasted a hole in that so equipment could get through. As I was crossing the beach, there were two six by six trucks standing by the beach, and four or five soldiers standing in between them, talking. And 88 shells came over and landed right in between those two trucks and when I looked back, I didn't see any soldiers any more.

We had to get off the beach in a hurry, so we couldn't dilly-dally and look at the scenery.

All the mine people had stretched some tapes along, so they had cleared a mine path for the trucks and the foot soldiers to get through, and we had to stay within those bounds, otherwise we might step on a mine. And when we got clear of the beach, the trucks and other equipment used the roadway, causeway, that ran across a flooded area, and we had to wade across this flooded area. There was no room for us on the road.

That flooded area was in some places almost up to your waist. The irrigation ditches in some places were over your head. Some brave souls would swim across the irrigation ditches and throw toggle ropes back and haul the rest of us across.

That flooded area was, I would guess, about a mile long. And we waded and waded and waded, and an occasional sniper shot would be fired and didn't hit anybody. We were mostly interested in keeping from drowning, because in some areas, the bottom was very slick and the footing was very touchy. You could slip down and fall down, and maybe drown yourself. But we all made it across that flooded area.

And I now began to see dead bodies. I guess some of the Germans were killed by some of the bombardment of the ships, and some of the holes they were blowing in the ground and in the road they were huge.

After about a half a mile beyond the flooded area, we met some paratroopers returning to the beach. We came to a crossroad, and the Germans evidently discovered us as they began dropping artillery shells on us. But most of them landed in the field alongside of the ditches we were hiding, and there were no casualties from that.

After the Germans stopped shelling, we got up and proceeded to round the bend and through a field. We got to the other end of this field and we were told to dig in. We all started digging slit trenches, and we no more than got them finished when word came down that we were moving again. We cursed a few people out for wasting all that energy.

The next field we got into, we began to see paratroopers, gliders all broken up, parachutes hanging from the trees. I thought for a while we got lucky and found a brand new jeep, but it wouldn't run. That's probably why the paratroopers left it, the Airborne Infantry, rather.

With all the parachute silk that was hanging around from the trees, I managed to tear up some of it and tried to clean up my mortar after walking through all this water, but silk is not the thing for soaking up water! But we did the best we could. My pistol needed a little cleaning too, so I cleaned that as well.

About this time, it must have been around noon or 1.00 pm; we finally wandered into a farm yard. I was hiding behind a pile of manure, and I was watching the Airborne Infantry come over. Another big wave of Airborne Infantry came over, in gliders towed by C-47's, and they started jumping out of the airplanes; and the sky was full of parachutes. It looked like a mushroom field. It was interesting watching them. I don't know exactly where they were going, but they were just a little bit south of us. They didn't land exactly in our area.

But it was a wonderful sight to see all those parachutes floating down through the air.

Typescript recollections, the Eisenhower Center for American Studies at the University of New Orleans and The National D-Day Museum, New Orleans, USA

PRIVATE RALPH DRAGOO
I Company, 22nd Infantry Regiment, 4th Division, US Army

We were lucky. I came off the landing craft onto the beach. I stepped in water with one foot. We were supposed to be in reserves, but one of our platoons wasn't there, so Lt Dan Crolin said, 'Come on, men, let's go!' so we did. We were scared to stay on the beach, but there was only one way to go – inland. We had to keep moving inland to contact the paratroopers. They were running short of supplies.

I had a flame thrower on my back. It weighed 100 pounds. The gun and holster weighed 13 pounds, at the time I weighed 135 pounds. A .45 pistol and a gas mask. We had trained to get over a 12 foot sea wall, but we could step up on it. We went in on Utah Beach. The Germans came out of the pillbox, one had his hand up with a rifle in his right hand. He was

American troops and vehicles at Utah. US Signal Corps/Ken Pugh Collection

ready to shoot me. I told my assistant to shoot it out of his hand. He did. We didn't want to kill them. We got off the beach and dug in. 'L'Company went through to take the next pillbox, they got the Germans out of it. We moved out and they marched some Germans past and they came at me like they were going to walk over me. I pulled my .45 and pointed it at them and they walked around me. You had to watch the SS Troopers. They were mean. They knew we were the first time under fire, but we got mean too, we had to, to live.

Typescript recollections, The Eisenhower Center for American Studies at the University of New Orleans and the National D-Day Museum, New Orleans, USA

PRIVATE FIRST CLASS RAY A MANN

Assistant Radioman, G. Company H.Q, 2nd Battalion,
8th Regiment, 4th Infantry Division, US Army.

After the meeting on the deck, where we listened to the talk, I went below to my bunk and seriously got my gear ready for landing. The compartment was a mess. Everybody was getting rid of excess baggage that they had been carrying along. The equipment was checked, straps were tightened and weapons examined. One fellow almost had an accident with a hand grenade. He had just adjusted the pull pin on the grenade to make it easy to remove, and then dropped the grenade on the floor. The jar falling on the floor almost caused the pin to pop out. Lucky he was able to grab the grenade and secure the pin just in the nick of time. After an equipment check, I took a shower, and I still remember looking at my body, each leg, each arm and I remember asking myself what I would be willing to sacrifice, if necessary, to get through the invasion alive.

For the invasion we were given gas-protected clothes. Mechanical protection made the clothes almost waterproof which gave the clothes kind of a greasy feel. Later on I learned to appreciate the clothes, because we slept out in all kinds of weather and often without blankets and sometimes the protected clothes offered additional weather protection. For landing, we were issued an assault jacket, simply a jacket with a large pocket in the back to hold a blanket, and to their surprise, we wanted to carry it. We had four pockets in the front for rations and equipment, and one pocket each side of the jacket would carry hand grenades. In some ways, the assault jacket was much more comfortable than the traditional infantry pack that we had carried up to this point.

After dressing, I rested for some time, and then during the night, we were given Communion and were fed. At about 4.00 in the morning, we were alerted to start boarding the landing craft. At this time, we were loaded into craft at deck level, and then the craft was lowered into the Channel. Ordinarily, the craft was boarded by climbing down a boarding net. This is a tough job to do when you're carrying a lot of equipment and trying to get into a ship that's bobbing up and down into the water. Anyhow, as soon as the landing craft hit the Channel, it started bobbing up and down. I got seasick. The craft was dropped into the rough Channel, and we took off to find our assault group. We circled in the Channel without much excitement until finally the time came for the ship batteries to open up and they started to fire with all their might. We saw the rocketship fire, with a little bit of the amount of the bombing from aircraft on the beach taking place, and then finally order came through for us to head for the beach. By this time, I was wet, seasick, and almost anxious to get going.

My boat had no problems with the underwater obstacles, and these were nothing more than large steel garrets that were placed so they would be just under the water, and each prong that stuck up had a teller land mine attached to it so that any landing craft that was lucky enough to hit it would be blown up. Our landing craft stopped in water almost waist deep, and we jumped out into water just about the time when our company commander said that we apparently were not on target, but what actually did happen was the error did work in our favor.

Our team rushed out of the craft and headed across the beach in small groups, just like that about 15 or 20 feet across the beach, shells started to fall. The first few landed in a group just ahead of me. Up to that point, I felt like this was almost like previous manoeuvres in Florida, even Slapton Sands. But when I saw our wounded men agonizing in pain and heard them scream, I knew that we were playing for keeps. A second group of shells landed near my group, and hit apparently our First Sergeant. Never saw him again. The company clerk was also hit and I took his bags and material he was carrying, and from that time on, I was acting First Sergeant, and finally became the Company First Sergeant. The Company Commander, when he found out that we were off target, surveyed the situation, and apparently there was only one German pillbox on the beach in our sector. This was defended on the hill by perhaps 10 or 12 men, and I was shocked to see that some of the prisoners that came from those pillboxes had oriental features, and I was told that they were Russians. We joked about it because we were wondering if we were landing on the right beach.

I finally reached the seawall and the German pillbox and paused to get my bearings. Even in the short time between my landing and the time we got to the seawall, I was shocked by the number of men who were landing and the number of wounded that I saw spread out over the beach. I saw a chaplain here and there praying over dead men. I was shocked by the amount of wreckage on the beach, and was shocked to be watching the water and then see tanks come up out of the water.

Le général Eisenhower s'adresse aux peuples des Pays Occupés

PEUPLES DE L'EUROPE OCCIDENTALE:

Les troupes des Forces Expéditionnaires Alliées ont débarqué sur les côtes de France.

Ce débarquement fait partie du plan concerté par les Nations Unies, conjointement avec nos grands alliés Russes, pour la libération de l'Europe.

C'est à vous tous que j'adresse ce message. Même si le premier assaut n'a pas eu lieu sur votre territoire, l'heure de votre libération approche.

Tous les patriotes, hommes ou femmes, jeunes ou vieux, ont un rôle à jouer dans notre marche vers la victoire finale. Aux membres des mouvements de Résistance dirigés de l'intérieur ou de l'extérieur, je dis : " Suivez les instructions que vous avez reçues ! " Aux patriotes qui ne sont point membres de groupes de Résistance organisés, je dis : " Continuez votre résistance auxiliaire, mais n'exposez pas vos vies inutilement ; attendez l'heure où je vous donnerai le signal de vous dresser et de frapper l'ennemi. Le jour viendra où j'aurai besoin de votre force unie." Jusqu'à ce jour, je compte sur vous pour vous plier à la dure obligation d'une discipline impassible.

CITOYENS FRANÇAIS:

Je suis fier de commander une fois de plus les vaillants soldats de France. Luttant côte à côte avec leurs Alliées, ils s'apprêtent à prendre leur pleine part dans la libération de leur Patrie natale.

Parce que le premier débarquement a eu lieu sur votre territoire, je répète pour vous, avec une insistance encore plus grande, mon message aux peuples des autres pays occupés de l'Europe Occidentale. Suivez les instructions de vos chefs. Un soulèvement prématuré de tous les Français risque de vous empêcher, quand l'heure décisive aura sonné, de mieux servir encore votre pays. Ne vous énervez pas, et restez en alerte !

Comme Commandant Suprême des Forces Expéditionnaires Alliées, j'ai le devoir et la responsabilité de prendre toutes les mesures necessaires à la conduite de la guerre. Je sais que je puis compter sur vous pour obeir aux ordres que je serai appelé à promulguer.

L'administration civile de la France doit effectivement être assurée par des Français. Chacun doit demeurer à son poste, à moins qu'il ne reçoive des instructions contraires. Ceux qui ont fait cause commune avec l'ennemi, et qui ont ainsi trahi leur patrie, seront révoqués. Quand la France sera libérée de ses oppresseurs, vous choisirez vous-mêmes vos représentants ainsi que le Gouvernement sous l'autorité duquel vous voudrez vivre.

Au cours de cette campagne qui a pour but l'écrasement définitif de l'ennemi, peut-être aurez-vous à subir encore des pertes et des destructions. Mais, si tragiques que soient ces épreuves, elles font partie du prix qu'exige la victoire. Je vous garantis que je ferai tout en mon pouvoir pour atténuer vos épreuves. Je sais que je puis compter sur votre fermeté, qui n'est pas moins grande aujourd'hui que par le passé. Les héroïques exploits des Français qui ont continué la lutte contre les Nazis et contre leurs satellites de Vichy, en France, en Italie et dans l'Empire français, ont été pour nous tous un modèle et une inspiration.

Ce débarquement ne fait que commencer la campagne d'Europe Occidentale. Nous sommes à la veille de grandes batailles. Je demande à tous les hommes qui aiment la liberté d'être des nôtres. Que rien n'ébranle votre foi — rien non plus n'arrêtera nos coups — ENSEMBLE, NOUS VAINCRONS.

Dwight D. Eisenhower

DWIGHT D. EISENHOWER,
Commandant Suprême des
Forces Expéditionnaires Alliées

Z.F.1.

One side of a leaflet air-dropped for French civilians. Ken Pugh Collection

101

We had landed and slowly we worked along the seawall to a causeway across the flooded land to meet another fortification of about 10 or 14 Germans. This incident was near a road that led to Ste. Marie du Mont. Inland, just a few farms from the beach we found perhaps 50 to 100 dead Germans who had been riding bicycles who were heading for the beach. They were apparently surprised by paratroopers during the night. It goes without saying that I was awfully glad that they didn't make it. *Typescript recollections. The Eisenhower Center for American Studies at the University of New Orleans and the National D-Day Museum, New Orleans, USA*

GUNNER JOSEPH S BLAYLOCK
20th Field Artillery, Baker Battery, 4th Motorised Division, US Army

We went up topside, and waited for our LCT to come in. We climbed down the rope ladder, down the side of the boat, and got onto the LCT. It was kind of rough at that particular time, which I remember because I had a hard time with the waves getting onto the boat. We got on, and with everybody taking a position, we started circling. I don't know how long we circled, but we made a big circle and kept going around and around and around. After a while, all the boats had gathered and we had taken off from the circle and started in towards Utah Beach. All of us were pretty quiet at that particular time. There was not much going on, and I think everybody was thinking about what their reaction was going to be on the beach and what was ahead of us, and if there was anything said , it was said in a nice, quiet voice.

As we were going on the way in, we could see the ships firing and see the paratroopers dropping from the 101st Airborne and the 82nd Airborne. The troop ship planes that were coming back were skimming the water about five or six hundred yards off of the sea. As we were going in, one of them got shot down right in front of us, about three of four hundred yards, so we all voted to see whether we picked them up or not or kept going in. The coxswain got outvoted and we decided to pick up the three people that had gotten on a rubber raft and carry them on in with us. We figured that that would only throw us off maybe six or eight minutes, so you're talking about a happy group of pilots. They were real happy that we stopped and picked them up, and then we proceeded on in. Everybody again was quiet. Every now and then we'd take a peep over the front or over the side to see what we could see.

During that time, I went back to the back part of the ship and ran into a can of coffee which I put into my pack, because coffee was precious at that particular time. For that first three days, we only had three chocolate bars, and I happened to get one package of K-rations off the kitchen truck.

As we continued on the way in, we got to I'd say about three or four hundred yards from Utah Beach. He let down the ramp and Lieutenant Fitzpatrick asked me to get off and see if I could feel any mines. I thought to myself that we had twenty five assault troops from the 101st Airborne who were fixing to come off anyway, so I got off. But I learned to tread water in Black and Red Creeks in Mississippi, so I got off and treaded water and told them no, there wasn't anything – no mines or anything, so to come on off. So, the 101st Airborne came off. They were about up to their shoulders as far as water is concerned, but the reason for this was the coxswain did not feel like he could go in any further because he was afraid that he would get hung up and couldn't get back out.

So the 101st airborne assault troops proceeded on in. Then next came the jeeps, and the first one that went off, went right on down to the bottom. Then the other two came off and proceeded on in towards shore. In the meantime, I had lost my carbine and wondered what I was going to do for a gun when I got in. Anyway, I hung on to the back of the jeeps, kind of pedalling and pushing the jeeps on in towards the shore. There were some 88's and some ack-ack and some mortar shells coming in, and as we got into the shore, the jeep proceeded on ahead towards the causeway. Bieganski and I ran to the sand dune and got up against the dune while we caught our breath a little bit.

After a while, we moved on down to the causeway, which was about one hundred yards from us and moved down to that and went up the causeway, then turned right and went about fifty yards and we ran into Manning and Lieutenant Fitzpatrick. We were getting ready to have a meeting with Gen. Teddy Roosevelt and as he started talking, a German fighter plane came over and started strafing. I dove into a foxhole and just as I went down, I started praying. About that time somebody dove in on top of me and just knocked the devil out of me in the back and knocked the breath out of me. He asked me did I mind, and I said, 'No, the more the merrier', you know. So after that was over with, that was pretty shaky at that particular time during that strafing. So we got together there with General Teddy Roosevelt, and he said, 'Men, you've landed about 2000 yards south of where we were supposed to have landed, and this is the co-ordinates'. He gave the co-ordinates, and each battalion commander found their places as far as their co-ordinates were concerned. He said, 'We will start the war from here'.

So, Lieutenant Fitzpatrick and Mike Bieganski and Tom Manning and I started down the causeway. There was some sniper fire, some 88's coming in at that particular time, so we went on about three or four hundred yards inland. Lt. Fitzpatrick told us to get off and wait here for the battery when they came in, and then he would come back and get us and take us to the bivouac area where we were supposed to put our guns. Mike Bieganski and I moved about fifty yards into the field and got up next to a hedgerow. We decided that our impregnated clothes we had on were beginning to burn us, and that was a good chance to change our impregnated clothes. We took off our wet fatigues and put on some clean fatigues and burning the impregnated clothes next to the hedgerow. At that particular time, we got a real good look at the war that day, and as it proceeded there were a lot of planes coming over, and a lot of our P-47's checking the beaches and so forth. It kept you looking up all day trying to figure out whether they were yours or whether they were theirs, and I remember that there were several German planes that flew over that really got the ack-ack guns at them, and then there was a Piper Cub that came over, so they really gave that one fits and shot that down.

Bieganski and I sat right there all that day looking at the war. We watched the troops as they came down the causeway. Then, later that afternoon the 90th Division began to move in. So that was a pretty long day for Bieganski and me, and we had several encounters there. First was that we had moved away from the hedgerow and had gotten about fifteen or twenty yards out in the field and were looking around and were trying to see what was going on. We kept hearing some fire and something go by us, and later on we figured out it was a sniper firing at us, so we moved back to the hedgerow. Later that afternoon, we kept looking for these planes and saw that one had spotted us and I guess he was trying to search us out as to whether we were German soldiers or American soldiers. As he came in on us to strafe, Bieganski and I dove on the other side of the hedgerow and he went on by. But we had another plane the same day to do the same thing, so they were patrolling the causeway and protecting our troops all day that day.

I was thinking about the war and if it was all going to be like today I felt like they could give it all back to the Germans because we were all so nervous that day, and excited, and scared. Bieganski and I used some of that coffee that we had gotten off the boat and fixed ourselves some coffee and stayed there all day D-Day. *Typescript recollections. The Eisenhower Center for American Studies at the University of New Orleans and The National D-Day Museum, New Orleans, USA*

LE COURRIER DE L'AIR

APPORTE PAR AVION *LONDRES, LE 10 JUIN 1944*

Le Jour "J"

Le 6 juin 1944 restera gravé dans l'histoire comme la date du déclenchement d'opérations militaires sur une échelle jamais connue jusqu'alors.

A l'aube du 6 juin les puissantes avant-gardes du Corps Expéditionnaire allié — parachutistes, troupes aéroportées, génie et infanterie — protégées par une formidable couverture aérienne effectuaient les premiers débarquements sur les rivages de la France.

Ainsi furent mis à exécution par le général Eisenhower, Commandant Suprême allié, les plans concertés des Chefs des Nations Unies concernant la première phase de la libération de l'Europe.

Ce numéro du Courrier de l'Air est consacré à un recueil, dans leur ordre chronologique, des déclarations faites par des chefs alliés et par des personnalités françaises pour marquer l'ouverture d'une nouvelle époque dans la lutte des peuples libres pour écraser décisivement la tyrannie allemande.

Quand nos amis et alliés français recevront ce Courrier, les événements auront déjà évolué rapidement. Néanmoins, ils reliront avec intérêt les paroles qui leur ont été adressées par des chefs militaires et par des hommes d'Etat.

Air-dropped newspaper for French civilians. Ken Pugh Collection

2ND LIEUTENANT WILLIAM R WINTERS

Battery C, 29th Field Artillery Battalion, 4th Infantry Division, US Army

There was very little enemy fire getting to the beach although there was an occasional artillery round coming in and we could hear some machine gun fire. I know I was very close to being seasick and I was glad to have my feet on solid ground.

We moved up to a sea wall and sprawled there temporarily. I remember taking my .45 out of the holster and unwrapping it and firing it into the ground to make sure it worked. We had wrapped our .45's in waterproof material. We then went over the sea wall and started advancing inland and within a short distance we ran into a lot of land mines and several of our men stepped on them. From that point on we advanced very slowly and walked very gingerly. About half an hour after we had landed, two armored tanks landed and moved up to where we were. We advised them of the land mines so they advanced in front of us and we followed in their track marks until we got out of the mined area.

Up to this point there was very little enemy fire although there was an occasional artillery shell coming in and sporadic machine gun fire and rifle fire. At approximately 9:30 my Radio Operator told me I had a call from Lt. Hurst, who was the Executive Officer of Battery C and he wanted to talk to me.

I got on the radio and said, 'Hi Jim, glad you got in. How's things going?'

He said, 'We are in position, but we did have sad news coming in.' He said, 'Our B Battery (which was approximately one and a half miles off the beach) hit a marine mine and all 59 officers and men, as well as our four self-propelled 105 artillery guns and some jeeps were lost.' He then said, 'How are you doing?'

104

Edward G L Slonaker's portrait photograph sent to a Women's Land Army girl. Edward, soon after D-Day, was sent to the American beach-head as a replacement officer. Sadie Greaves (later Hall)

I said, 'Fine, although I don't have much to do with no artillery to fire up from this point and am pretty much tagging along with the infantry and keeping my head down.'

He said, 'Well get me a fire mission so I can see if these big babies still work.'

I told him I would do what I could and get back to him as soon as possible.

It wasn't too long later that we suddenly ran into a lot of machine gun fire and rifle fire. I got on the radio and said, 'Fire mission co-ordinates such and such, fire number one only for adjustment.'

Very shortly they gave me 'on the way' and I picked up the round and radioed back, '100 over 100 left.' They gave me 'on the way' and the round was in the target area. So I said, 'Fire for effect.' They gave me 'on the way' with all four guns and we ended up shooting three rounds and I said, 'Cease fire, mission accomplished.'

We started advancing and I fired four or five missions and at about 4:30 we reached our objective, which was Ste. Marie du Mont, where we relieved elements of the 101st Airborne. At approximately 5:00 o'clock, planes started coming over towing gliders. When they cut the gliders loose they would land and were unable to stop in time and run into a hedgerow at which time the front end of the glider seemed to explode and equipment and men came out of the front. These gliders were made from plywood and Normandy is certainly hedgerow country with every field almost completely covered on both sides, top and bottom by hedgerows.

We were then ordered to move out towards Ste. Mère Eglise. Our casualties had been light up until this point, but on the way towards Ste. Mère Eglise we ran into hotly contested action finally getting to the outskirts about an hour later. We stopped at the last hedgerow looking into Ste. Mère Eglise and stopped at that point. There was a lot of machine gun fire and rifle fire coming in and shortly some artillery on our right flank started coming in rather close to us. I knew this was our own artillery and immediately took a yellow hand grenade from my pistol belt, pulled the pin and threw it out and yellow smoke came up which meant friendly. Very shortly the firing ceased.

Our paratroopers were in Ste. Mère Eglise and I was afraid to fire any missions because we did not want to injure any of our own men, but I did select three areas where I knew I would not hit any of our men and fired one round in each of these areas. This was merely to let the Germans know we were in very close, and we did have artillery. At dark we settled down behind the hedgerows and for the first time we had a chance to relax, and we ate K-rations which was really our first meal that day. None of us slept very much that night.

Typescript recollections, The Eisenhower Center for American Studies at the University of New Orleans and the National D Day Museum, New Orleans, USA

PRIVATE GEORGE L WALTER

Wireless Operator, 4th Infantry Division, US Army

We carried our M-1 rifles and wore gas-treated fatigues over our army uniforms. We loaded into landing crafts and then headed for Utah Beach. We landed on the beach and it was very busy. Some engineers were in and some infantry shooting was all around us, and some men hit and calling for the medics. We dropped our equipment and left it on the beach. Engineers were probing for mines and removing them. Wire was cut and more troops were landing.

Then we got off the beach and moved inland through the hedgerows of Normandy. It was terrible fighting in the hedgerows and we found a lot of the paratroopers, still in their harnesses, in the trees. We cut them down. *Typescript recollections, The Eisenhower Center for American Studies at the University of New Orleans and the National D-Day Museum, New Orleans, USA*

LIEUTENANT PETER LAWRENCE RNVR

Senior Radar Officer, *HMS Black Prince*

By scrounging spare parts from stores office we managed to improve the radar technically and increase its range. Our work had been on night patrols against German ships but it was now to direct the guns against targets on the beaches and on the Cherbourg peninsula. We were provided by the Admiralty with charts which showed the radar reflections that one would get off land. Now the D-Day landing we were involved in was the northernmost amongst the Americans, Utah. We were not just to target the German heavy guns but also smaller emplacements.

Transcript of tape-recorded recollections.

Peter S H Lawrence shortly before D-Day.

GUNNER WILLIAM L KING

Radioman 44th Field Artillery Battalion, 22nd Combat Team, US Army

About half an hour later I started hearing the ships talking back and forth. I was in communication – or supposed to communicate with the British cruiser *Black Prince*, the American cruiser *Tuscaloosa* and the American destroyer *Hobson*. And I could hear these ships talking, then I heard the infantry say that they had landed and I think it was somewhere around 7.30 in the morning when I heard the first transmission. So I called, and I don't know who answered whether it was the infantry who answered me or the ship answered me, and I told them I was in a position where I could copy both the infantry on the shore and I could also hear the ship and if they needed a relay I'd be glad to make the relay. So I was very happy to hear that I did have the right crystals in the radios and the communication was going to be good.

I hollered up the bridge and told the lieutenant that I was in communication with the infantry and the ships and we started our run into the beach. Along the way, we passed a couple of huge floating mines. They had spikes sticking out of them, and if we had hit one, it would have really blown us to kingdom come.

We started our run into the beach, and the shore batteries I think on Pointe du Hoc started zeroing in on us. They were coming within about 50 feet of us. They were throwing water all over our heads.

Then we landed. I think it was along about 8:45 am. I had put my watch in a condom and tied it into a knot and stuck it in my pocket, so I periodically checked the time.

Once we were landed, we were in a traffic jam, and couldn't get off the beach. My jeep was second from the end and the bottom of it was loaded with sandbags in case we hit a mine, also in each sandbag, we had a lot of food left over from the kitchen. And when we landed, we couldn't get off, so here I was sitting about halfway into the water, another buddy of mine, a fellow by the name of Jim Martin from Charlotte, North Carolina – was in back of me. He was in a command car, and he didn't have the same radio I had. He had a bigger radio, a more powerful one. I hopped out of my jeep and I honestly don't remember where the lieutenant was. I know the driver disappeared, and I grabbed my shovel and Jim Martin hopped out of his car and said to me, 'What are you going to do, Bill?' I said, 'Well, I don't know about you, Jim, but I'm going to dig a foxhole.'

HMS Black Prince *in the River Tyne approaching Swan Hunter, Wigham Richardson's Yard for replacement of her gun barrels after Normandy service.* P S H Lawrence

So I went a little way up the beach towards the sea wall and started digging a hole and I got down about six inches when it filled right up with water.

Then I remembered that we were told that if General Rommel was on the beach at that time, he would bring his tanks right up to the water's edge and shoot us off. And if General Von Rundstedt was there, he would allow us to come in and then he would pound us to pieces once we got in: so I thought, well, I'm sitting here in my foxhole, I'm getting wet, I might as well get up and stand along the side of my jeep. I had three radios in the jeep, two of them voice radios and one code radio.

So I got up and stood alongside my jeep and salvos of four rounds were coming in quite often. I thought that it was coming from a battery of four guns that were 88's. There was a loud explosion, and I heard shrapnel go around my ears, and the air go out of the tires of the jeep, and I felt something warm in my foot, and I looked down and I had a hole in the side of my shoe and I said, 'Ha, Purple Heart,' and I ran over and jumped in my foxhole again.

I looked and there was a medic near me and he was up against the sea wall in a foxhole and he was treating different fellows that came over to him. I told him that I'd been hit and he said he'd be over to take care of me in a minute. I said, 'Well, don't come down here where I'm at. It's not real safe down here because all the shells are landing down here'.

So I went up and jumped in a deep foxhole right next to him, and I kicked the sand down in between the two foxholes and took my shoe off and put some sulfa on the wound and put a bandage on it. I had shrapnel just under the ankle bone. He said, 'Boy, are you lucky,' and I looked at him and said, 'Lucky? How can I be lucky?' And he said, 'Well, you've got a million dollar wound. A lot of fellows shoot themselves to get a wound like this. You're

going back to England.' I said, 'Oh heck, just put a band-aid on it and I'll keep on going.' He said 'If we don't send you back to England you're going to lose your foot in a couple of days.' I said, 'Well, where do I have to go?' he pointed up the beach where a First Aid Station was located.

There were more shells landing up that way than down where we were. I said, 'I don't really care to go up there,'and he said, 'Well, you've got to go up there to be evacuated.'

So I headed up the beach. I had my rifle in one hand and the shoe and gas mask and every time a salvo of four shells would come in, I'd hit the deck and every time I got up, I'd leave one more item, and when I arrived at the First Aid Station, I don't think I had a gun, a gas mask or shoe.

I checked in at the First Aid Station, and they put a tag on me. I sat there all day long because there was a 20 foot drop in tide and they had to wait until the tide started coming back in before they could take any more wounded off the beach. There were more people being injured in that First Aid Station with those shells coming in there and hitting all those fellows who were just lying there out in the open on stretchers. I was one of the lucky ones. I could get up near the sea wall and sit in a foxhole.

Along about 7.00pm, one of the medics came up and told me that they were going to start evacuating and did I want to evacuate. I said, 'Yeah, but you'd better take the other more seriously wounded ones first and then I'll go later.' They had a jeep with a framework that would hold four litters, and they would drive down the beach a ways, and then out to a LCT that had dropped its anchor two miles out in the Channel in the deep water.

About 9:00pm they came to see me and said, 'This is the last load going down. If you're going down to the ship, you'd better come on,' so I hopped in and sat alongside the driver.

When I got down there, the water had come up high enough that there was about 150 feet of water before I even got to the LCT, and I started walking out to the LCT and all the fellows on the ramp were hollering at me and giving me words of encouragement to come on, hurry up, and that I was going through these underwater obstacles, these crossed pieces of iron, and not thinking that any minute I might step on a mine. I just kept trying to force myself through the rising tide that was coming in so rapidly it would almost knock me down.

Finally I got almost to the LCT and some hands reached down and pulled me up. The commander pulled up the end gate and used his winch to pull us off the beach. *Typescript recollections.*

JOHN C RHODES
US Navy Armed Guard, USS LCF 22

Contemporary notes

June 6, 1944, invasion of France – in first wave – 22 boys killed when sister ship was sunk on beach run. Fired (many) rounds on beach head. No one on ship was hurt. Thank God! *Ken Pugh collection.*

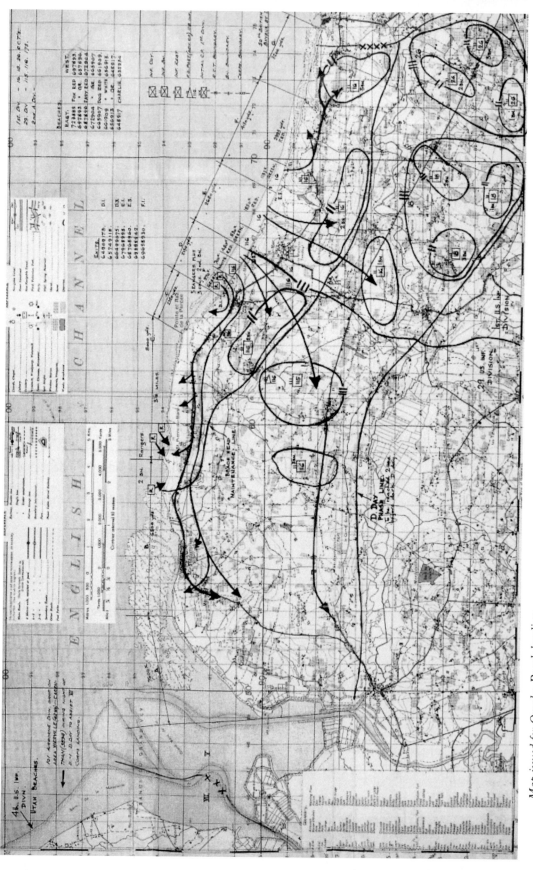

Map issued for Omaha Beach landing.

CHAPTER 7

Omaha

The six-mile long, crescent-shaped beach stretching beyond Vierville-sur-Mer in the West to Colleville-sur-Mer almost to Port-en-Bessin in the East, designated Omaha, and for American assault, was formidably defended by both man-made and natural obstacles. A thousand men would die on this off-shore mined, obstacle-strewn expanse of beach with its shingle high-tide bank leaving but a few yards at high tide to a sea wall of variable construction and up to four metres in height. Then, behind this and its promenade road and an anti-tank ditch was a marshy area behind which there were cliffs which at either end of the beach were virtually perpendicular. For vehicles the only possible access to the plateau behind the cliffs lay by one of four ravine roads inland. From clifftop entrenchments and concreted emplacements German defenders had a commanding view far closer and more dominant of their target than the Turkish positions overlooking Suvla Bay in August 1915 and it might be mentioned that in both American and British pre-war military doctrine the British and Commonwealth Gallipoli experience of amphibious operations against a defended enemy shoreline, more particularly in April 1915, had served as a warning of what the attackers could face.

The assault troops at Omaha had a desperately difficult task, but rendered essential because the Cotentin Peninsula and Cherbourg were objectives in the days immediately ahead - hence Utah – and the unquestionable necessity of linking inseparably the allied front from West to East.

As may be judged from the German defenders' accounts which follow, nowhere near did the Germans match the invaders in number but their geographically dominant position, their armament in 88mm, 75mm and 20mm guns, their machine-guns and emplacement protection, gave them for some hours a critical advantage despite the punishment they were to take from naval shelling and bombing the accuracy and destructive effectiveness of which was always going to be difficult to achieve when, or if, such specific targets were intended.

The losses in the first assault waves at 0630 were catastrophic – 96% of one company almost on disembarkation. The shattered remnants of units huddled up against the sea wall materially and spiritually bereft of what it took to overcome problems which seemed unanswerable. Then the incoming tide concertina'd forward anything which still had the capacity to move, men, vehicles, guns, armour, or human and material wreckage which floated. Targets for German gunners became more concentrated still. A particular tragedy lay in the premature launching of the amphibious tanks which on one flank led to their foundering with the loss of many crews.

The situation was saved by the movement of destroyers close inshore, their guns blasting the cliff top and then the resurrection of leadership and morale in a few, and then, more, men. The sea wall sheltering was now spurned and the cliffs assailed, no attempt being made to go for the ravines with their roadways. The trenches were cleared and the gun emplacements attacked from the rear. Three villages, Colleville, Vierville and Saint Laurent-sur-Mer, were cleared too and the gun position to the West at Pointe du Hoc was taken.

Linking with the British to the East was not achieved and the planned extent of the first day objectives had not been reached, but disaster had been averted in a tremendous recovery, sadly at heavy cost overall, with more than four thousand men killed, wounded or missing.

MAJOR LOGAN SCOTT-BOWDEN RE
Special Forces Combined Operations Pilotage

I was embarked in a headquarters ship with Admiral Hall, who was commanding Force O, which was the Naval force supporting the Omaha Beach reconnaissance. The headquarters ship stopped and the LCTs, which had been going a bit astern of us, came up with the amphibious tanks on board and the pilot boat was lowered and we scrambled down and got into it and off we went, just in front of two columns of the DD tanks for the right hand side and the same thing was happening on the left hand side, the 29th Division and the 1st Division. We were on the right hand side and we led them correctly in, not that there was any real difficulty, but there might have been had the visibility been bad or something like that. Then they deployed line abreast and so we then stayed alongside the left hand one quite close, almost shouting distance, but you couldn't hear above the sea and all that. The Major who was commanding that group of tanks gave sort of hand signals we could see quite easily. Then the Flying Fortresses dropped bombs which were meant to pulverise the beach defences. This is what the soldiers had been led to expect, and not a single bomb landed on the beach defences. (It never was intended that they should, I found out subsequently, but they were bombing behind the ridge on the artillery positions.) I know that the American soldiers, because I attended various briefings, were expecting the beach defences to be thoroughly bombed and they never were – the actual beach defences in front.

Anyhow everything you could think of was firing at them, and as we went in, in this little boat – it had a crew of three – a Lieutenant, regular officer of the US Navy who was doing his fourth amphibious landing and he really knew what he was about. A very good Coxswain he had, who also dealt with the engine, and they had a multi-barrelled pom-pom. Four barrels mounted on the front for anti-aircraft purposes but also it could fire horizontally. And there was a little Mexican with this gun, this multi-barrelled gun, who I got to know. He had gone across the border of Mexico and volunteered to join the American Army. Marvellous little chap, and then we had three little rockets on either side and I had to let off three on one side and the Captain let three off on the other. They were just to add to the weight of stuff going in, which was absolutely stupendous. By that time Battleship *Texas* was broadside in firing its main armament, and the crescendo was simply enormous. And then we got closer in, and then inevitably these landing craft beached. They were terribly heavily laden with, I think, four tanks in each which had everything on them they could have. They had any amount of spare ammunition and all the rest, and they were DD tanks to swim. But this Major with them line abreast had indicated to us, and the decision was with the Naval Lieutenant who I was with, that they did not want to be launched out at whatever distance it was. I can't remember, it might have been 1 or 2,000 or 3,000 yards anyway, because they couldn't possibly have swum in this heavy sea in the time to be there in advance of the

Infantry. And, to our absolute astonishment, we looked to the left and saw that they had stopped on the left and were launching their amphibious tanks and they sank twenty-six of them.

Now the beach, there have been two enormous changes of the beach since D-Day. One, there has been over half a century of sand piled in, plus some subsidence on the British beaches because the Plateau de Calvados extends out for two kilometres opposite the British beaches, and it was known as a plateau and it had a deep shelving edge to it which is on the charts to this day.

The other is that there were these two transverse runnels up to – oh, I suppose – two feet deep. One was deeper than the second one, which was further out, and the result of that was that stuff could get drowned, so to speak, in these runnels, and some of these DD tanks had considerable difficulty in getting ashore, and then they were shot up by a concealed 88 millimetre gun. A huge emplacement which is now totally visible if you go to Omaha Beach, because of the rock fall that has occurred over fifty years. It was completely concealed, and these DD tanks did get in but then were badly shot up and, of course, the Infantry took tremendous casualties on that right hand sector.

(And we could see all this). We actually rescued a couple of the crew of one of the tanks which had been hit, and the oil had come our way and I was wearing battle dress actually at the time but I got it so covered in oil that I had to abandon it later on and borrow some American kit, which I had to wear for the next three weeks. Literally hundreds of Americans were killed and a lot of them were killed actually at the back of the beach in the little boulders that were there, and then others were killed before they got there, and when the tide receded they got trapped in this water runnel and there were literally scores and scores of dead Americans just along there to our right. By that time the assault landing craft with Infantry had come through and as they returned empty we were able to put these two chaps on board and off they went to probably a hospital ship or something. But we, our orders were to stay around to see what happened, exactly what happened and report back to the Admiral. Well, the Admiral had come in so close he could see what had happened when we got back eventually after about four hours when things had gone right by then. We saw this wonderful American Brigadier General, who was second in command of the Division, get up to this pillbox with this embrasure, which by then had been silenced, and encourage the American soldiers to get through this bit of wire, which wasn't all that broad because the beach and the cliff converge more on the right hand side. They are a bit wider away to the East, and they then started getting at the emplacements in the ridge, which were colossal actually. I mean you look at it now and there is a nice sort of plain ridge with a hillside with a bit of scrub here and there, but then it was an absolute maze of emplacements, and so they had a very tough time indeed. And then The Rangers came in on the right and they got up the cliffs on London fire engine ladders. They got them most of the way up. Anyway they were well enough trained to be able to cope with the rock climbing at the top if they didn't. And then they came in and seized this emplacement that had been such a damn nuisance and other defences in the immediate vicinity of Vierville. And then, of course, things opened up and the American Engineers were quickly at work- it was thought one of the reasons for not bombing was they thought that they would make such a mess of these little re-entrants – particularly the Vierville one – with heavy bombs that they wouldn't be able to get through. They were in a certain amount of mess, but the American armoured tank bulldozers got cracking and they soon had routes going through. A decent route going through Vierville and up these other re-entrants to the left as well. And so it was – it then turned into a complete success. But great the advantage to Omaha was that once you got the ridge, which was only 130 feet high, you denied the Germans observation, and that was a great advantage.

Well, I went back to the headquarters ship for a while and reported to the Admiral and told him what little he might not have known. But I think he was so well informed by then that our reporting back didn't really matter.

The shambles going on on the left, due to the most disgraceful decision to launch the DD tanks from all that distance out, that was the tragedy. They had never been able to swim themselves in in time to be there ahead of the Infantry, and in any case they drowned twenty-six out of thirty-two. Absolutely insane. Thirty two tanks were put ashore on the extreme right, with trouble, but they got ashore. *Transcript of tape-recorded recollections.*

STAFF SERGEANT VICTOR MILLER
E Company, 5th Rangers, US Army

I carried an M-1 rifle, so I wore a rifle belt with all of the ammunition for the M-1. I had binoculars, I had wire cutters on the belt. I might add that I strung my binoculars on the back in-between pouches of M-1 ammunition rather than carrying it on a strap over my shoulder. I had the wire cutters attached on one pouch. I had a grenade launcher in a pouch hanging on the belt. I had my canteen on my belt. I had a compass on my belt. I had the first aid pouch on the belt. We had fighting knives. I always wore my fighting knife on my trousers' belt rather than on my rifle belt. And I had a bayonet, I'm sure, but that went on the pack. We were carrying light packs as I recall, without our bedrolls. This is the basic equipment I was carrying anyway. (I missed mentioning a most important tool – a shovel for digging slit trenches!). We did have to take gas masks and we had those and as we started out then – I might say that we had 17-jewel Hamilton watches issued to each man, and we had switchblade paratroop knives that would flip the blade open at the touch of a button.

Of course, in the pack, we had our raincoat, mess gear. And then we put on Mae West life preservers, and ultimately got into our LCAs and, as I remember, were lowered down and set sail for the coast. We were each issued 2 puke bags, and to the best of my knowledge, in our boat of 30-some men, there were only two of us who did not use them. Probably most of them used both. But they certainly were well used, and I might say that when you were crammed in that craft, there was no place – you were front to back solidly, so that if one was sick, if they didn't have a bag, it would simply have gone down the neck of the person ahead of them but that wasn't very good.

So we set sail, and it was quite rough. The boats pitched quite a bit, and this of course, was a great contributor to the seasickness that assailed most of the people. So we headed for the coast, and as we approached it, it didn't look like we thought it should. It was obscured by smoke. The grass apparently was burning there from

Staff Sergeant Victor J Miller (Special Weapons Section) nicknamed 'Baseplate'.

the many shells that had landed on it, and as we got closer in, it didn't look very promising either, in that we could see tracers going down the beach, and that meant people were shooting on the beach, and if they were shooting, somebody was going to get hit and we were the ones going in. Anyway, as we got closer and closer, we could see more and more detail. There were the obstacles, these triangular pieces of steel sticking up there with mines dangling from them, and this looked a little formidable.

And, of course, as I say, the bullets are still flying along the beach. You can see the tracers and the shells coming in, and so as we proceeded shoreward, we ultimately got to a point where the British coxswain on our boat said, 'I'm aground, I'm aground!' he dropped the ramp and the Lieutenant in ours, I believe Lieutenant D. Anderson, said 'All out' jumped and disappeared beneath the waves, and some in the front of the boat reached down and dragged him back in. I believe it was Sergeant Charles Vandervort who simply put his tommy gun in the ribs of the coxswain and said, 'I think you had better get us ashore!' I might say that our boat under those circumstances, probably got closer to the actual sand beach than any other, because we were able to get out without getting in water more than to our knees! I don't really blame the ship's crew; as soon as we were out, they could retreat and get away from this rather dangerous spot.

Meanwhile we all unloaded from our LCA, and having no trouble so far, but we promptly moved up and sprawled out onto the rocks that we were now on above the sand, and we were instructed to stay there until the officers got together to decide just what our next move should be.

There were quite a few wounded men who had been scattered along there, where they had been hit. Some of them were out some distance, and the tide is now coming in, and the little sand is now becoming sandbars, which are getting smaller and smaller as the water rises, and they were crying out in the hope of succor from someone. There wasn't much that could be done for them, certainly from our standpoint.

Finally, the officers did decide what we should do, that the perimeter sector had not been acquired by the infantry troops that came in an hour before. They were still right there on the beach instead of having the beachhead, including the road along the top that we were supposed to have gone out through, and they said that our mission should be changed to taking a beachhead. So someone put a Bangalore under the barbed wire that was strung along – there was a kind of seawall and a fence with many strands of barbed wire and ultimately, they put the Bangalore under there and blew a breach in that, and we started our ascent up this very steep hillside, which was still obscured by smoke. And so we began to go up that, hesitantly of course, not knowing what life was going to bring. Life may be bringing death! Anyway, we began to go up that, following paths. There were signs all over the area: 'Achtung! Minen!' – and it was very possible that these were mined and we would blow ourselves up if we proceeded. Yet, we had to go.

Suddenly, I missed one of my squads – they were both with me at that time, the two squads of my section and I missed one, and I went back down the hill and I found them. 'What are you doing down there?' 'Well, they tell us that there is a minefield up there.' I said, 'That's tough, let's get up there!', and so we continued up, and suddenly, I saw – I wasn't sure what it was. It was really a dead German, but I had never seen a dead person like that before. He was lying there in his uniform and his waxen skin, and I thought, that must be a dummy someone has rigged up there. If I touch it, it will probably explode. It is a booby trap.

But we continued up and got on top of the hill, finally. We reached the road that was the coast road running through Vierville-sur-Mer and St. Pierre du Mont. And so we're there for a bit, and we suddenly hear this whoosh! whoosh! whoosh! whoosh! and 1, 2, 3, 4 rockets fly over us, which are then landing down on the beach, and an LSI (Landing Ship Infantry) is there, and they're disembarking down the stairways on each side of it, and then suddenly that's engulfed in flame.

They kept shelling the beach, and these flights of rockets were going down there, and we were so happy to be above it, because it was far more dangerous than it was on top, and so we continued on and we crossed this coast road. I'm the kind of tail end of the Company. The Company had 65 men at full strength, so that wasn't a very big Company, so it isn't strung out too long, but they were moving up a kind of a ditch along a hedgerow and I'm kind of at the back with the special weapons. About that time the Battalion Commander, Lt. Col. Schneider, arrived there and, as I listened to him, it was quite interesting. We were apparently supposed to have an artillery group of some kind supporting us, and some Lieutenant reached the Colonel at this time and reported to him that they had only gotten one gun ashore, and he said, 'Fine – let's have some fire right up here.' And pointed at the hedgerow across facing us, and the Lieutenant says, 'Sorry, Sir, but that's too close. We can't fire that close a range. We have to fire further.' So that didn't help any.

And then they called for some mortar fire, and so one of our mortars was set up and fired a few rounds up there, and there supposedly was a counter-attack coming up there and so this at least helped repel it, and then they said that we should go in and take the town of Vierville-sur-Mer, and so we moved. We were east of that, as I recall, and so we moved towards Vierville and went through the town trying to find any snipers or other Germans that were hidden in there, and we really finished the day doing that operation. We ended up on the other side of the town on the west side in a kind of a perimeter, and at that time, it was getting dark, and we were told to dig in there for the night, and so I dug a fairly deep slit trench that night and bedded down. *Typescript recollections.*

CAPTAIN J C RAAEN Jr
5th Rangers, US Army

As we came in Colonel Schneider, seeing the heavy casualties being suffered by the first troops on the beach, shifted the whole two waves from Dog Green to Dog White where resistance seemed lighter. To shift 1500 yards to the left when only a thousand yards from the beach was a problem the British did well. We didn't lose a single boat, we didn't get mixed up and as we came into touch down we still had perfect formation.

Schneider's wave hit first, we were minutes behind him and apparently to his right. By now the noise was deafening. An LCM or LCT was hit on our right by artillery and burst into flames. A minute or so later we were in the obstacles. LCI91, 50 to 100 yds. on our right was hit by artillery. The boat ground to a stop. The ramp dropped. Sullivan jumped out with me right behind him. The water wasn't as high as my boots. The coxwain had done well by us. Ten yards of shallow water amid the damnedest racket in the world. You could hear the bullets go screaming by. Somewhere a twenty or forty was beating out sixty rounds a minute. Rifle fire came from our right as did most of the MG fire. A DD tank let fly a round.

There was the beach. And then a runnel of water. An MG burst chewed the water as I jumped in. The dry land again. The beach must have been about 30 yards wide at that time. I can't remember clearly, but I remember reaching the sea wall. It was packed with men two and three deep. You couldn't dig in because the rocks were 6 to 8 inches in diameter and piled deeply. The sea wall was made of wooden logs two or three feet high, with breakwaters running back toward the sea. Those breakwaters prevented good lateral communication on the beach though they gave us protection from the flanking fire that poured down the beach from our right.

I tried to get my life preservers off. They wouldn't come. I rolled over, still no luck. I couldn't go on like that so I stood up and still no luck . I looked around. It was my first look at men in combat. They were huddled in against the sea wall, cringing with every bullet. Artillery fire was churning the water's edge. To our left I saw LCI92 touch down...Wham! An artillery round caught the starboard ramp. Must have hit a flamethrower there, for the whole side of the ship burst into flames and spread to the deck. I looked back at our LCA, men were still coming out. There was Father Lacy, the last man coming out. He wasn't ten yards from the boat when Wham! Our engine compartment was hit by artillery. I don't know what happened to the crew. They'd done their job well – too well, for the cox'n was too hard to the beach to back off.

By now my men were dropping around me and in the adjacent bays. I yelled to a radio man who stood up and

John Raaen, on the left, with the Rangers Padre, Joseph Lacy, in Normandy. The Catholic priest whose physical fitness was questioned by the Rangers at his late appointment and was readily acknowledged by Lacy, served with complete disregard for his own safety on the beach, tending to the wounded and ministering to the dying at the water's edge.

cut my preservers off. 'Anybody hit?' 'Yea, [McCullough] got a slug in the back of his leg.' One man, my messenger, only two behind me hit. Not bad for thirty-three men.

I called for Sullivan. 'Over here, Red.' He was in the next bay. I slipped over and made my report, one casualty and the rest of HQ dispersed in these three bays. [A marginal note adds here: "Sully, for God's sake do something.' He was right, etc.] We passed the word for Col. Schneider. He was 50 yards to our left giving orders to the company commanders. However, I remained on the left [right?] while Sullivan went over to Schneider.

I began checking the men, making sure they still had their weapons and ammo, getting them more collected for the next move, while wondering what it was to be.

Apparently some infantrymen or Rangers had worked their way off the beach and up the hill [side, for] there was a fire fight to our right, up on the bluff.

The terrain was different from the maps. The high steep hill was 100-150 yds in front of us, covered with smoke and flame from a grass fire to our right. The terrain was flat from the foot of the hill to the coast road in front of us. With a battered little stone wall and then the wooden sea wall. Wooden sea wall!! Christ!! It was supposed to be stone! We were on the wrong beach! We couldn't be to the right of Vierville because there'd be cliffs in front of us and the Pointe de la Percee on our right. Therefore we must be to the left. The next sea wall was Omaha Dog White. I looked round more carefully. The sea wall ended three or four bays to my right. I could see farther down to the right one, perhaps two D.D. tanks of the 743rd backing down to the water and then slowly coming across the beach, each time giving five or six men cover to cross the beach. Back and forth, but that was 200 or 300 yds away.

Not ten yards to my right a grizzled old Engineer Sergeant set a heavy MG tripod down in a hole in the sea wall. He then went back to my left. A moment later he returned with a heavy gun. A thin Engineer Lieutenant in a green sweater was carrying ammunition. Together they very calmly set up their gun in that exposed gap in the wall. The Sergeant very methodically began to traverse and search the hill to our right where the fire fight appeared to be. The Lt., and I'll always remember the disdain he showed, turned around with his hands on his hips, surveyed the men huddled at the sea wall, spat out something to the effect, 'and you men call yourselves soldiers.' He tried to organize his men. Then the 116th. But to no avail.

By now, Col. Schneider had given the word to advance. The gap in the wire was to our left, HQ to follow one of C Company's MG sections. Van Riper [1st Lt. Howard E. Van Riper, my Exec and Commo Platoon Leader] and I drifted to the left with the Company, leaving the Engineer Lt. with his hands still on his hips looking disgusted. (I heard he was killed a half hour or so later)

We found the gap. A line Company was going through. Some Heine was firing from the right along the coast road. There was a shattered stone building, probably a pill box just across the road. C Company was moving through now. I tagged on, rushed across the road. Lying stomach down on a stone slab on the left side of the pill box was little Vullo, the smallest man in the Battalion, having general repairs on his buttox. He hadn't crossed the road fast enough. We trotted down a little path and then the column stopped, hit the dirt. It was[n't] to[o] comfortable there in the opened [open?] so I shifted my men to the left into a small gully or ditch. The column moved again, stopped, moved. There was heavy brush at the base of the hill and a flagstone path leading through. About six stone steps, and then a path leading up to the right. The column stopped as I reached the last step. I sat down and looked back toward the beach. Men were still coming through the gap in the wire, probably 116th. Boats were still coming in. As far as [the] eye could see, our gap was the only one through the wire.

The column moved on, up the steep slope, the smoke was getting bad. After about 50 yards we were gasping for breath and gulping in smoke, our eyes were watering and we couldn't see ahead. I passed the word for gas masks. We had the new assault masks with the canister on the face piece. Mine wouldn't come out. I put my helmet between my legs. Finally got my mask on – took a deep breath and almost smothered. I had forgotten to take the covering plug out of the canister. I felt like I was smothering to death, I couldn't get the plug out. I ripped off my mask, my helmet slipped from my legs and started to roll down the hill. Sgt. Graves stopped it. Now I was choking with smoke. I finally got the mask and helmet on, took three steps and was out of the smoke. I was so furious, I kept the mask on for fifty feet more just to spite myself.

We'd left the path now (it curved back to the left past a little shack) a[nd] continued to the top of the hill. We saw our first German, a dead one. He was lying in a little hollow just below the crest. He was sort of greenish yellow, looked like wax. Before we knew it, we thought he was a wax booby-trapped dummy. It wasn't till much later that we realized that that was the first dead enemy we'd seen. In the hollow, we paused for breath before crossing a tiny stone wall into the hedgerow country.

At the top of the hill we paused, looked over the scene again, etc. and then moved to the right (WEST), parallel to the beach. C Company's 81mm mortars and a light M.G. section were emplaced in the far western hedgerow prepared to fire parallel to the beach. I dispersed HQ behind in the field, behind the mortars and left a non-com in charge. Just as I left Van Riper came up with the rest of HQ and dispersed them in the same field. There was scattered fire to the WEST and south of us and some low velocity artillery was passing close overhead heading for the beach. Captain Bill Wise, C Co, C.O., told me I'd find Maj. Sullivan and Col. Schneider at the southern end of the hedgerow but not to go into the open field beyond because the enemy was to our front, I found Sully & Col. Schneider at the gate end of the field.

Unfortunately there was no <u>known</u> situation for Sullivan to give men. All he could say was that he had seen a patrol move off to the SW along a fence toward the far hedgerow. He had me move out along the fence to see if I drew fire, because that would be the best route to move the portion of the battalion that had not displaced along the crest. I zig zag[ged] about 75 to 100 yds before I reached cover. I had drawn enough fire to mention most of it friendly anyway. There was a dead German in the hedgerow. *From an account written in 1944, never finished but published in a military magazine. The phrases in brackets were added later and the piece as it stands was sent to Peter Liddle by Major General J. C. Raaen late in 2003.*

FIRST LIEUTENANT JAMES W 'IKE' EIKNER Sr
Second Rangers, US Army

We were all volunteers who went into the Rangers with eyes wide open and willing to accept the most arduous of physical training and with the understanding that we would quite probably be assigned the most dangerous of fighting missions. We who survived the initiation disciplines were really much more than just specialized infantry, we were professional fighting men – gung ho and ready for action.

We did not go into battle all weepy and full of fright, but straining at the leash with confidence that we could defeat the enemy in any circumstance. We were atypical soldiers.

I was the Communications Officer in my battalion and as a member of the headquarters group, I was involved in the planning, training and execution of our D-Day mission – the destruction of the enemy's 6 – 155mm guns atop the cliffs at Pointe du Hoc.

The guns were there – hidden away in an apple orchard and all ready for action. The enemy had moved them due to intermittent bombing raids. They were more dangerous there since they could have been fired from there without suffering counter-fire at least for some time. The enemy had placed telephone poles in the gun positions to fool the look from the air. Had we not been there the big guns would have opened up with devastating effect on D-Day morning.

James 'Ike' Eikner.

About daybreak on the sixth, we were all straining our eyes trying to discern the shore and it shortly became apparent to some of us that we were headed to the wrong Pointe – we were just off Pointe Raz de la Percee about 3 miles short of our designated mission at Pointe du Hoc. It was Col. Rudder who took the decisive action to get us back on course. This navigational error lost us the element of surprise that we had counted so much on to get up the cliffs. But we were not about to chuck it in – so in we went picking up enemy fire along the way. I remember when the first rifle ball hit our craft – BANG! Someone yelled out, 'what was that!' and I replied that we were under fire: 'Heads down!' So here we were under fire bailing water with our helmets to stay afloat, and some seasick from the rough water.

I was the last man off my LCA and had agreed to bring off a cloverleaf of 60mm shells- as I ran off I stepped in what I thought was shallow water but turned in to be a covered over crater- I went in overhead, climbed out with the shells, put them under the cliff and immediately started up a rope. About one third way up the enemy was leaning over throwing down grenades – I shouted up to two fellows ahead of me, 'They are throwing down grenades- faces in, butts out!' About that time there was a loud explosion and here comes an avalanche of dirt and rocks – I was knocked out for a while, and it was pain in my legs that brought me to – I dug my Tommy Gun out of the mud, took aim on an enemy, but 'snap' it was all clogged.

I spied a man in the cave under the Pointe with a radio, went down and sent off the first messages – then Commando Lt. Col. Trevor directed me to where the rest of my communications fellows were – we then established the CP in a large crater facing the sea on the cliff top. My fellows and I were constantly trying to make contact with our fellows at sea or on the beach at Omaha but could not raise anyone. We had to depend on the Navy for our support – they were delivering gun fire on the enemy when called for by our spotters – later when a Naval shell hit the side of a bunker where our observers were operating, several of our people were killed and wounded and radio contact with the Navy was lost – I then set up signal lamp communications with the Navy and we continued to call down a direct gun fire against the enemy.

I believe The Ranger Force, the Second and Fifth Ranger Battalions, commanded by Lt. Col. Rudder, made outstanding contributions to the success of D-Day. We were the first American Unit to complete their mission – by 9:00 am at Pointe du Hoc and quickly shut off a terrific fire down on Omaha Beach and also anchored the entire western Omaha flank.

Our greatest disappointment at Omaha was the lack of bombing of the enemy positions. I understand this was deliberately planned. There were no craters on Omaha Beach or in the roads to hinder progress, and the French gave us friendly waves so they had not suffered, but what there was, on Omaha Beach, was a huge number of American casualties.

The D-Day Rangers did one Helluva fine job of fighting on that historic day! *Typescript recollections.*

PRIVATE G M ANDERSON
2nd Battalion, HQ Coy, 16th Infantry Regt, 1st Infantry Division, US Army

That final evening we had a meal, another review of our mission, a final check of equipment and weapons. One could hardly believe the load we were asked to carry on this journey. All of us had a special gas mask carried on the hip, two or three days of cold food rations and our regular amount of ammunition. Some carried extra pack charges of TNT, mine detector equipment, Bangalore torpedoes, flame-throwers and extra Bazooka and machine gun ammunition.

My particular unit boarded the Landing Craft at about 4.45 am and joined the other six or seven boats of our section. We were scheduled to hit the beach in the 2nd wave at 7.00am in an area of Omaha called Easy Red. The sea was rough, as our Landing Craft continued to circle many of our troops became seasick. In what seemed like an eternity we finally headed towards the beach. I was standing near the front of the Landing Craft next to a Captain from Div Artillery with a pair of field glasses trying to observe what had happened to the first wave. As we approached the last few hundred yards we began to draw intense small arms fire as well as mortar and artillery fire from a couple of well concealed bunkers. The ramp finally was lowered and we began to evacuate as quickly as possible into waist deep water. Almost immediately we began to suffer casualties from the severe small arms fire. We had at least a hundred yards to go before getting to the sandy beach area and at least two hundred yards of sand to reach the cover of the rock and shale bank. All along the way we were trying to keep the seasick and walking wounded moving as we felt it was sure death to remain in the water. About 30 of the troops in my boat reached the safety of the shale bank, many of them wounded and some others so sick and exhausted they could hardly function.

After what seemed like several hours our unit had cleared a path through the minefields and reached the top of the bluffs above the beach area. In looking back at the beach area, unless you were there, you could not imagine the destruction of boats, vehicles, equipment and the bodies of the dead and wounded. *Typescript account.*

CAPTAIN BERNARD S FEINBERG

Regimental Dental Surgeon, 116 Infantry Regiment, 29th Division, US Army

At about 4am we debarked down rope ladders, fully equipped, 65 pounds on our backs. Gas masks, first aid kits, Red Cross Brassards on arm, no rank on shoulders and so forth into our LCI. Litter bearers had litters (ie. stretchers)

We circled for about an hour or so, moving closer to shore then straightened out and went in. We landed 20 minutes after H-Hour which was 6 am.

We were taking constant fire from batteries and pill boxes on shore. Our LCI was extremely lucky. No casualties. From what I saw others were not so lucky – men (and material) in the choppy water, drowning, dying, yelling for help.

Our ramp dropped open and we ran off in disciplined order, no panic. Training paid off. Waist deep in water. Rushed into the beach, which was strewn with our dead and wounded, plus those floating in the water. Our medics became busy immediately, giving First Aid and so forth. Coming off the LCI, our radio man, Private Jerry Greene, was shot through his thigh muscle, upper arm muscle, and nevertheless with his radio on his back dragged a wounded buddy into shore and saved his life.

We all tried to get to the bottom of the hill for protection. We were being fired on with

Looking over Pointe du Hoc, Omaha, a few days after the landing. A photograph taken by Andrew Huxley.

everything conceivable, witheringly, from above, also enfilading fire from above and to the right and left.

Meanwhile, we could see to the north of us Pointe du Hoc, the steep cliff on which our 29th Rangers were assaulting. For the first few minutes or so, they and our infantry were exchanging fire until communications sorted that out.

We were pinned down for about five or more hours.

About 12:00 noon or so our first tanks came ashore. What a beautiful sight. About 2:30 pm saw first German prisoners – another beautiful sight. Also more men and material all up and down the beach were arriving, the remainder of our regiment.

Meanwhile, Brigadier Dutch Cota, our Assistant Divisional Commander, was all over the place after shouting those famous words, something like this, 'No sense dying here, men. Let's go up on the hill and die.' And with those words, he started to tap soldiers on their butts and said, '29, Let's go!' – our divisional yell. And I was one of them.

We went up the hill on the way to Vierville-sur-Mer. Saw many German dead all the way.

We arrived at liberated Vierville-sur-Mer and spent the night in trenches about five and a half feet deep evacuated by retreating Germans. *Typescript recollections, The Eisenhower Center for American Studies at the University of New Orleans and the National D-Day Museum, New Orleans, USA*

PRIVATE JOSEPH DOUGHERTY

M Company, 116th Infantry Regiment, 29th Infantry Division, US Army

From the *USS Charles Carroll* we embarked into small landing craft about 30 soldiers to a craft. The water was very, very rough. I used both my vomit bags and borrowed another.

(The Naval Officer in command of our craft got us into shallow water before letting the ramp down and staggering through barbed wire we waded up the beach). Bullets started flying and landing right in front of us. It looked as if someone had thrown big hands of gravel at us – the bullets were hitting just in front.

When we got under an overhang of the cliffs we felt safer; then, away from the beach,

With the tide up, the narrowness of the beach in front of the cliffs is captured in this photograph of US 1st Infantry Division troops at Omaha. US Signal Corps/Ken Pugh Collection

Awaiting evacuation. US Signal Corps/Ken Pugh Collection

we had to go through a grassy field full of mines and up a hillside sewn with oats (giving cover.)

My number two gunner carrying the barrel to my tripod did not reach this point as quickly. I saw on my right, a D Coy boy with a barrel but the tripod man didn't get in. I waved him down and we put his barrel on my tripod and we shot into the aperture of that huge pillbox that we weren't far away from. Of course we didn't hit anybody but it kept them from shooting too much at us. *Transcript of tape-recorded recollections, The Eisenhower Center for American Studies at the University of New Orleans and the National D-Day Museum, New Orleans, USA*

PRIVATE WILLIAM E PARKER

D Company, 4th Medical Battalion, 4th Motorised Division

We had the Company Commander's jeep and we were supposed to go inland and locate our area where we were supposed to set up a clearing station to evacuate the wounded but we couldn't get off the beach.

So immediately we started to help to take care of the wounded that were there on the beach. Everywhere you looked, in the water, and on the beach, was the wounded and the dead. I don't guess there was any wounded still lying in the water. We didn't bother with those, but we worked our way up and down the beach, putting in sulfa drugs, giving sulfa tablets, and bandaging those that were wounded, some were wounded real bad to where you could take and stick a bandage in their side or somewhere, it was so bad, to stop the bleeding and try to save their lives, but there was a lot of them that didn't make it. So, anyway, we stayed on that beach all day on Tuesday June 6th, till about 11 or 12 o'clock that night. We decided we'd get over there in the little ol' hole, in one of those sand dunes, and try to get a little sleep. We put our blanket up over us and got a little sleep. *Typescript recollections, The Eisenhower Center for American Studies at the University of New Orleans and The National D-Day Museum, New Orleans, USA*

LIEUTENANT AUSTIN PROSSER RNR
Landing Craft Tank 1171

We were at Saltash on the *Tamar* and attached to the Yanks. We actually landed in St John's on the other side of the river for D-Day – then it was postponed and we came back to Cawsands Bay and then sailed again. We had got six Sherman tanks, two half-tracked ambulances and two half-tracked ammunition lorries as our load and the Yanks lived on board. We let the officers use our small wardroom and you can imagine how cluttered we were. They drank all our booze before we sailed – so we had none left. But they had brought up neat alcohol from their ambulances and drank that.

We got off Portland and this is one of the most fascinating things – I still see it in my mind now – we were told to 'hove to', which in our language is pull off to one side and let the fleet through. The American Fleet came through, and it was the most fascinating sight I have ever seen. It was led by one little minesweeper, then followed by their destroyers and cruisers and what not, and the whole battle fleet came past, and we still didn't know what was going to happen. All we were told, we had to go to this beach. After they went through we sailed off. Got off to St Catherine's Point, where all the convoys were meeting.

We found out we were going on Omaha Beach. There was no question it was going to be the nasty one, and one of the flotillas came down with us peeled off to Utah. We were due at 8.30 to land our first tanks. Because when we got there we were in exactly the right place, I mean it's hard to describe, but there were ships everywhere and merchant ships everywhere and balloons flying and God knows what, and it was rough. Tanks wallowing around in the water and we got there at 8.30. Couldn't get in anywhere. It was all cluttered up with junk, which my job in Sicily would have been clearing that junk, but it was broken down landing craft, assault craft, broken down tanks – we couldn't get in. And the Beach Master was screaming at us through his loudhailer – had we Engineers on board. They wanted Engineers to get up to blow things up, the Yanks had got their loading wrong. The Engineers were still at sea. So we were told to push off down the beach and see if we could find somewhere to beach. And we eventually went in, and there was some broken down Yankee assault craft there. We went in stern first and hooked them on and pulled them off out of the way so we could go in and land the tanks. But we had to clear bodies away, and that was at ten o'clock we eventually got them off. We got the tanks off.

There were blokes running around in assault craft, which were the small craft, and we gave them lines. They went in and hooked onto these broken down craft and we just towed them into deep water and dropped them off. So, then we turned round, but when we went in we dropped the big, what we call a 'kedge anchor' and we got in on this kedge anchor. You drop that off about half a cable out and you go in on the kedge anchor. So when you have unloaded you can pull yourself off with it, because you can't run your engines because you would suck the sand in. It's highly technical stuff.

The beach itself was chaos. I mean it was just a mass of moving things and then we were being shelled from a bunker. We were being shelled from both ends. I was there when that destroyer went up and blasted (defence emplacements). Went close up, I was right by the side of it – I have a deaf ear now from it. We were under these heavy guns being blasted by the Yankee battleships. Every time they fired, I think, we lifted out of the water. You weren't scared because you were so busy but we watched our tanks go off up towards the gully they were trying to get up, and they were all shot up before they got off the beach – all the tanks we landed. We saw them all shot up. We were told, we had instructions by radio not to leave the beach because they thought they would have to evacuate Omaha Beach and we were told to lay off the beach because we were carrying a balloon. We laid off the beach, our flotilla – about twelve of us landing craft – behind the battleships and our balloons there and we stayed there that night and we didn't sail until the next day. *Transcript of tape-recorded recollections.*

GEFREITER FRANZ GOCKEL

3rd Company, 726 Regiment, 716 Division, *Wehrmacht*, at a machine-gun post in defence of emplacement WN 62, Colleville sur Mer, Omaha Beach

Letter: Saturday, 10 June 1944

Dear Parents, brothers and sisters.

Best wishes from your son and brother Franz. I'm fine but for my wound. I hope the same can be said of you.

On Tuesday 6th June there was an attack, the like of which no-one, not even those who fought on the Eastern Front, had experienced. The Americans bombed us on both estuaries – the left and right. In full expectation of everything that could hit us, we waited by our weapons. About four o'clock in the first grey light of morning we saw the first big boat units. We had no sooner noticed them than in rapid succession there were flashes on the boats. Soon the first shells came screaming towards us. There was scarcely a square metre, where either a bomb or a shell hadn't fallen. In five minutes the house was going up in flames. My gun was in a dugout some forty metres from the house which was hit by several shells. It stood up against the first few, but as the first landing craft came in, it too went up in flames. The machine gunner got several bullet holes in his jacket. A few shells came at us – 7.5's and grenade throwers right in front of the gunports with the result that half of the fortification collapsed... It was with great difficulty that I was able to get out of the rubble. Then I ran into the communication trench. Then it took a direct hit and yet again I landed up under rubble, once more scarcely able to free myself. Right next to my head lay a 7.5 shell.

Then the slaughter began. The water was about 250 metres away. Many landing craft were destroyed by heavy fire, but many more kept coming. Now for the Americans it was all about getting over 250 metres of sand and that was disastrous for them. It was also a miracle that with all the shooting not one of our section was either killed or wounded. By now the Americans were starting to get a taste of us. Although we were shot at from the landing craft, our twin and four-barrelled guns continued unrelenting fire. Soon the beach was covered in Americans

Franz Gockel, 17 years old, Holland 1943.

Franz Gockel's pre-war post-card view of Vierville sur Mer onto which he has marked German strong point positions overlooking Omaha.

caught by our firepower. Only a few reached the safety of the gravel bank. Many also remained uninjured lying on the sands. But as the water came in, they too had to move on. In turn we opened fire on them. Beyond the gravel bank was the fire curtain for our grenade-throwers. These created heavy losses amongst the Americans. We couldn't understand how they, despite such heavy losses under such a hail of fire, could still come on. Around midday they had broken through on our left. Then we also began having our first wounded, but not severely wounded. All were able to get back into town themselves. Around three o'clock I was

German strong points above Omaha Beach (Franz Gockel was at Number 62).

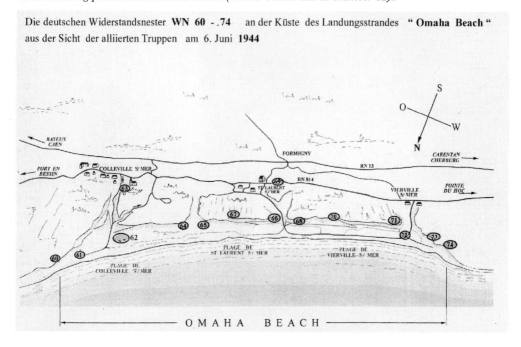

Die deutschen Widerstandsnester **WN 60 - .74**   an der Küste des Landungsstrandes **" Omaha Beach "** aus der Sicht der alliierten Truppen am 6. Juni **1944**

wounded by a sniper on the flank. He was about twenty-five metres away from me in a ditch. Until then I hadn't noticed him, otherwise he wouldn't have managed to shoot. So then I too went back to be transported off with several comrades. Kaiserling and Platz were similarly wounded, but I've heard no more about them. I'm now 120 kilometres away from the coast, but it's all still going on...

It's estimated our unit has accounted for between 2,000-2500 dead and wounded as well as fifteen to twenty tanks destroyed. In addition about twenty small to medium landing craft and a large tank landing craft have been destroyed. We seem to have offset the massive superiority in numbers.

I fired over 400 shots with my rifle, getting about 300 hits and at a distance of about 100-250 metres.

But that's enough for now. Best wishes, John and brother Franz.

Recalled later:

Once again I inspected the ammunition belt. I attempted to concentrate on my weapon to take my mind away from the impending events. In a recess of my gun position stood ignition switches for two flamethrowers which were aimed at the beach and the tank trench. Also within reach was a pile of hand grenades.

The bombers were suddenly over us, and it was now too late to follow through with the plan to spring into the prepared dugout for cover. I dived under the machine-gun as bombs screamed and hissed into the sand and earth. Two heavy bombs fell upon our position, and we held our breath as more explosions fell into the ground behind us. Debris and clouds of smoke enveloped us. The earth shook. Eyes and nose were filled with dust. Sand ground between teeth. There was no hope for help. No German aircraft appeared. This sector had no anti-aircraft guns, and unimpeded the bombers could drop their deadly load upon us.

An endless fleet lay before our sector. Heavy warships cruised along as if passing for review. A spectacular but terrifying experience for those of us who survived the Naval gunfire.

0600

The heavy naval guns fired salvo after salvo into our positions. At first the ships lay well offshore but the range slowly decreased. With unbelieving eyes we could recognise individual landing craft. The hail of shells falling upon our position grew heavier, fountains of sand and debris rose in the air with the impact. The mined obstacles in the water were partially destroyed. The morning dawn over the approaching landing fleet exhibited for us approaching doom. Bombs and heavy calibre shells continued to slam into the earth, tossing tangles of barbed wire, obstacles and clouds of dirt into the air. The explosions of naval gunfire became mixed with the salvoes of rapid fire weapons.

Our heavy weapons were pre-set on defensive fire zones, thus we could only wait, and continue to wait. It appeared as though the enemy would land in the approximate beach centre. We had planned on the enemy attempting a landing only at high tide, in order to drive the boats over the open beach. But now was low tide, the waterline lay about 300 metres distant.

The shells and bombs had destroyed many of our positions, but we had not suffered heavy casualties. We used every available minute to retain contact with one another throughout the rain of shells. Along with warships of every description we could see troop transports, landing craft and assault craft preparing to set the invading army upon the beach. Suddenly the rain of shells ceased, and a strange quiet enveloped us. But only for a short time. Again explosions of gunfire from the ships could be heard, and again shells slammed into the beach. Some of the log obstacles were splintered, some burning; slowly the wall of explosions approached, metre by metre. Worse than before, a deafening torrent of smoke and dust rolled toward us, cracking, screaming, whistling and sizzling, destroying everything in its path. We crouched small and helpless behind our weapons. I prayed for survival, and my fear passed.

The first shells of this barrage landed among us, but miraculously no one was wounded. Over us and within our positions the explosions pounded and rattled. Hissing and screaming the shrapnel and splinters flew through the air. They slammed against concrete or thudded into the ground. Suddenly it was again silent.

Now with great speed dive bombers approached our positions at low altitude, weapons rattling, bullets whistling and popping around us. There was six of us in the position, and still no one was wounded. A comrade stumbled out of the smoke and dust into my position and screamed: 'Franz watch out! They're coming!'

The sea had come alive. Assault boats and landing craft rapidly approached the beach. The first closely packed landing troops sprang from the boats, some knee deep in water, others up to their chests. There was a race over the open beach toward the low stone wall running parallel to the waterline which offered the only protection. The defenders sprang into action. It had been futile to attempt to defend against air and naval bombardment, and until now we could only attempt to save our own lives. Now we heard the first machine gun bursts. Within seconds the first waves of assault troops collapsed after making only a few metres headway. Assault craft careered leaderless back and forth on the water.

I had opened fire with my heavy machine gun with short bursts aimed at the landing boats, when the sand-covered ammunition belt caused it to jam. I tore the belt from the feed tray, shook it clean, and slapped it back into the tray. At that instant the machine-gun was torn from my hands and I don't know how I escaped this blast without injury. The ignition switches for the flame-throwers had been destroyed by shell splinters, only the remains of the cables hung limply in place.

A comrade fired round after round from his 75mm gun, and soon return fire came from the oncoming assault craft. His position was covered with smoke and dust from exploding shells, a round from a tank struck the aperture of his gun position and put the weapon out of commission, the gun crew escaping to safety with light wounds.

On came the second wave of assault craft. Again a race across the beach. Again the defence positions opened fire. The resistance from the defenders grew weaker. More and more comrades were killed or wounded. The tide came slowly forward, the waterline creeping up the beach. With the incoming tide the open area became shorter for the assault troops. Tank landing boats dropped their ramps and the tanks rolled onto the beach, shooting as they moved.

The battle raged back and forth for some hours, the beach became strewn with dead, wounded and shelter-seeking soldiers. Anything that could move on the beach sought shelter, with many falling victim to the defenders. We began to notice our own losses. The lightly wounded were bandaged and sent to the rear. The seriously wounded were carried to a sheltered area. Dead comrades were left lying where they fell, there was no time to look after them.

Some of the assault troops reached the low stone wall, seeking protection from our gunfire. The safety offered here was temporary. Our mortar crews had waited for this moment, and began to lay deadly fire upon pre-set coordinates along the wall. Mortar rounds with impact fuses exploded on target. The shell splinters, wall fragments, and stones inflicted casualties upon the troops. Hour after hour boats and tank landing craft assaulted the beach, attempting to gain as much ground as possible upon the flat sand. With great confusion and haste soldiers, weapons and equipment were pushed onto the beach. Soldiers attempted to organise. Despite constant fire upon our positions from naval guns of all calibres and heavy machine-gun fire, the waves of attackers broke against our defences. The tide continued to rise, the unprotected stretch of beach became more narrow, and the surf brought a gruesome cargo to shore. In the swells wounded soldiers fought for their lives, the dead troops floated and tossed in the water, the waves dumping them onto the shore. The incoming tide had reached the low wall at midday, and the landing craft with shallow draft lay approximately 100 metres before us. With rifles we continued to attempt to stop the onslaught. Landing craft were fired upon, and a large transport filled with soldiers took hits upon the decks and bridge. Over the confusion we could hear commands shouted over a loud speaker or through a megaphone.

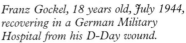

Franz Gockel, 18 years old, July 1944, recovering in a German Military Hospital from his D-Day wound.

We continued to replenish our rifle ammunition from the belts of my machine-gun. Each of us had a case of MG ammunition next to our position. After a few moments a big troop transport turned without releasing the troops and sailed past. We believed that the Americans were initiating a withdrawal, but the heavy gunfire began to fall upon us again.

About mid-day, some comrades and I made our way to the upper position. A final jump into the bunker was possible under covering fire from Paul Haming and Helmut Kaiserling (both of whom were killed shortly thereafter). A half ration of bread and a mess-tin of milk offered a welcome respite. In a water glass swam the dentures of Heinrich Kriftwirth. A comrade reported that Heinrich had been killed by an artillery round in his casemate while serving as a gun crew leader. He had broken his identity tag and had brought half of it with him. Moments later Heinrich Kriftwirth suddenly appeared in the trenchline covered with dirt, creeping towards us with torn uniform. An exploding round from a naval gun had thrown him against the concrete wall, and he had remained unconscious in a corner for a long time.

From the upper command position I once had an overview of the entire beach from Colleville to Vierville. On the sea were even more large ships than observed earlier, and between these ships and the beach was heavy traffic in boats of all description. Also seen were burning and torn apart landing craft in the surf and on the beach. Dead and wounded lay everywhere, especially in front of WN 62. A tank was burning near the *Steinbrecher,* and numerous tanks were knocked out between WN 61 and 62. Weapons and equipment were seen in the tide. A large number of ships flew barrage balloons for protection against aircraft, but they also made a good target for our artillery batteries behind the coastline.

The landing troops had first captured those positions to the west and east of us which had suffered heaviest damage and casualties through air attacks and naval gunfire. From these captured positions they penetrated further inland, making it necessary for us to defend ourselves from attack from the rear. We had no supplies or reinforcements. A messenger was dispatched to the company under orders to bring reinforcements but was not seen again. The enemy continued to land more troops. Our resistance became weaker. About midday two landing craft struck mines attached to the 'Rommel asparagus' anchored in the sea. Heavy explosions ripped through the boats, leaving only wrecks behind.

The pressure from the assault troops on our flanks grew stronger. The first enemy soldiers penetrated our position, surprising us while we were concentrating on the landing craft on the beach.

I saw our position commander, *Oberfeldwebel* Pye, crawl wounded out of the line of fire. With two other comrades I had taken over covering the left westward side. We still had our rifles and one light machine-gun. While changing locations across the torn ground a comrade received a fatal wound. A few minutes later I, too, was hit in the left hand. The Americans had entered our network of trenches and were suddenly only 20 metres from us. A comrade who later bandaged my hand stated that it looked like a good *Heimatschuss*, a home-for-sure wound.

Crawling and running with my rifle clamped tightly under my arm, I rapidly made my way towards Colleville-sur-Mer. In Colleville there was already fighting, and the machine-gun and rifle fire could be clearly heard. At the outskirts of Colleville at our company command post I again linked up with wounded comrades from my position.

Here I learned that the enemy had penetrated the village some hours earlier. The landing forces had quickly crossed onto land between Colleville and St. Laurent-sur-Mer, and were moving inland. During a surprise attack from the landward side before noon our commander and other members of the company had been killed near the command post.

For us wounded this location no longer offered any protection. Aircraft continuously overflew at low altitude, putting all possible targets under fire. About fifteen of us climbed aboard a truck for transport to the rear, accompanied by a captured American. We drove at breakneck speed over an open road to Ste. Honorine. To our left was the sea about 2 kilometres distant, and once again we could see the invasion fleet, part of which still flew barrage balloons.

The route was blocked at the entrance to Ste. Honorine. Ruins of bombed houses covered the streets. Dead cattle lay in the pastures and along the road. The supply units had also suffered their share of casualties, giving mute testimony to the deadly effects of the landing preparations. Many of the supply units had become immobilized through the systematic destruction of road intersections and village crossings. It was not possible for the vehicle transporting us to proceed any further, and those of us with light wounds proceeded on foot in an attempt to reach the city of Bayeux. En route a horse and wagon was requisitioned from a French farmer, after which we made better time, despite our fear of aircraft. Frightened civilians continued to appear along the edge of the road. Many of them during the first hours of the invasion had lost all belongings and their homes.

In Bayeux the field hospital had already been evacuated. With a truck we passed destroyed and burning vehicles on the way to an assembly point in Balleroy. This route ended at the entrance to the heavily damaged and still burning city of Vire. Almost the entire city had been destroyed by air attacks, and progress with the vehicle was once again impossible. We established quarters in a farmhouse at the edge of town, the inhabitants having fled the premises at the beginning of the bombardment. Food remained on the table, and we helped ourselves to bread, milk, butter and eggs. A cask of calvados was discovered, from which a few bottles were filled and taken with us. *Translation of typescript account.*

130

GEFREITER GOTTHARD LIEBICH

8th Company, 916 Infantry Regiment, 352 Division, 7th Army, *Wehrmacht*

I was seventeen. Our company was in tents in an orchard inland of Vierville, one end of Omaha, with Colleville at the other. Rommel had ordered much improved fortifications but they weren't finished by the *Todt* Organisation at that time.

On the actual day of the landing when the noise of bombing or bombardment of the coast was continuous, at about four o'clock in the morning our Officer said, 'Pack your bags, get ready, we're off' and we cycled off towards the coast, our baggage following by horse and cart – we never saw it again. I think we reached Formigny and hearing shelling much closer we ditched our bikes and went on by foot. When we reached the cliffs, perhaps between 10 and 11 in the morning, from there we could see a mass of balloons and ships beyond imagination. Somehow and from somewhere we had taken our first American prisoner. We searched his pocket and found chewing gum.

Gotthard Liebich, 17 years old, an infantryman in France, 1943'44.

We hoped we would get artillery, *Panzer* or air support but got nothing. We only had rifles and machine guns. We tried to send a message back but he kept coming back: 'Can't get through, soldiers all over the place behind us.' By midday we knew we were surrounded, I think it was Vierville where they had got through. I remember the spotter planes which seemed to be able to report any movement by us but we were not seen. It was a long day and night. (Liebich was captured the next morning.) *Transcript of tape-recorded recollections.*

Gotthard Liebich, an 18 year old prisoner of war in the United States.

PRIVATE JOHN H MacPHEE

E Company, 2nd Battalion, 16th Regiment, 1st Infantry Division, US Army

We boarded APA 45, the *USS Henrico*, ate Navy chow which was like the Waldorf Astoria compared to what we normally had. Desserts every day, home made ice cream and as many American candy bars as you wanted...

(We disembarked into landing craft for our destination, Easy Red on Omaha Beach.) We were all wearing the new sleeveless combat jackets, with all kinds of pockets. Everything was impregnated against the eventuality of a gas attack. This included long johns. I did not wear mine that morning. I figured if I'm going to die, I'm not going to go scratching myself.

I was a rifleman – demolition man. I estimated that I had approximately 85 lbs on my person.

When the ramp went down, I inflated my Mae West and I went down. It was up to my neck. The weight on my body was not balanced so that my body was on an angle. That together with the current made it very difficult.

The beach was mined at low tide with those jumping mines that detonated when you stepped on them. There were mines floating on the surface too. They were setting these off with automatic weapon fire and shelling from 88s and mortars. There were many yards of water to get out of. Many were hit in the water and many drowned as a result.

At one point, I found myself trying to take cover behind one of those fence post type obstacles. I must have looked like an ostrich hiding. But believe me, at the time it looked like a wall. I was sea-sick and exhausted and scared to death.

I made it out of the water and there must have been 100 yards of open beach. At least it seemed so. I could see a small wall up on the beach that offered some shelter. Physically exhausted I fell and for what seemed an eternity, I laid there. At that point, the wall became very personal. I was wounded three times at very short intervals. Once in the lower back, smashed and paralyzed my left arm and two bullets through the left leg enlodged in my right. That did it. Call it shock, facing reality or whatever. I lost all my fear and knew I was about to die, made peace with my Maker and was just waiting.

I could not move. Confusion all around. I guess if anyone saw me they figured I was dead. After what seemed like an eternity, I was seen by two of my buddies. I had almost made it to the shelter, so close and yet so far. They did a very brave thing. They exposed themselves under fire, came down and dragged me up to the wall.

I ended up in an abandoned pillbox, which must have been the first field hospital. I eventually was put on a DUKW with some other litter cases and ended up on a Navy AKA out in the Seine Bay. The ship was the *USS Achernar* Command Ship for the First Army and Ninth Air Force. This was the first time I lost consciousness. Between all my wounds, loss of blood and all the pieces of shrapnel, my whole body was affected. I thought I was dead. It still feels like yesterday in my mind. *Typescript recollections, The Eisenhower Center for American Studies at the University of New Orleans and the National D-Day Museum, New Orleans, USA*

A casemate at Pointe du Hoc hit by a heavy shell, probably from a battleship.
A Huxley

Bomb damage, Pointe du Hoc.
A Huxley

Shelled casemate, Pointe du Hoc. A Huxley

PRIVATE H PANKEY
26th Infantry Regiment, 1st Infantry Division, US Army

When I got off this LST and hit that beach my heart jumped in my mouth after I seen these bodies and I said to my buddy, Jimmy Sweats, 'Man, will we ever see the sun come up, I mean tomorrow or the moon,' and I said, 'I don't know how we are going to do it.' It was that terrible. I mean we were scared to death, I was completely shocked, but we got over it.

So I hit (the beach) about one o'clock, I think, in the afternoon. But the bodies were floating around from the 16th and 18th Infantry and maybe the 29th. By the time I got in (we got off by half track) there was no fire coming in at that time. There were a lot of bodies lying around and the waves were in and taking them out. We went to the bluffs, but we were pretty lucky that they wasn't firing down on us at that time. We dug in, and it was a mess. *Transcript of tape-recorded recollections.*

ENSIGN CALHOUN BOND
US Navy, Stores Officer on LST 498, to be used as a Hospital Evacuation Ship

We took aboard jeeps and trucks for the 29th Division and men of the 115th Infantry Division. Our commanding officer went out of his way to make everyone comfortable on board. There wasn't enough sleeping quarters. They were in trucks and ambulances and people were taking turn sleeping but the cooks were busy and there was plenty of food.

As we approached the beaches things became fairly confused. We were supposed to land, I believe, somewhere to get out people on the beach somewhere between eight and ten in the morning. For reasons I couldn't see, the LCIs were acting as traffic control ships, and we would get within about a mile of the beach, and we could see an LST burning on the beach. We could see people having an awful time to get up the cliffs. It was quite an experience to have the capital ships in back of us. It sounded like railroad trains as the shells would go over us. There were lots of bodies in the water, floating in dress blues.

Navy ships had sent their small boats in and they had not been able to get ashore, the beach obstacles were too bad or else there was confusion at the beach. Where we were, within a mile or a mile and a half, we just knew we couldn't get in; the cluttering up the beach just couldn't be cleared and so they kept on postponing bringing our people in.

As I recall, Col Smith and his aide and a couple of others went in first in one of our small boats. (Then another went in) one small boat came back, maybe five or six in the afternoon and we sent quite a few of the infantry and our boats and other boats down the landing nets. We could see them going in (but) really there was so much confusion and smoke on the beach. We know that they got in there, we know we got our boats back, but we still had a lot of vehicles on board. *Transcript of recorded recollections, The Eisenhower Center for American Studies at the University of New Orleans and The National D-Day Museum, New Orleans, USA*

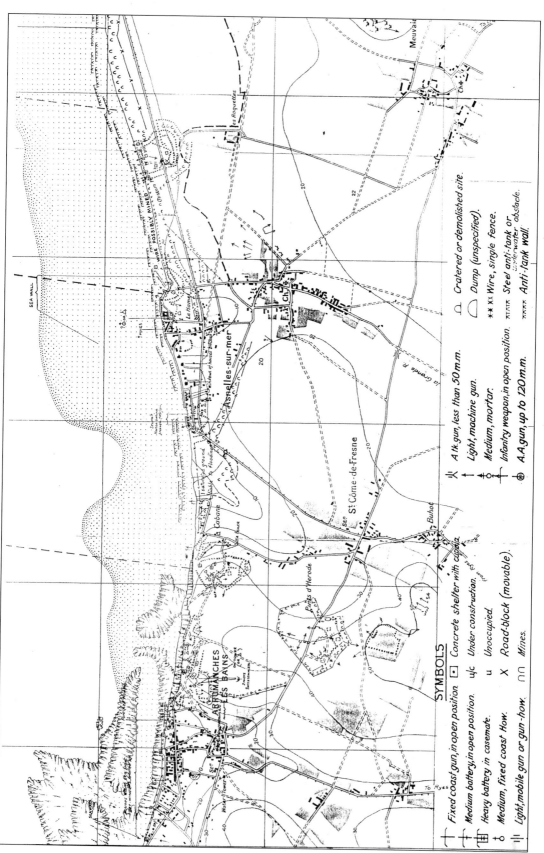

A section from a map issued for the assault of Gold Beach identifying known and conjectured hazards.

CHAPTER 8

Gold

The most westerly British invasion beach, Gold, from Port-en-Bessin, nearest to Omaha, to Arromanches, le Hamel and La Rivière, its eastern border adjacent to Juno, the Canadian landing area, was ten miles across but only its eastern half was free from a rocky shoreline backed by cliffs. The landings were to be concentrated in that sector with its gently shelving sandy and clay beach. In contrast to the relative absence of coastal development behind Utah and Omaha, Gold with Arromanches, and then Juno and Sword still more so, had linked villages to be assaulted. Street fighting was to be expected. Specialised fighting armoured vehicles were to be on hand to assist in this – 'Flails', 'Petards', Bridging and 'Crocodile' tanks.

The objective here was to break through to take Bayeux, nearly five miles inland and the higher ground which on both sides flanked the ancient town. Wind and tidal conditions intruded additional factors, holding back the landing of armour. Casualties among senior command aggravated the problems for the 1st Battalion Royal Hampshire Regiment whose H.Q. radios were destroyed too, denying the battalion the rescue means of calling specifically for naval gunfire or air support in front of Le Hamel. Three out of five landing craft taking commandos in to Port en Bessin were sunk on submerged obstacles and the reduction of this small task-force for a key objective frustrated achievement on that day. (After an outflanking assault it was taken on D+1).

To the East better progress was made. The landing and employment of 'Flail' tanks in beach and off-beach mine clearance, and the all-purpose armoured engineer assault vehicles (the AVREs) hugely assisted infantry progress inland from the beaches but again not without loss.

The 50th (Tyne and Tees) Division secured Arromanches, vital to allow installation during the afternoon of the first elements of the artificial [Mulberry] harbour for the British and Canadians. From this division, furthest East, the 6th Battalion Green Howards had soon taken their immediate objectives but the 5th Battalion East Yorks and supporting AVREs were in difficulties against incompletely destroyed emplacements at La Rivière. Progress during the day was made in most sectors aided by the landing of armoured fighting vehicles and self-propelled guns but it has been suggested that there was an excess of consolidation rather than relentlessly pressing forward though this was certainly not comparable to the inertia and its consequences in August 1915 at Suvla Bay on the Gallipoli Peninsula.

LIEUTENANT MICHAEL IRWIN RNR
in command of nine Landing Craft Assault

We had these sixty pound Spigot bombs to put onto the beach at H Hour minus one minute on Gold Beach at La Rivière to blow up the beach obstacles before the tanks came in of course and we had a crew of myself, the engine room chap and another. We were towed across the Channel by LCFs, Landing Craft Flak and LCT, Landing Craft Tanks but the

The composite photograph issued to Michael Irwin to help identify his beach. H M Irwin

A glimpse of PLUTO as the landing craft leave the Solent. PLUTO was the pipeline to be laid to supply oil to the beach-head. H M Irwin

An LCT with engine trouble, 5 June. Note the 'in distress' signal ball. H M Irwin

'An LCF which towed us but suffered engine trouble in mid-Channel. We cast off tow and proceeded under our own power'. H M Irwin

'Crossing the Channel under her own 'steam' but needing a jerrycan of petrol from a destroyer to keep going'. H M Irwin

Less than thirty minutes before zero hour and the camouflage netting is taken off an AVRE Flail Tank on an LCT. 'This Flail was destroyed at the landing.' H M Irwin

Coming out from the beach. 'Note two Spigot bombs still in position after firing as a result of water in their electronic ignition system'. H M Irwin

'The grave of my friend, Bruce Ashton, killed alongside me three minutes before zero hour.'. H M Irwin

weather was atrocious and my towing LCF broke down. We cast off and went in under our own steam and so did the rest of my flotilla.

As we passed the destroyers which were bombarding the Germans, men cheered us. Then there was an awful tragedy, one of my LCAs (with my friend, an Australian, Bruce Ashton aboard) was rammed by an LCT following and the whole lot were drowned.

We were now being machine-gunned but I dispatched the Spigot bombs. Two didn't go off because of wetness. We had been given Sticky Bombs to put on top of the Teller mines and I tried this but they all fell off. I then saw the East Yorks, a wonderful Regiment, doing the actual assault and that was a pretty horrifying sight because a lot of them were killed and we were laying off. And I always remember one chap who was hit, I could see him, and I can see him now and it's so vivid... I could see him. He got up, ran forward, fell, ran forward and dropped dead, it was like a rabbit. I didn't know but there were then the troops under the sea wall at La Rivière. The tide

Michael Irwin

was coming in but one chap very bravely jumped over the wall and the others followed suit so they were saved. But the two tanks went in and the tide was up. The flails worked. They knocked out a lot of the beach obstacles and then both of them caught fire, and they were knocked out by this eighty eight millimetre gun just as they came into sight. But fortunately shortly afterwards a tank went in and blew up this eighty eight millimetre gun. And then I thought, 'well, we've had enough,' and so we came back four miles to a Landing Ship Infantry, which then took us up and I went to sleep and woke up the next morning in harbour. *Transcript of tape-recorded recollections.*

COMPANY SERGEANT MAJOR STANLEY E HOLLIS
D Company. 6th Battalion, Green Howards
Holder of the only Victoria Cross awarded for D-Day

We made sure all our weapons were working right and the Company Commander came to me – Major Lofthouse – who was also a very good friend of mine. We had been through a lot of the war together. We had a good working relationship and he gave me a square box. He said 'Give one of these to each of the men Sergeant Major'. So I opened it and it was a box of French Letters. 'Well', I said, 'what is to do, what are we going to do. Are we going to fight them or fuck them'? They were for (waterproofing) the Bren guns anyway and they did work. They did work very well, because in fact we landed waist deep in water.

Stan Hollis of the Green Howards. The Green Howards Museum, Richmond, North Yorkshire

Well, we had to go down scrambling nets into the landing craft and the sea was rough and the landing craft coming up and down. It was a bit awkward getting down with our equipment. We had big Bren pouches sticking out and rifle butts and Sten gun butts, and I can remember going down those nets and thinking to meself 'There must be easier ways of earning a living than this'. However, we got in the landing craft – about eighteen or twenty men to a boat – we cast off from our transport, *The Empire Lance*, and we cruised round and round in circles until the whole company was afloat, and then we set off in line abreast for the shore. A Company on the right – five boats. B Company, five boats line abreast on this side and we came in. These things did four or five knots and it took us about an hour, an hour and a quarter, to get in. After we had been in the landing craft for about half an hour everything in the world opened up from behind us. Twenty-five pounders firing off loading platforms, floating platforms firing thousands of rockets in one salvo, and cruisers, destroyers, everything opened up.

When we got to the shore, I was stood in the front and I saw this shelter. There was, in fact, a railway running (right down to the beach) and that was a waiting room or something for this railway and I thought it was a pillbox. As we were coming in I lifted a stripped Lewis off the floor of the landing craft and I belted this thing with a full pan of ammunition. It was then that I received the most painful wound I had in the whole war. I lifted the stripped Lewis off and it was white hot and I got a bloody great blister right across my hand there. It was as big as my finger and that was very painful. Well, as I say, we landed about waist deep in water and the man in front of me, Sergeant Hill, he had been a very good soldier all through the war. A real fighting man. He jumped out first and he jumped into a shell hole under the water. The landing craft went over him and, of course, he couldn't come up with all the stuff he was carrying. The landing craft went over him and the propellers cut him to bits.

On reaching the high water mark we lost one of our very important officers. We lost the beach-master. He was the man that was supposed to say 'right, you go that way, you go that way'. So he was out of action. By this time shells and mortars were dropping. We were getting no small arms casualties yet. The plan was for me, the Sergeant Major, to have two, two inch mortars from each Platoon and two Bren guns from each Platoon, dash along the beach about a hundred yards and then straight up to the high water mark and lay down with my troop and drop smoke bombs over on the far corner of the minefield, and also open up with the Brens on to these hedges to keep their heads down. If anyone was there, there were chaps coming through the minefield. As we were coming over the beach this tank blew up and there was a scare patch on it – some sort of a door – it blew off and it bowled along the beach like a hoop right through the company. It never touched anyone, because if it had that would have been curtains. At the same time the one and only German aircraft I ever saw from here to being wounded later on came along the beach and he opened fire just above us, and I think it would be the East Yorks that got the benefit of it. But that was the only aircraft of the enemy I saw.

Well, we dashed over the beach. A lot of the boys had been seasick and they were only too glad to get out of those boats. We ran up to the top (of the beach) and along the ridge where there was just rolled wire. Well, an Irishman was alongside me, and believe it or not, there were two or three birds sat on this wire and this Irishman, Mullaly, he said to me 'No bloody wonder they are there Sergeant Major. There is no room in the air for them', and he was killed a few minutes later going up the road.

Well, up to now things had gone pretty well and we had expected far heavier casualties than we had had.

The minefield (was extensive in area). The Platoon of D Company were led through by the Assault Pioneers of the Battalion. They went ahead with their 'Hoover' things and laid the white tape behind them and we trod on the tape. Two Platoons came over the minefield to advance over the field just beyond the hedge over the Meuvaines Ridge to the Mont Fleury gun battery. The other Platoon of the company, the company headquarters, with me came up this road. When we got through the hedge we started getting small arms casualties. This is where that man Mullaly was killed. We knew the fire was coming up from up there somewhere but we didn't know exactly where. When we got to where the crossroads are now – this was just a track then – the fire was, of course, a lot closer and we were getting more casualties. So then we got down and we crawled. We crawled up this hill and when we got (to the top) Major Lofthouse and I came forward to see what we could, and we were laid down there and we saw where the firing was coming from. Major Lofthouse said to me, he said, 'There is a pillbox there Sergeant Major'. Well, when he said that. I saw it. It was very well camouflaged and I saw these guns moving around in the slits. So I got my Sten gun and I rushed at it just spraying it hosepipe fashion. They fired back at me and they missed. I don't know whether they were more panic stricken than me, but they must have been, and I got on top of it and I threw a grenade through the slit and it must have sickened them. I went round the back and went inside and there were two dead, quite a lot of prisoners. They were quite willing to forget all about the war. There was a communicating trench from that pillbox to another one further along, and I could never understand until a couple of years ago how I got so many prisoners. I got about eighteen or twenty prisoners. But we found out later that this was the command post for the Mont Fleury gun battery, which is just over the brow of the hill and this explains where all these chaps came from. Well, we didn't bother with escorts for prisoners we just pointed the way back down to the beach and they were quite happy to go by themselves.

Well, as we came over a field to advance to this Mont Fleury gun position, and it was at the top of that field that I looked back and I had been firmly convinced that the Green Howards were the only people fighting this bloody war. But when I looked back I couldn't see any water at all (for boats and landing craft) and it was then that I realised that somebody else was helping us, and it gave us a great feeling of confidence. Anyway we advanced towards these positions and as we appeared the Germans ran out of them – the back of the pillboxes. Ran out and over a wall into the wood. Well, D Company had got behind a mound. Colonel Hastings had come to see us in these things and saw that we had got them and so that everything was going alright. It's now about half past nine in the morning. We got behind the mound. These chaps were starting to shoot at us from behind the wall and I saw a man running along the top of the wall. Why I don't know, but he was running along the top of the wall, and I borrowed a rifle off one of the chaps and I took a shot at him, and to my amazement I hit him. I had never been known as a good shot. If I fell down I couldn't hit the floor, sort of thing, but I knocked that man off the wall and at the same time I got hit in the face. Not a lot of damage. A lot of blood. The firing ceased then. We went over there and we found a German soldier – had been just that minute killed so I assume it was the one that I had knocked off the wall. The Company then advanced. The whole Company advanced round the edge of a wall into the next village.

By that time I was in charge of 16 Platoon. Lieutenant Kirkpatrick of 2 Commando had been killed. He had his arm broken on the beach and he had walked about until now, which was about two o'clock in the afternoon, with a broken arm, and he was killed just outside the village. I took 16 Platoon over and coming through this village Major Lofthouse ordered the different Platoons to search and clear out different farmhouses along the road. This was the particular one he picked on for me and 16 Platoon to come in and clear. We came in the gate.

The house was locked, so I broke the door down. I went up the stairs into the various bedrooms and I burst into this bedroom here and there was a small boy about ten or eleven years old. He must have been pretty frightened. I was covered with blood and he must have been terrified. I am convinced that he thought I was going to kill him. Anyway there was nothing in the house. I came down again and I decided to have a look to see if there was anything round the back of the house and there didn't seem to be anything going on out there, and that is where I was, I think, the most frightened I have ever been in my life.

I looked round this corner and straight away a bullet knocked a lump of stone off the wall. I was very lucky to get away with that. I saw two dogs in the gap in the hedge. They were dancing about wagging their tails, jumping up and down at somebody, and I knew full well we were forward troops so I knew there were no mates of ours that were there. On closer inspection I saw a field gun, or what appeared to me to be a field gun, so I went back and told the Company Commander what I had seen. He told me that we would see what we could do about it, but before I went back I told seven or eight of 16 Platoon to dash out across and engage whatever was in that hedge. Just open up with Bren guns and shoot that hedge up. Well, they ran out and immediately all seven or eight of them were killed – stone dead straight away. Well, I thought 'there is not much future here', and I went back, as I said, to report to the Company Commander, and he said to me 'Well, get a PIAT gun and a couple of Brens and crawl forwards through the patch of rhubarb' which I had described to him. Well, I got my PIAT gun and Bren gun – I had two Bren guns – and the three of us crawled through this rhubarb to the forward edge. We got to the forward edge of the rhubarb and I poked the PIAT gun through and had a shot. Well, as was usual with me, I missed, and then the field gun fired and blew the top off the building. Well, there was bricks and stones and masonry flying all over the place so I thought we better get out of it and leave it to somebody that was better equipped than we were to deal with it.

So I crawled back out, walked back up the road to join the Company about a hundred yards up the road and told Major Lofthouse what it was. He said 'Well, we will leave it and let somebody else deal with it'. Then we heard a terrific racket coming from ahead of us and somebody came and told me that the two Bren gunners I had brought in were still in the rhubarb. They were pinned down and couldn't get out. I said to Major Lofthouse, 'Well, I took them in. I will go and try and get them out'. Well, I came back with a Bren gun and I waited until there was a lull in the firing and I ran straight out across there and just straight ahead for the Bren guns. We quietened them down and I was able to shout to these two lads to get out and come back and join me, which they were able to do, and we came back and rejoined the Company.

There was C Company on the left and A and B on the right. We advanced up (and came upon a tank), and the tank went on ahead of us up the hill. It was pouring down and the lane was in a hell of a mess. It had been churned up by tanks, and as we were going up the slope – Seventeen and Eighteen Platoon on this side, Company Headquarters behind the tank, Sixteen Platoon with myself on the left hand side going up, we heard a lot of banging going on either side. We couldn't see, of course, what was going on, but we knew someone was catching it. And then the tank stopped. Well, we were crawling up by then and we started getting casualties from somewhere up the top – small arms and machine gun. Why the tank stopped I don't know. Maybe the tank commander could see over this hedge and see there was a tank knocked out in that field and could see it there and he knew what was going to happen down there. I think that must be why he stopped. He wouldn't go any further on.

It was also here that I committed an unpardonable sin. I had been all day back at the orchard where we formed up getting the troops fully equipped with ammunition and seeing everything was right and making sure everybody had as much as they could carry and still be mobile. Well, we got here and we were down on our hands and knees and I could see that the firing was coming from a tree and this side of the lane was getting casualties. So I was laid down here and I could see these two Germans who were getting up, firing a burst down that side of the lane and then getting down. I watched them for – I suppose it was only a few seconds. It seemed quite a long time. They would bob up, fire and get down. Bob up, fire and get down.

So I thought 'Well, we will have to see what we can do about it', and I turned round to the chaps and I said 'I am going to have a try at this'. So I felt in my Bren pouch for a grenade and when I put my hand in I had a pair of socks and a shaving brush in me doings – in me Bren pouch – and this after I had made sure that everybody had their equipment and ammunition. Anyway I turned round to the chap behind me and said 'For Christ's sake give me a grenade', and I waited until I got the rhythm of what they were doing – bobbing up and down and shooting. Bobbing up and down and shooting. And then the last time they bobbed up I threw this grenade, and I could never throw a grenade like the Army taught you. I used to throw them like a cricket ball. So I threw the grenade. The Germans saw it coming and got down. Well, I followed the grenade up straight away. I ran right behind the grenade. When it landed I hadn't pulled the bloody pin out. Now, of course, the Germans didn't know that and they kept down waiting for it to go off. By the time that they had realised it wasn't going to go off I was on top of them and I had shot them both.

When we arrived at this point my Company Commander came to me and said that he would take two platoons up this hedge and I was to take what was left of 16 Platoon – by now about fourteen or fifteen men – up this hedge. It's a double hedge. A ditch in the middle – ideal cover. So I took my Platoon up here. We were crawling all the time in the water. It was pretty uncomfortable and we could hear a lot of fire coming from the top – not at us because they didn't know we were there. We got up to the hedge and I called everybody forward with the automatic weapons – the Bren guns and Sten guns – and we opened up with everything we had on that top hedge from where we were in this ditch, and I would like to think we caused a few casualties because the firing immediately stopped. There was a tank in this field that was in good order. It was running about alright and Major Lofthouse sent a runner across to me to say that we had to come back. On the way back I and Sergeant Major Moffat – he was B Company Sergeant Major – picked up one of our Captains, a Captain 'Bolo' Young. He was a very good officer and we put him on this tank. He had been badly wounded and he was brought back through this gate and taken away back there. We had completed our job. We had done what we set out to do. We had quietened the thing. Whether we had killed anyone or not we don't know but at least we had either shifted them or we had knocked them off – one of the two.

You must understand that I came from Middlesbrough where everybody is connected with Green Howards in some way or other. The families, they are all connected to the Green Howards, and, of course, the Green Howards are the 'be all and end all' of the British Army, and I was very proud to be a Green Howard. The best moment in my life, the proudest moment in my life, was when I was made a Sergeant Major. (I thought that) there is nobody better than me in the Army then when I was made a Sergeant Major. Apart from that all these fellows were my mates. I had lived with them. Apart from the fact of being in the Army I had lived with them in civvy street before. We knew, well, everybody knew everybody else, and there wasn't only me doing these things there were other people who were doing them as well and the things that I did. If I hadn't done them somebody else would have done them. There is no doubt about it. It was just not a case of who would do it, it was just when (it would be done). *Taken from a recording made of Stan Hollis when he was on Sword Beach speaking to a party of Instructors and Officer Cadets from Camberley Staff College. The Green Howards Regimental Museum, Richmond, North Yorkshire.*

CAPTAIN G M WILSON

7th Battalion, Green Howards

The next spot of bother came when I realised that my two alternative wireless links to Brigade were missing. The big half-track truck had apparently failed to get ashore and the Signaller with the second set in a hand-cart was nowhere to be seen.

Stepping rapidly over a number of bodies and wounded I made my way with our boat party towards our RV a walk of about a mile. We kept to the beach (which appeared to be un-mined) for fear of mines and it was very heavy going in soaking clothes and heavy equipment... The first job was to collect together the various men who had travelled piecemeal. One by one they filtered in and again luck was with me – I had not lost a single man. I was sat there scarcely believing it when I was brought to my senses by a burst of Spandau fire which plunged into the bank a few yards away – instinctively we dashed for the far side of the road where a brick wall would at least cover us from view...

It now dawned on me that in the excitement of everything I was failing miserably to execute the job in hand – communications. It was essential to let the Brigade (who were still in the water) know the position. The Company sets back to me were working fairly well so we knew how things were going with them; they had taken the first objectives, some big guns a few hundred yards inland. All but one battery had been knocked out by the RAF early that morning and this one contained 40-50 very bomb-happy Germans who failed to fire a shot. So far so good if the news could be got to Brigade. I was just despairing when a hand-cart wireless set came into sight and in no time the vital news was through...

...we set off (towards our final objective) and we met our first civilians. They must have been either bomb-happy or pro-German because we were mostly received with stares and stony silence. Some admittedly seemed mildly pleased and brought out some frightful cider to quench our thirst and some few waved to us. It should be said in all fairness however that not only are these people of a very dour and quiet nature but most of them have lost relations in the bombing and fighting and had had their homes destroyed and often livelihood ruined. This would not make for a great welcome neither would the fact that the Germans (as we later learned) had not interfered with their lives to any great extent. Still, the reception was to us, at the time, very disappointing after what we had conceitedly expected. *From an unpublished account written soon after the war. The Green Howards Museum, Richmond, North Yorkshire.*

CAPTAIN ROBERT J KILN

Hertfordshire Yeomanry, 341 St Albans Battery, 86 Field Regiment, RA (50th Division) aboard an LCH (Landing Craft Headquarters) with responsibility for maintaining a ship to shore bombardment as the guns of the Regiment approached the beach.

I was asked to maintain the bombardment for an extra ten minutes and this was actually valuable because it meant that our gunfire was still coming down on the main German battery at Mont Fleury, which was our main objective in the centre of our beach, and we were still firing on that when the infantry were across the beach and getting towards it. The great object of all this was to keep the German heads down. It's quite interesting because that Mont Fleury battery never actually fired a shot. We kept the bombardment going until we were within two hundred yards of the battery, so by the time they got up from below where they were sheltering, we were on top of them. Then I could see that our AVRE tanks got ashore first, I think, with the Shermans of the 4/7th and with the infantry, and there was one

German gun right in front of me which was firing and had knocked out three or four of our vehicles, three or four of the tanks. We could see where it was but he was in a pillbox, and I remember getting a naval gunship to come in to try and silence it. We hit it. I looked at it afterwards, when I got ashore and there was about ten foot of concrete. We could never have knocked it out. It was knocked out fairly shortly after that by an AVRE shellman who came up and fired straight through the gunport and knocked it out. The landing I watched, and it was my job to bring in naval gunships and knock off any strongpoints, but quite frankly, it went very quickly. The East Yorks were up through the beach, bypassing the little fortified village, it was of Victorian/Edwardian type stone houses on the beach front. They were very heavily fortified. They bypassed that and captured the lighthouse at Ver-sur-Mer, which was about a thousand yards inland. They captured that by eight o'clock, within half an hour. On our right we could see the Green Howards who were the right hand assaulting battalion, going up the main road to the Mont Fleury battery, and they captured that very quickly. That was where Company Sergeant Major Hollis won his V.C.

I stayed on the LCH all through D-Day. On the morning of D-Day the East Yorks on the left of our beach had to clear the little town of La Rivière, and during the morning I was firing naval ships to help them advance along the sea wall to the left to clear the town. That was quite difficult because you couldn't see where on earth they were. I remember we had to tell them to hang out the yellow flags over the sea wall and to let off yellow smoke so that we could see how far they'd got. I spent the morning doing that and I'd really finished that by twelve o'clock. The afternoon was quite quiet. *Transcript of tape-recorded recollections.*

CAPTAIN R H E HUDSON
7th Battalion, Green Howards

(Approaching the beach) I had for a long time nursed a secret thought that the mighty Atlantic Wall would have fire as one of its defences – that somehow they would have set the sea alight and how pleased I was that this was not so. Indeed we had a wet landing as when some way off shore, perhaps one hundred yards, the craft scraped the bottom and jarred to a halt – it refused to budge. A few words with the Royal Marine Captain, down with ramp and out I went with the signallers and a few more. It was a sandbar – we were soon up to our shoulders, the radio equipment was completely drowned and one of the signallers was nearly so. A little man and a determined one, he nonetheless got ashore together with his set. The exodus of a number of us from the LCA lightened it sufficiently to allow it passage over the sandbar and it next gently pivoted about 110° about an underwater obstacle alive with its shell. We in the water tugged and heaved and with the additional skill of the RM Skipper, the craft moved off and beached whilst we waded ashore. The Battalion was about 400 yards to the right of its intended beach – we moved along the water's edge to the correct position and many were still being sick or trying to find 'landlegs'. What a war!

Ronald Hudson.

We moved inland beyond La Rivière – were shot at from close range and then from some high ground could clearly see some German soldiers dismantling a machine gun. Dispersed them quickly with the excellent Bren and passed on. The sun came out – it was warmer weather than we had experienced for some time. My battle dress was drying nicely and steaming. My cigarettes, although in a tin carried safely through North Africa and Sicily, were ruined, brown and ugh! We came to a farm – roses climbing over the buildings. Cattle dead, legs stiff and pointing skywards. No people. The lowing of a cow in pain – she stands unable to move, just lowing. Her udders so swollen it seems impossible they can be stretched. What is to be done? A Corporal volunteers to milk her where she stands – permission given, his section remains on guard. Farm searched and six German soldiers found cowering in the remains of an outhouse.

My Company with squadron of tanks becomes a mobile column and we ride on the tanks. Move fast and a German staff car with driver and two officers approaches. Mistakes our tanks for his own – not until twenty to thirty yards from leading tank did he screech to a halt – must have seen the gun pointing – one officer attempted to run but all occupants killed. Marked maps found in car. Column later on road to Villers-le-Sec, where on long straight road and at 300 yards distance, old man at entrance to old peoples' home stood in centre of road waving us to stop. He was shot dead from behind – astride the tanks we gingerly approached, moved the body of a very old man and soon discovered the reason for his warning. Just beyond the field and behind a large number of stacks of corn lay armed German soldiers – spotted pairs of feet from the top of the leading tank – the machine gun opened up just by my head (nearly scared the wits out of me) and fifty or more Wehrmacht quickly gave themselves up to be marched back towards the beaches. *The Green Howards Gazette, (June 1994)*

2ND LIEUTENANT J MILTON
B Company. 6th Battalion, Green Howards

We had to climb down this netting from our transport, the *Empire Mace* into our assault landing craft. This was one hell of a job. I shall never, never forget it. Then we had to jump from the bottom of the netting. The landing craft took just a platoon, thirty or so. I was in command of a platoon in B Company, going in about 20 minutes after A and D assault companies.

(Abiding impressions): the ships, ships and ships everywhere and until we got close inshore, the noise of the shelling; then it seemed to stop. I was very keyed up and scared, very apprehensive, then when we landed all that disappeared. You just got on with what you had to do and whatever may happen to some people, it won't happen to you.

We were landed at exactly the right place and we had hit no obstacles. We were very, very lucky. When the ramp went down we saw a house with a circular drive ahead of us

John Milton.

– just where we were supposed to be, and we went slightly to the left of this, D Company having gone straight for it.

On the beach we saw huge signs in German about the mines but we just had to go through there. No one struck a mine, so whether the signs were untrue, or we were dead lucky, I don't know. Yes there had been flail tanks there but we couldn't literally follow their tracks inland off the beach, only off the beach up a lane across a road to the house with the circular drive could we do this.

It seemed to me that there was no confusion; there were so few of us, our other

Behind Gold Beach and the danger of mines. J G H Gritten

companies being ahead. There were just tanks, Flail Tanks and us. I didn't see any casualties and it was only later that I learned of Stanley Hollis in one of our forward companies taking a vital pillbox just behind the house with the circular drive and as a result winning a VC.

We went round the left side of this (neutralised) pillbox, went further on up to the village of Crépon, seeing wounded Germans gasping for water and the temptation was to stop, but of course there was a fear there as well that they might be fooling you and might just put a gun on you or a bayonet, but anyway, we didn't have time to do that sort of thing.

A Flail Tank with its whirling drum of heavy chains designed to explode mines in its path. Ken Pugh Collection

At Crépon, Stanley Hollis won the other part of his Victoria Cross by clearing out a German machine-gun from an orchard and then returning to rescue two of his own men left in the orchard and with the anticipation that the other side of the orchard was still commanded by the Germans. Hollis was a very nice, straightforward sort of person – a very intelligent person. You don't become a Sergeant Major in the Army unless you have a lot about you – more so than the Second Lieutenant.

We finished up about a mile short of our objective, St. Leger, but I believe we were the furthest forward British or Canadian troops. However we had to pull back a little as we were too far forward in relation to the battalions either side.

We left a Bren gun carrier ahead which got knocked up, and so I had to go out to try to see if we could get it back and so I had a part in that. Eight of us, I think. We went out and we managed to get this carrier back. Fortunately we didn't come across any opposition so the Germans must have done a bit of retiring as well at that time. But the thing I remember more than anything of D-Day – it was a lovely day, but in the fields there were the cattle that had been shelled from presumably the day previously and so on because a lot of them were sort of lying with their feet up in the air, and it really was quite dreadful. But some had obviously been killed very recently so I happened to have a butcher in my platoon. So I said to him on the evening of D-Day, I said, 'Right, let's have some steak for supper. The platoon will have steak for supper. Get on with it.' So he did. I can't say the steak was absolutely brilliant because it was cut straight from the hindquarters of the beast that had just been killed by shellfire, but anyway, we did have steak. Our platoon had steak for supper on D-Day.

We were very tired on D-Day night, that was the overwhelming feeling and it is reflected in my letters home. *Transcript of tape-recorded recollections.*

CAPTAIN PETER L de C MARTIN

'A' Company Commander, 2nd Battalion, Cheshire Regiment, 151 Brigade

The assault wave was due to go in at twenty five past seven on our beaches, and we were due to arrive two hours later, or two and a half hours later – ten o'clock. And so I went up on to the deck with Major The Viscount Long, The Brigade Major, and we surveyed the scene in front of us, and it was an incredible scene all round us with all the shipping. We had, or at least I had, seen a very similar sort of display in Sicily when we landed there, but this was even bigger and there were all these rocket batteries firing off from landing craft and even twenty five pounder guns firing off from LCMs – Landing Craft Motor. I don't know what the M stood for now but small landing craft. And the RAF was very busy, and there was a great thunder of noise. The smoke palls everywhere. Obviously there was landing craft sort of broached too on the beach. Some of them burning. It all looked, on the beaches, chaotic. Out to sea it was very orderly, barrage balloons flying, but on shore it all looked pretty chaotic.

However, we came in exactly on time. The Green Howards and the East Yorkshires had done their stuff. We were landed on the right beach, unlike in Sicily where we all landed on the wrong beaches, and we moved to, we left La Rivière. We marched up through Ver-Sur-Mer up on to the Meuvaines Ridge, which is the high ground beyond Ver-Sur-Mer which was to be the Brigade assembly area.

Peter Martin.

147

And there we waited for our transport, which was all coming on different ships to ourselves. And it was fine and sunny and very pleasant lying on the rich Norman grass and there was the odd, very odd, mortar shell, and there was the odd ping of a sniper's bullet, but really very peaceful and quiet. We could hear the racket going on behind us over our right shoulders where 231 Brigade in the Le Hamel, Arromanches area was still fighting it out, but in our area it was really pretty quiet. All the transport arrived absolutely on time, absolutely complete, and by midday we were ready to go and there appeared to be nothing to stop us going straight forward on to the Divisional D-Day objectives on the Caen-Bayeux road.

So we started off from the assembly area with a couple of mobile columns based on the 6th DLI, I think and 8th or 9th DLI, each sending their reconnaissance platoon. And one of my machine-gun platoons and one or two odds and so on went forward and we went across country. We didn't stay on the roads at all. We came across the odd German. Most people were going the same direction as we were. They were all elderly. Some of them were obviously foreign. When I say 'foreign' – not German [but] Russian, Poles, people like that. I collected a very nice Luger pistol and a very nice pair of binoculars from one gentleman. The Platoon Commander got shot by a sniper and wounded. One of our machine-gun carriers, a bren gun carrier with a machine-gun on, was run over by one of our tanks coming through a hedge, and we had two men wounded slightly by a mortar splinter. By the end of our advance we had encountered no opposition whatsoever. There was still fighting going on on our left, which was the Green Howards in Crépon and places like that – villages – but we were not in, we were avoiding all the villages. We were going across country, and it was really one of the quietest days of the war.

So we got on to, or very close to, our objectives and then we were ordered to stop. We had to wait for everybody else on our flanks to catch up. Knowing that by the end of the day I was due to be setting off with 8th Armoured Brigade to Villers Bocage, and knowing that time spent on reconnaissance was seldom wasted, I decided to go and have a look at the Rucqueville assembly area, which was forward of us a bit but not very far forward, and to see what the area was that we were going to form up in. So I went forward towards Rucqueville – absolutely dead quiet. All the villagers had locked themselves in their houses. No Germans could be seen whatsoever. So I drove forward in my jeep with my driver on to the Caen-Bayeux road and absolutely dead quiet. Not a sign of a soul or anything. So I turned to my driver and said, 'What about popping down to Bayeux and liberating it', and he said, 'Good idea Sir', and I imagined that hearing the radio report that 56th Brigade are moving inland rather towards Bayeux, by the time we got down there that they would all be occupied anyhow. So we went zooming down the road and we started going a bit slower when we got to the built-up area, and then there was a Frenchman on a corner who whistled and said, 'Boche, Boche'. So we stopped and turned round and thought that discretion was the better part of valour and we went back again. As we did so an American fighter plane came zooming down low strafing the road because we weren't supposed to be there so we were fair game. So my driver and I got in a ditch very hurriedly, and he fired a burst of machine-gun at the jeep but all he did was hit one tyre. So as soon as he had gone by we changed the wheel. It was a very edgy situation with the Germans about. We got back to 151 Brigade to discover that our operation had been postponed.

So that night it started to be brutal slightly, but I can remember a general feeling of euphoria. We had expected this ghastly jam on the beach and it really had been a very quiet day, certainly compared with other battles we had been in. So we were all on top of our form.

Transcript of tape-recorded recollections.

PRIVATE LES PLEWS

1st Battalion, Royal Hampshire Regiment

My task as first out of the boat was to run up the beach carrying a Bangalore torpedo to be placed under the barbed wire entanglements. A few yards up the beach a macabre sight greeted me – a man's torso.

I glanced back briefly, men were falling, some still in the water. I pressed on. Later, in a pillbox, I retrieved a photo from one of its defenders. *Typescript recollections.*

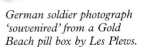

German soldier photograph 'souvenired' from a Gold Beach pill box by Les Plews.

CORPORAL GEOFF STEER

'B' Company, 1st/4th King's Own Yorkshire Light Infantry

The ship stopped, the beach was 50 yards away, the doors were opened and the catwalks were lowered. Out we went in about 8 feet of water, swimming a bit. I was fully clothed, with a full pack and a Bren gun resting on the pack with pouches full of ammo. We hit the beach and we were approaching the breach in the wall when a Marine officer ran to meet us. He said to the officer in charge of us, who was Captain Keebles, that they were going to blow up a booby-trapped building, could he get the men back on the boat. Captain Keebles' reply was to blow the bloody building up, the men had seen and heard explosions before. Everybody lay flat on the beach, there was a dull thud and pieces of masonry and lots of dust about, then we were waved on up the road. The Captain commented there was more noise from a bloody hand grenade.

We moved on up the road. Our destination was a field at Coulombes, a small village where we could change our trousers, our dry trousers were round our necks. The reference number was 123456 for the field. The whole battalion had their trousers down. Off we went towards Bronay which was in contact with the enemy. The enemy withdrew and we dug in for the night, or as it turned out, for a couple of days, while the 25-pounders and the RAF softened up Cristot. *Typescript recollections.*

Les Plews, 1945.

Geoff Steer (on the left) with a friend, Frank Williams.

Deactivating and detonating different types of mines and booby traps attached to obstacles on Gold Beach.
J G H Gritten

SUB-LIEUTENANT J G H GRITTEN RNVR (Sp)
Official Naval Reporter aboard LCT 903

Notes made en route to shore

White Verey light goes up opposite us, meaning capture of battery. Heavy lowering cloud. Occasional Lightnings (American aircraft.)

8.35: 2 cruisers bombard shore from stbd stern quarter.

8.50: Shells bursting all along shore as we approach. Destroyers pounding shore as they pass along coast across our bows. L 35 and Polish destroyer L 78. Houses along coast – shambles. 4 shells burst near LCT on Stbd side. Shell firing (Sic- bursting) among LCTs but we proceed inshore.

9.15: Shells seem to fall in same spot and short. Destroyers opening up. Shore mass of smoke. Pass LCT with hole blown in stbd side... it's our flotilla.

9.30: Shells burst near us and pass overhead to fall to stbd. Teller mines are choc a bloc with craft disgorging masses of equipment and men. Beach only about 5 yards of pebbles. Beyond this, green fields. Anti-tank ditches now empty and rising cultivated ground. A stream of our tanks are now pushing up the slope and halt beneath the ridge while destroyers laying off-shore and tanks on beach put up a barrage.

Airborne and Sea power: Gliders being towed towards their drop-zones, passing over allied warships including the battleships Warspite *and* Ramillies *engaged in bombardment of the German defences. This picture was taken by one of the Admiralty Press Division's Official Naval Photographers.* J G H Gritten

Some German photographs and artwork 'souvenired' by J.G.H. Gritten. Note the German soldier searching the French cart.

CORPORAL JIM BROWN

6th Battalion Green Howards, M/T Section,
driving a jeep, one of two vehicles available for Brigadier Knox

Unfortunately I hit a shell hole under the water and it decanted my vehicle over and though I was revving like hell I wasn't making any progress but there were some tanks on the beach edge and they hooked me up to one of them and pulled me out and the waterproofing did its job. Then my job was to go up to the de-waterproofing place. They had already put mesh down on the beach to help vehicles ashore because it was quite soft sand.

There were some terrible sights – men with their guts hanging out. The advanced dressing stations had not yet been set up. It was a rough day altogether. *Transcript of tape-recorded recollections.*

LIEUTENANT CHARLES FARRELL

3rd Battalion Scots Guards

I was chosen to go out on D-Day to report on the fighting in the early days and the tank fighting in particular, and come back and talk to the officers of the three battalions of the Guards Brigade on the lessons to be learned before we came out. I was honoured and pleased. My job was as a liaison officer of 30 Corps HQ but they knew what my real role was. Curiously we left from Felixstowe, I just had a jeep and a sergeant, Sgt Fisher, and a wireless set. We landed at Arromanches. When the ramps went down, my jeep was the first to go off and it was quite an alarming little jump as it was on to the flat steel platform called a Rhino ferry – it was just a large flat platform with two small engines on the back.

On the beach there seemed to be little shelling. It seemed almost like an exercise of which we had done so many, and being guided by the Beach Masters. However, we didn't really reach the beach because our Rhino impaled itself on one of the German tripods. We skewed round on this and were swinging round on the tide. We waded ashore and had to wait for the tide to recede to get the equipment off. It wasn't for some hours that this was possible and then I drove off with my sergeant to the advance HQ of 30 Corps which was being set up in an orchard near Bayeux. *Transcript of tape-recorded recollections.*

An emplacement at Mont Fleury under construction. A Huxley

The destroyed Longues battery. A. Huxley

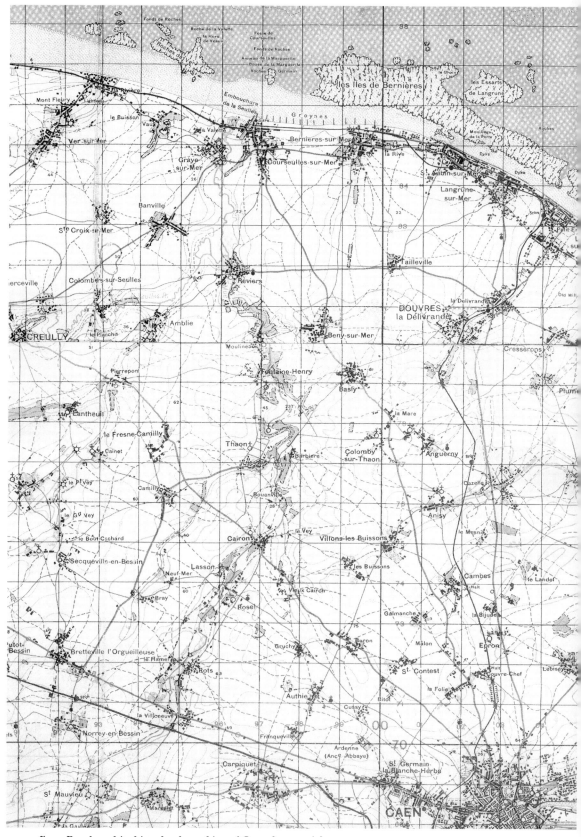

Juno Beach and its hinterland: outskirts of Caen, bottom right.

CHAPTER 9

Juno

Juno Beach, selected for initial assault by Canadian troops and in support by Canadian and British troops, extended for six miles east from the eastern boundary of Gold Beach at La Rivière to St Aubin-sur-Mer. Royal Navy, Canadian and Free French warships were to be in support here.

The coast in this sector is comprised of a series of almost linked holiday resorts considerably adapted into concreted defence emplacements. Rocky outcrops, mined obstacles below and above the waterline, a stiff wind and a swirling tide combined to cause serious problems for the assault craft crews and the troops they were carrying through the swell.

Delays, in terms of many landing craft, and for some, disasters, and a consequent degree of confusion, were the result here – troops were killed or wounded and many were drowned when their craft exploded mines, soldiers out of the landing before they had landed. A rapidly narrowing beach with no mine-cleared passages off it caused further delay and offered the defenders concentrated targets.

Immediately behind the beach, street fighting and trench clearing were the order of the day because neither the bombing nor the naval shelling had neutralised German defence. Positions were taken right along most of the line and in fact Canadians in the sector facing Caen advanced inland further than troops anywhere else on D-Day, but Courseulles-sur-Mer was not taken till mid-afternoon and with the heavy swell delaying the landing of Canadian armour and artillery for some time, another key objective, Carpiquet airfield, nine miles inland, was not taken on 6 June. Furthermore a gap was not cleared on the left flank adjoining Sword Beach so that it could not be said that success was evenly achieved above the shoreline. The Canadian and British achievement was considerable but not yet conclusive.

LIEUTENANT JOHN D McLEAN
'B' Company, Queen's Own Rifles of Canada

Suddenly the ramp went down and the men jumped into water up to their armpits. I was the seventh man out. Bullets whizzed around us and smacked into the boat and into the men. Being the centre craft, we were in the zone of concentrated crossfire. Men were being hit and disappearing under water. The chap in front of me, who was rather short, was carrying the heavy bangalore torpedo. When he jumped, he went under at once. Not knowing whether he had lost his footing or had been hit, as soon as I was in the water, I leaned over to haul him to the surface. At that moment, I felt as though someone had struck me with all their power with a baseball bat and I was knocked flat into the water. My left arm would not work.

I started swimming for the Beach. I had dropped my Sten gun so my hands were free. My main thought was to save my life. I remembered advice Jack Wreyford had given me: 'Don't try to be a hero. Duck when the going gets tough and you may come back in one piece.' Before being hit I had shouted to the men to return the fire from the shore. It was a normal reaction to strike back. Now as the adrenalin pumped into my system, time seemed to slow down drastically and I became much more perceptive of everything going on around me. Returning fire under such conditions was like spitting in the ocean. So I called to the men to stop firing and head for the protection of the wall as fast as possible.

It was a slow swim. The undertow was quite strong and I dug my toes into the sand to keep from washing back out to sea. I was in no hurry as I knew I would need all my strength to make the dash across the open beach where little spurts of sand showed where enemy bullets were hitting.

The Platoon got ahead of me, at least those who had not been killed or wounded in the water. I could see splashes of bullets coming across the water, and from time to time I submerged in order to swim under what looked like fixed lines of fire. As I got closer to the Beach, I saw one of my men, (I think Westerby), sitting propped up against one of the big obstacles made into a tripod out of railway tracks with a mine sitting on the top. I yelled to him to get to the wall, but he only smiled sweetly, and said he had had it. I yelled again that it was an order, get moving. At that moment, another burst of MG bullets pumped into him. He gave a great convulsive movement and his head flopped over to one side.

Just before I gathered my strength to run for the wall, I saw my batman Norris lying on the open beach. He looked in bad condition and I thought he was dead. Months later, I met him again, much to my surprise. He had been patched up and although still limping, he was doing full batman duties at Corps or Army Headquarters.

It surprises me to this day just how many I saw being hit as they crawled out of the water. There were gruesome sights which even now I do not wish to record. At the time, they were just part of the action. Afterwards, they reminded me that they were firsthand examples that war is hell.

I ran at a low crouch as fast as I could across the beach, possibly 20 yards and collapsed face down against the foot of the seawall. All sorts of things were going on around me, but at that point I was exhausted and not interested. I heard someone say that our Company Commander Major Charlie Dalton, had been hit. Later, Charlie told me he thought I was dying. Then one of the men came up to me and asked if I could get the pin out of his grenade. It is interesting that, even though I was obviously wounded and out of action, the men still expected me to solve their problems. My left arm was nearly useless, but was able to extract the pin with my teeth, and then I persuaded him to let me throw it over the wall from where I thought the rifle fire was coming. I could see he had his doubts. It showed in his eyes, but he let me do it anyway. Then he took another grenade from his belt, pulled the pin himself, and went off to join the fighting.

A short time after this, a Stretcher Bearer came up to me, cut off my webbing and eased off my jacket and shirt to expose the large hole in my shoulder. He worked quickly and gently, literally covering the wound with sulfa powder and then using the bandage from my steel helmet to bind it up. As he did so, he turned me over and propped me against the sloping wall from where I had a ringside seat to watch what was going on along the beach...

By afternoon, the Beach Party was brewing tea and not having eaten since 6 a.m., I welcomed a mug. German prisoners were being rounded up. It annoyed me to see them being loaded on the returning landing craft before the wounded. As someone explained, though, it was important to have them out of the way and also to get them back to England fast for propaganda purposes.

During the long afternoon with the fighting moving farther inland, a medical officer came by and checked each one of us. He had set up an emergency medical centre in one of the empty pillboxes and those who were stretcher cases were taken over there immediately. My wound was not considered serious, so I was one of the last to be given attention. He redressed it and put my arm in a sling. My shoulder ached badly, but I was still mobile. I lay in the sun getting used to the buzzing flies around the dried blood on me and others, the smell of the dead and of cordite, and listening to the sounds of battle in the distance.

In the later afternoon I was told to report to a stranded landing ship on the beach where I would spend the night. *From 'We Were There: A Record for Canada' The Army, Volume 2 by Jean Portugal (from pages 614-618).*

LIEUTENANT HECTOR RUSSELL
'B' Company, 10 Platoon, Canadian Scottish

All our ranks were now well briefed as to where we were to land; who would be on our flanks; our objectives; and our opposition. We had proper maps, French currency and an unlimited supply of condoms for anything that required waterproofing – watches, compass, paper money, pay books etc. I noticed some of the more optimistic types stuff a few extras in a convenient pocket...

We had been practising our drill for exiting LCAs for about a year. So the routine was pretty well rehearsed. When the ramp came down, the centre section was to go, followed by the right section and then the platoon commander, followed by the left section. The head of the centre section took off as soon as the ramp came down.

In retrospect, the section leader, centre section, left the craft as soon as that ramp was down; the next two privates behind the leader were hit, rifles and shovels blocking the centre and right sections. Anyway with those two areas blocked, the ramp down and gunshots coming from all directions something had to be done FAST. It was my job so remembering old movies, I shouted back to No 3 Section 'Follow me!' and took off. The unit had such *esprit de corps* that my troops advanced into the shellfire.

As I was about to jump/step off the ramp, there was a shattering cracking explosion and everything turned red, and almost simultaneously, a blinding white hot searing in the area of my right eye.

The run-in to the beach at Juno Mike Red to the West of Courseulles. The coxswain is behind the screen, the soldier is on lookout and the remaining troops with their bicycles are covered by the tarpaulin. The choppiness of the sea is clearly evident. I D Campbell

After travelling about 12 feet in the air, and landing in the shoulder-deep water, I surfaced face to face with a German Teller mine attached to the railway track tripod jack. It was about 16 inches in diameter, black and covered with barnacles and very ugly.

Trying to stand up and wade to the beach, I found that my left leg was not working as it should, there was a bad break in the femur between the hip and the knee. As I was floundering around, I saw the rest of the platoon were following, in fact L-Cpl Kane who was second in command, 3rd Section, jumped in and landed right beside me, fortunately. Kane was 6 feet tall and well built and he picked me up by the web straps above the back pack and pulled me through the water to the beach. I am a fairly good swimmer, but with the rough seas and heavy boots, helmet and equipment, I sure appreciated the help.

As I was lying face down on the sand/pebble beach, I heard one of the platoon soldiers say: 'Cheez, did you see Mr. Russell? He had the whole side of his face blown off', – Not very encouraging for me.

I could see a steady stream of blood pouring into the sand so I knew it was time to assess the damage. First, I had to stop the blood flow. We all carried two First Aid Dressings in a special pocket built into our battledress. I could not unfasten the button of it, as there was something the matter with my right hand index finger. I was able to tear the fighting knife from its special scabbard on the lower right leg to cut open the pocket. Tying one dressing to my right eye around the head, I kept the other tied to my index finger. The bleeding was stopped (I hoped). No one took that band aid off my finger for a month.

I should mention that what happened to me was completely unanticipated, almost inconceivable; We, the 3rd Canadian Infantry Division were known as the 'Death or Glory Boys', so none of us gave a thought to being wounded. Either we made it or we didn't. Toss a coin.

I had been dropped right at the water's edge and the tide was coming in. With water creeping to knee level, I had to move, but with my lower left leg lying boot flat in the sand, it was like an anchor. When I tried to arch my back to get hold of the leg below the knee I could only get hold of a piece of battledress and pull. I could hear the grating as the bones came back together. I had moved about 3 inches forward.

I could see about 15 yards ahead, Cpl. Norman T. Green with six or seven men huddled behind a shallow dune, but still in the intense bombardment area. I shouted, caught his attention and gestured him to come to me, which he promptly and bravely did. I told him to gather up his section and move straight forward out of the 'beaten zone' and get off the beach. But first pull me forward a yard or two. It was a relief to see them move out of sight over the dune, and to be out of the rising tide, at least for a while. *From 'We Were There: A Record for Canada' The Army, Volume 4, by Jean E. Portugal, (from pages 1935-1938).*

GUNNER W T JONES
3rd Canadian Anti-Tank Regiment

Our gun, H1, was to be the first towed gun of the regiment to land. We were to land on Mike sector of Juno and proceed to our Assembly area for a speedy de-waterproofing. Splash shields off carriers, breech blocks degreased, and condoms off the telescopic sights. This was the plan, but what action goes according to the plan? On our run in to the beaches about three miles from shore, we were ordered out of the landing order and fell back about five miles. Here we circled for hours, which seemed like days as the seas were rough and we weren't sailors. We had been told our beach exit was plugged and closed to vehicles. Finally our turn came and in we went. The tide, however, was now not suitable for a direct landing (i.e. Ramp down, drive off) as we had rehearsed for many months. Major Ev Scott informed the gun sergeants we would be landing on a small 'Rhino' raft. This was the first time we had heard about Rhino rafts and we sure weren't crazy about the word 'raft'. There were the usual derogatory remarks about the Canadian Brass. We were assured that four Bren gun carriers and guns could fit on these rafts, 'if properly handled'. Out from the beach puttered our raft, a low slung affair, with steel decking and no railings, powered by two outboard motors and crewed by two REs who looked about 40 years old! Needless to say, it was quite a feat for the RN and REs to get the LCT (Landing Craft Tank) ramp down and chained to this postage stamp-sized raft, with such a high surf running. How they did it without loss of life or limb, I'll never know, but they did. As we were H1 we had the dubious honour of being the first to drive down a ramp that could be coming up, onto a pitching raft and hope the steel tracks of the carrier would hold on the slippery deck of the raft. With driver, Jack Kennedy, and myself, we drove on, quickly followed by H2, 3 and 4. 'H' troop set sail for shore.

About five hundred yards from shore, one outboard quit and we proceeded to go round and round in slow erratic circles, much to our dismay and to the alarm and terror of all traffic near us. On examination of the motors I found they were 'Johnsons' and manufactured about a mile from my home in Canada. A combination of my cursing the War Workers and the REs calling for the wrath of God, brought it to life. Once again we headed for the beach. Our orders were to drive off with the gun crew running behind in the water, and not to stop on the beach. As we drove off, the gun crews' parting words were, 'By J....., you'd better wait for us!'. Once on the beach we slowed down and tried to pick up the crews, but because of the high splash shields they couldn't get in the carriers on the run. So we stopped. As soon as we stopped a Canadian Provo (military police) came roaring up on a motorcycle, yelling at me to keep moving. As he went by us he drove right into a shell hole about 12 feet in diameter and so deep there was water in the bottom. As H2, 3 and 4 guns passed, they all offered free advice and comments to this hapless Provo. Once we got free of the sand, we poured it on and up the road to Graye-sur-Mer. *Taken from an article by Stan Medland, 'Confrontation in Normandy: The 3rd Canadian Anti-Tank Regiment on D-Day' published in Canadian Military History, Spring 1994, Vol 3, Number 1, pages 56 57.*

CAPTAIN W R HAIR
Regimental HQ, 12th Field Regiment, Royal Canadian Artillery

My group and the men of the Inns of Court got on the beach and were heading for the safety of the dunes. We started across the beach and I could hear the MGs, so I dropped down twice before I hit the dune. I had about 30 seconds while they changed the gun direction to our right. Once at the dune I was safe. The pillbox could only fire at the beach, not the dune. The Inns of Court never got off the beach – the ones who were to get off and whistle up to the Orne River – since both exits were plugged. My officer friend had a jeep, but the rest of the company had bikes and they couldn't go anywhere. They remained on the beach from between 8 or 9 am till about 3 pm when the major exit on the left had opened and the gun on the right had bagged off.

We worked our way back then to the pillbox to try to winkle out the enemy gunners. But one of the LCTs came in with a tank on. It was supposed to be a DD tank but hadn't come in earlier and they decided to send them in anyway. This one came in and as soon as the ramp was lowered it started firing at the pillbox and fortunately one of his rounds went in the slit. He fired about four rounds before he hit it. That put the pillbox out of action.

The first thing when I got across the beach I hit a trip wire. Someone had tripped on it and I saw only half a body. I just went right on up to the dune. That was the first casualty I saw. After we got to the dune and I was moving back and forth in its shelter trying to find gun positions, I saw another body lying on the beach and as I went past, his eyes kept following me, though he didn't turn his head. When I came back, his eyes picked me up again and he'd obviously been hit somewhere in the chest. There was no blood. I went back across to the end where they were setting up the RAP. I told the Padre that there was someone there and he was gathering the Stretcher Bearers etc and he went back out with me to where this chap was lying and he knelt beside him and turned and looked up at me and just shook his head. I realised there was no hope, sure enough, the next time I went past, he was dead; just the Padre going to him and shaking his head, shook me. These were the first two casualties I saw...

Because of the blocked exits we never did get off the beach till 3 pm or so. Space was so jammed that when my guns came ashore there was no place for them to go. They just lined up nose to tail there and were firing inland I would guess up to 8,000 or 9,000 yards (4 or 5 miles) supporting the infantry trying to establish their bridgehead.

We fired about three hours from the beach and by this time we had some mortaring, but not much. I was sitting with Battery Commander Gib Goldie looking out over and beyond the dunes and I saw this wounded Corporal crawling back on his hands and knees from maybe 50 to 100 yards beyond us and he was a Canadian Scottish chap. Without thinking, I got up and just walked to him and picked him up, but he wouldn't let me leave without his rifle. The Scottish were a magnificent outfit and he dragged his rifle back with him. The state of training of the Canadian Scottish was superb. They were great. I dragged him back to the RAP just below us *From 'We Were There: A Record for Canada' The Army, Volume 4, by Jean E. Portugal, (from pages 1835, 1836).*

ROSS MUNRO

Canadian Press War Correspondent

I had a grandstand seat from the *Hilary*. It was terrific. The ship was close in, and with binoculars I could see a hell of a lot that was going on on the battlefield. As the running reports were coming in to Gen. Keller over the wireless from shore, I met him on the deck which was serving as the HQ OP (observation post), and he gave me the text of his brief message to Gen. Crerar, the Canadian Army Commander, back in England: 'It is hard fighting, but our troops have broken through the initial beach defences and are on their way to the intermediate objective, probably 2 miles inland.' Then he told me: 'I'm committing the Reserve Brigade now and it is landing at Bernières where the best beach exits have been made.' At this point the first wounded were being brought aboard as the first battered landing craft pulled alongside. Bleeding and badly hit, they were carried to the Sick Bay and the emergency dressing station and the doctor worked over them.

Some destroyers which now had run out of ammunition were returning to England and by good luck and chance, a story of mine got out ahead of any other correspondent with the ground forces. In it I had told of the Canadian success in securing the beachhead in two and a half-hours of fighting, and had quoted Keller's message to Crerar.

All night and morning I had been writing my head off in the wardroom, trying to describe the incredible invasion scene. I had minute by minute information flooding in over the wireless from shore. How different from Dieppe! I knew exactly how the fighting was going and could see much of it from the ship's deck. But I was not permitted to use Naval

German prisoners being gathered at the shell-damaged railway station at Bernières.

Troops pass casualties awaiting evacuation, Bernières.

The drawings of Corporal Eric Earnshaw, 5th Battalion, The Royal Berkshire Regiment, whose artistic skill led his officer, Peter Prior, to instruct him: '*You are not here to kill Germans but to draw what you see.*'
Peter Prior

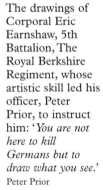

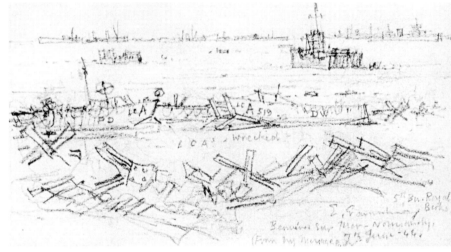

Bernières-sur-Mer: disabled landing craft

Canadian troops coming ashore with bicycles.

A Canadian Official photograph presented by General Crerar to Lieutenant Peter Prior who is marked by an arrow giving movement instructions to German prisoners.

wireless to England to get the story out. I had to rely on any ship going back to England.

Sometime between 10 and 10:30 a.m. I went ashore, not with the assault platoons, but with Tac HQ made up of Gen. Keller and a handful of Staff Officers, two of whom were going in to set up an advance HQ on the beach.

Smoke was still pouring up from St. Aubin and there was gunfire on the slopes behind Bernières and over by Courseulles. But we ran right up on the beach, skimming past a line of hedgehogs with mines still attached and Tac HQ splashed ashore as the craft grounded.

I had expected to have very heavy shelling on the beach, but there was very little shelling or mortar fire there, and we walked into Bernières with the Reserve Bde infantry which had just come off craft. Small groups of French civilians cheered our men as they passed by, and a girl handed me a crimson rose. With tears in her eyes she told me that her home had been ruined by the initial bombardment. 'But' she said, 'the Allies are here! Canadians are in our village, and now the Germans are gone'.

I got into the centre of Bernières and started writing my pieces. There was a high stone wall in the town made of a sort of cobblestone material and it was about 10 feet high. I got behind that and figured it would be good protection against mortaring. I dug a trench and got my typewriter going.

My friends of the 13th Field Regiment, R.C.A., had landed and were in a nearby orchard and started firing in support of troops south of Bernières. The concussion from these SP 105s lifted the typewriter off my knees and I had a hell of a time getting that story done. It was the most difficult typing I've ever done. Did I have sore knees? You aren't kidding.

From 'We were There: A Record for Canada' Royal Canadian Air Force and Others by Jean E. Portugal, (pages 3403, 3404).

LIEUTENANT D J STRUTHERS

the Gun Position Officer of Dog Troop, 66 Battery,
14th Field Regiment, Royal Canadian Artillery

We opened fire at approximately one half hour before 'H. Hour' firing over the Infantry in the LCA's and covered an area of beach defences approximately four hundred by two hundred yards with four rounds per minute from each gun – a total of 96 guns. We stopped firing at 2,000 yards from the target and turned away from the beach to unshackle the guns and tanks and pitch the unused ammunition overboard. We touched down at thirty minutes after 'H. Hour'. I went ashore in the ammunition half-track as it was loaded in the bow and consequently it was first off. Some mortar fire was coming down on the beach. I saw an overturned Bren gun carrier with a human arm waving feebly and a number of bodies at the edge of the surf.

We bunched in front of Bernières-sur-Mer as there was only one exit over the beach wall where there was supposed to be three. The Queen's Own Rifles of Canada were still mopping up by the railway station. I was followed by one S.P. only as the other three were directed to a gun position just off the beach, unknown to me. When I reached the top of the sea wall some enemy machine-gun fire went overhead. The Engineer sergeant who was directing the traffic stepped back and there was an explosion and I lost sight of him as I was peering out of the slits in the armour of the half-track.

With my one self-propelled gun I followed the Reserve Company of the Queen's Own through the town. The first field south of the town was to be our first gun position. Two guns from A Troop and one from Charlie Troop were already in position and a director was already set up. I made my way towards the director when a red ball passed me and hit the first A Troop gun. The detachment was able to scramble out. I headed back to stop my gun from entering the field as it had had trouble with the narrow gate. The second A Troop gun was hit and the detachment jumped out. The C Troop was hit in the ammunition bay and exploded. No members of the detachment were ever found.

A German 75 millimetre anti-tank gun had destroyed three of our guns. The Germans had watched the whole Squadron of the Fort Garry Horse tanks go past before opening fire on us. German intelligence had obviously reported our AVRE's (the funnies). Our S.P.'s with their side plates for waterproofing and back decks piled high with anti-tank mines, mortar bombs and 303 ammunition, had looked strange to the Germans and taken for AVRE's. My gun survived as there was an earth bank between the anti-tank guns and my S.P.

We were then in the front line as mines had delayed the Fort Garry's. I collected five of our Regiments S.P.'s in a walled farmyard. In the afternoon we moved up to Beny-sur-Mer and were mortared out of our Battery gun position. *Typescript recollections,*

SERGEANT JIM PAISLEY

'A' Squadron, 5th Troop, The First Hussars
[6th Armoured Regiment of London, Ontario]

At the order, our LCT swung around astern to the beach and we prepared to launch. Our screens were up and the ramp extensions were put out. Our tanks then launched, but we had trouble due to having only three engines running properly. We had taken a fair amount of water and we assumed this had done some damage. Anyway we pulled out in third gear driving for the beach. We also got some screen damage above the water line from gunfire, but not serious enough to prevent us from gaining the beach. Lt. Little got us all out on the deck just in case, and we were steering from the deck tiller.

We pushed in until we were just off the beach obstacles when one of our LCTs fitted out as a rocket ship came in behind us and fired its broadside. It was a hell of a racket and the launch complete, it turned away from the beach and its bow wave came over us from the rear and we went under.

We were all pulled down and four of us soon surfaced, but Lt. Little did not appear for some time. When he finally came up, he was gasping for air. He had got tangled up in his headset and couldn't get free. We were all bunched around the dinghy when Bill came up.

Due to considerable beach fire hitting the water around us, we did not inflate the dinghy as it was a more inviting target. Within a few minutes, Hawken our Loader, was killed and we kept ducked down as low as our ETEAs (Emergency Tank Escape Apparatus) would let us. Several pick-up boats were in the area, but didn't come to us till later. Some time went by and Jimmy Spence our Gunner, being a non-swimmer, was very sick from the wave motion and the sea water he had swallowed. He insisted we inflate the dinghy and when we did, he crawled up onto it. He said: 'I'd rather be shot than drowned'. Jimmy had gone through all our DD training without being able to swim and we had to teach him to handle the underwater training, a pretty gutsy piece of business.

With Jimmy on the dinghy, and the other three of us hanging on the side, we floated around for what seemed like a couple of hours. I think it was probably 10 o'clock. Lt. Little prevailed on a pick-up boat to rescue us by threatening to shoot holes in the craft with his pistol!

We were then put on an HQ ship laying off the beach, nose in. This ship was used by beach control people, and early in the morning had taken a lot of fire from shore, and had casualties on deck. We were put aboard and were in reasonable shape except for Jim Spence. He had swallowed half the Channel. The crew got him cleaned up and warm, and he began to recover though still seasick from the rough water. We were all covered with oil and the crew outfitted us with some spare clothing. Spence and Copeland were dressed almost like Navy personnel.

Lt. Little spent most of the time trying to find someone to put us on shore, but apparently the orders were that no crews were to be put down without tanks. *From 'We Were There: A Record for Canada' The Army, Volume 3, by Jean E. Portugal, (from pages 1008-1010).*

LIEUTENANT PETER PRIOR
Intelligence Officer, 5th Battalion, The Royal Berkshire Regiment, 8th Beach Group

Soon we were only a few hundred yards off the coast, by a little village called Bernières-sur-Mer. My landing craft was the middle one of three, and we approached the beach in formation. The other two were unlucky, for the Germans had placed mines on wooden poles and stuck them in the sand. As we came in, the craft on either side had holes blown in their bottoms and quickly settled down on the beach. This didn't stop the men on them from getting ashore, however, except for one and I found his body later in the day in a broken-backed landing craft, to my great shock it was Tomlinson, (the Canadian officer).

Our craft had better luck, at our landing place there was almost no opposition. I struggled up the beach waist deep in water, holding my Bren gun high over my head.

The first necessity was the blowing up of a section of sea wall by the engineers to enable the tanks and lorries to get off the beach. In a remarkably short space of time this was done and we had a road built of seawall debris.

Men of the 5th Battalion, The Royal Berkshire Regiment on Juno Beach. The 18 year old soldier, with his hands in his pockets, was to be killed a few days after this photograph was taken. Peter Prior

Four men from Peter Prior's Intelligence Section of No 8 Beach Group: Eric Earnshaw, the artist of Juno drawings illustrated in this book, is seated, eating his lunch. Corporal Butler, on the right, was fluent in German and spoke French.

I went through some gardens on the far side of the village, and edged up cautiously to a point where three Canadian tanks and their supporting infantry were held up. I looked at the German positions, and at first saw no sign of life. Suddenly there was a flash and with a loud explosion the tank beside which I was standing burst into flames. The Canadians were well trained, but so was the German anti-tank unit. Nobody escaped from the tank and, for me, the war changed from an exciting excursion into a grim reality.

By noon we were still stuck in Bernières. Large numbers of vehicles had been landed – the traffic jam was almost solid. There were soldiers everywhere, and it was fortunate that there were no German aircraft about, for we would have provided a splendid target. But although there was a crush, there was not confusion; for everybody knew where they had to go and what they had to do.

By the afternoon, my Intelligence Section, having installed themselves in somebody's comfortable drawing room, were dealing with the first batch of prisoners and spies; the latter, of course, seemed more interesting.

In the first flush of battle, innocent local residents were arrested on the slightest pretext and delivered to us as 'spies': an old peasant women who was caught wandering about ahead of the forward troops; she was looking for her favourite cow: a girl who had been to visit her grandmother in the neighbouring village; she was making her way back home: a keen local patriot who had run up a home-made flag on the top of his barn – all of them were delivered to our door as suspected agents of the enemy. Before long one had to push one's way through a cluster of spies to get into Battalion HQ at all and in the end, the Colonel ordered them all off the premises. *Typescript recollections and transcript of tape-recorded recollections.*

CAPTAIN IAN HAMMERTON

1st Troop, B Squadron, 22nd Dragoons, Royal Armoured Corps,
79th Armoured Division

We were told it was going to be the fifth (of June) but in fact the weather was bad and we didn't leave until the evening of the fifth. And when we cast off, my landing craft was in a lead of a line, and as we went past Portsmouth, Gosport, and out past Spithead, I was asked up on to the bridge by the Skipper, Dutch Holland by name, and I looked back and it was a fantastic sight. We were followed by lines of landing craft. We were only the leading craft of one line. There were, I could see, four lines and as the further we moved out into the open sea you could see more and more craft coming out of all these basins. It was as if a giant was pulling them out on strings. And I remember passing one of the old Victorian gun forts in the Solent and at that point I gave up my dinner.

I managed to get down below and find the sandbag in which were maps for all the tank commanders, and there were as I say, maps. Not only quarter inch maps of the whole area of Normandy, of the beachhead area, but also a five inch to the mile detailed map with defence overprints showing the positions of ditches and wire and minefields and gun positions and so on. I dished those out. There were also some photographs taken by the RAF only weeks before, taken by planes low flying along a beach at low tide, so you could see all the obstacles uncovered by the water. There was also a picture taken, presumably pre-war, of a family building sandcastles on the beach, and you could see behind them the sea wall. So you were able to judge the height of the sea wall quite easily from that. In the sealed camp at Gosport before we left we had considerable briefing with sand tables and models and that sort of thing. We were very well briefed.

Our landing craft coming in scraped along the side of a rocket launching LCT which

Captain Ian Hammerton with men of his troop.

fired off volleys of hundreds of rockets. It knocked us off course slightly, but nothing dreadful. We landed alright and my flails flailed up to the wall. Unfortunately the Engineers bridge tank had the bridge shot down so we couldn't use that to get over the wall. It meant that we had to shoot our way through some steel gates called Element C, made of railway lines welded together and all tied up in barbed wire. I had to move my tank up to the base of a concrete ramp which the tide was just beginning to touch, and by aiming the gun, by looking through the barrel – the Commander had to do this – and when you looked through a seventy-five millimetres wide barrel it's extraordinary how wide it seems if you are thinking of something coming through from the opposite direction! Anyway, aiming at each joint, loading, firing, re-aiming at the next joint. Loading, firing, it took some time to reduce these gates to rubble. And then it was a matter of getting out, attaching the tow rope which was already shackled on to the front of the tank, to the wreckage, dragging it out of the way. A Churchill did try to go up the ramp and push it out of the way, but it got stuck. So I had to pull the stuff out into the sea – reversing back. My other two flails managed to get up the ramp and start flailing up on the top knocking off mines. And as we were about to go up I am afraid we were flooded. I had to blow the waterproofing round the turret ring, of course, to use the turret gun and we flooded. So we had to bail out, which we did. So we walked the tightrope along the edge of the jib and dropped off into five feet of water. We were carrying our machine-gun, Browning machine-guns, boxes of ammo, grenades, wearing – not only wearing our anti gas battle dress but overalls on top of it. It was a struggle to get out of the water.

169

The tank, I am afraid, was a write-off because it was sunk. It was recovered later and doubtless cleaned out and restored to use by someone else.

Initially I was sitting on the top of my Sergeant's tank. I should have explained that my first Sergeant's and one other flail had landed a few hundred yards the other side of the famous house at Bernières-sur-Mer, and they flailed along the parallel road to the seashore towards us. The two flails with me still flailed up to that road and then turned right to meet up with him. There was an anti-tank ditch in the way, which the Engineers managed to fill with a fascine, and then I was called to deal with a minefield the other side of Bernières, which the flail did. I travelled on the back of one of them.

Yes, well, as far as I know we were so pre-occupied in what we were doing that I don't know whether we were under fire and we must have had an easy time of it.

The Infantry were alongside us. Some of them had landed a little bit earlier. In fact, as we scrambled out with great difficulty onto the shore, there were a number of Canadian bodies there. Anyway, having dealt with the minefield we were then diverted to a field the other side of Bernières and asked to flail round the perimeter to prove it, in other words, to see if there were any mines there or not. And as we did so the DUKWs, the Royal Army Service Corps Supply Swimming Lorries, came up the shore, followed us round, and as they did so they dumped off their loads of ammunition and petrol. And we finished that job round about one o'clock in the morning – pitch darkness. And some of my chaps in my crew had gone back to the tank and rescued our waterlogged, sand-laden, oil-soaked blankets, and we rolled up in those and went to sleep. *Transcript of tape-recorded recollections.*

SERGEANT BERNARD UPSON
22nd Royal Dragoons, in command of two 'Flail' tanks

We were loaded into tank landing craft, two flails forward on each, RE tanks with various special tanks in support, we touched down in quite deep water it seemed, and rolled forward onto the beach and then toward the softer sand of the dunes. We flailed the sand but it had not been mined (in our path); the bridge tank dropped its bridge on top of the dunes down to the shoreline and immediately a shell took the top off that tank. We kept behind the dunes out of the line of fire and I went back to where I had seen my Troop Officer go up a break in the dunes.

By this time the Canadian Infantry were coming ashore. We were close to the dunes when a huge net was blown off a very large pill box which had not been visible previously. Small flashes were coming from slits in the concrete, infantry were running into this fire. I directed my gunner at these slits and he soon disposed of them – we were too close to the pill box's main armament for the barrel of the gun to be trained on us and we were able at point blank range to put five high explosive shells into the gun destroying it and its crew.

I now moved forward through the dunes to link up with my Troop Officer. On my way up I saw a church with a spire which I guessed was an observation point and gave Bishop, my Gunner, the order to deal with this. He did, with his second shot. A French boy, at the time, with his wounded mother sheltering in the church, later confirmed that the Germans using the observation point had been killed.

I moved alongside my Troop Officer's tank. They were being held up due to the bridge being blown. A Royal Engineer bridge tank had been called into action to drop a bridge. The bridge tank had run into trouble, the tank's crew had got out and been shot by a sniper. My Troop Officer's Gunner had got out to help them; he too was pinned down by the sniper. Fortunately he had taken his wireless speaker with him and was able to ask me to direct fire at a red-roofed house where he thought the sniper was. The air was full of mortar fire, they had the range and were giving the area a bashing. I then directed my Gunner to range onto the red-roof house. Up to now I'd not been outside of the tank, the lid was open but I was well inside.

The Gunner fired at the house. I came up to observe the shot, at that moment a mortar bomb dropped on top of the turret. A splinter of metal went under the flap and hit me in the head between my eyes. Blood flowed, I put on a First Field Dressing to stop the bleeding. The dressing could not contain the blood and I lost a lot of blood, and passed out.

When I came round, I was lying on the beach against the pill box wall that we had destroyed. The wind was blowing sand about so they had covered us with blankets. I had been given morphine, a large 'M' had been put on my forehead with indelible pencil. I was to have this souvenir for some time to come.

Later I was carried to a landing craft which took me out to a hospital ship which took me to Gosport. *Manuscript recollections.*

CAPTAIN I D CAMPBELL, RAMC
Medical Officer to a Beach Landing Party

We embarked well before 5 June at Southampton and as we were embarking on a former cross-channel steamer there at the gangway was Winston Churchill, Field Marshal Smuts and Ernest Bevin, and Churchill looked so sad. He was really just about weeping and all he was doing was the V sign and saying, 'Good luck, boys, good luck,' and giving some a pat on the back.

We were aboard ship for some days and it struck me how serious a factor was religion; the chaplains when they had a service had a full house.

We were to land at Juno Mike Red behind our Canadian friends, D Company of the Canadian Scottish with whom we had trained and exercised. An LCT picked us up and we landed at 10am.

There was a lot of wrecked boats and there was a lot of casualties on the beach. They were very similar to the fake casualties only they were real and our early, our first unit which was a big Beach Dressing Station had landed at 8.15 with the first assault and we contacted them and they were busy treating the casualties. Part of the beach group's responsibility was to have stretcher bearers to gather the casualties and take them to the Beach Dressing Station where they were treated. Now my responsibility was to report to the Beach Dressing Station and then to proceed to the village of Graye-sur-Mer, which was about 600 yards from the beach. *Transcript of tape-recorded recollections.*

Major Bob McEwan (on the left), in command of D Company, Canadian Scottish, severely wounded on D + 1 and treated by No 1 Field Surgical Unit. On the right, Captain Jack Bryden, 2nd in Command of the Company, killed half an hour after this photograph was taken on D-Day and who was to be awarded a posthumous gallantry medal for neutralising a pill-box. I D Campbell

German anti-aircraft defence: a 'souvenired' photograph. P Prior

CORPORAL JOHN BRIGHT

Wireless Operator, Royal Corps of Signals attached to 3rd Canadian Division

Our Rhino was eventually fully loaded and was propelled by its two engines at a sedate pace of about 3 mph. towards the beach. Everyone on board felt very exposed as they crept along at a snail's pace whilst all around there was noise, smoke and confusion. The Naval shells were still whistling overhead and the rocket launchers firing their broadsides together with the explosion of mines and shells against a backdrop of diving and wheeling aircraft. Added to this was the din of enemy gunfire but the Rhino still chugged serenely on. Nearer the beach the scene changed to one of much more urgency. Crippled landing craft at odd angles, abandoned tanks and vehicles, bodies on the beach and floating in the water, smoke and fires everywhere and above it all the noise, noise, noise. It was unreal under a clear blue sky. When the Rhino hit the beach, the two of us needed no second telling and picked our way off the crowded beach and through the exit and took a breather in a crater. Then through the minefields, along paths marked with white tape which had been cleared by the Royal Engineers, we made our way. After passing through the village of Bernières to the rendezvous area we quickly dug a slit trench and in spite of the uproar settled down to brew some tea and await the arrival of our wireless truck and driver. *Typescript recollections.*

French currency issued to John Bright.

John Bright (in the centre) with two comrades, 'Bunny' Williams and 'Hush' Harker, on leave in Trafalgar Square, London, May 1944.

SERGEANT J KITE

Special Forces, Army Commando

We had seventy-eight pounds of kit on our person. Firstly everyone had identification tags, one dirty green and one dull red colour, our Army number and religion, date of birth on one of these tags. It was buried with you if you were killed, the other was sent to the Records Office. We wore khaki shirt, very long, no vest, no pants and khaki trousers. Battle dress tunic, socks and boots. Inside our backpack we had to fold our overcoat square enough to fit inside. Our ground sheet and a blanket. This was essential for the blanket you were buried in if you were killed, and in the small valise we held our mess tins, 'housewife', which were needle and cotton etc, soap and rations for the next forty-eight hours. Ammunition pouches held as much as we could carry and we had normally our Sten guns, six Sten gun cartridges in each of our pouches – all my crowd had fully automatic weapons – no rifles. We had one Bren gun which the Second in Command, James Buck, carried. Every man carried fifty rounds for the Bren gun on top of their kit, because the Bren gun uses more

A family's war service: John Kite (top right) with his brothers and sister.

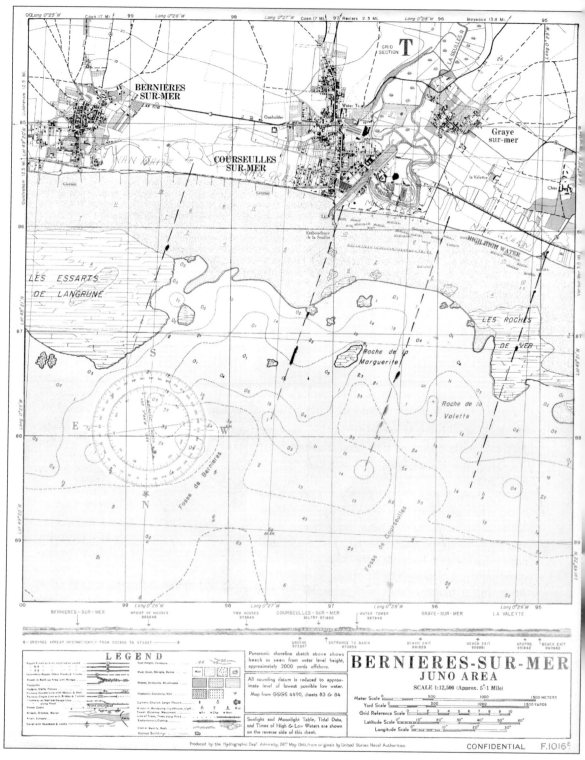

An original map issued to R.M. Bache for the Juno Beach landing showing the Bernières-sur-Mer and Courseulles sector.

ammunition than what we did. We carried a full water bottle on our chest and respirator. On top of that were the gas cape and a stupid little rubber tyre which was supposed to prevent us drowning.

With all these things we had to wade through the water and run up the banks and push on to our target. You can imagine how awkward it was. Up and down like yo-yos in the water, avoiding sniper fire to our left and to our right. They were all up in the houses at the top.

Our beach was Juno Nan and above the beach we had to climb a concrete wall. Assault Engineering had put tracking up against it to help us.

On reaching the shore I reported to Lieutenant Colonel Warden, who was about sixty yards away from our boat and all he wanted to know was how many men came off the boat. He said, 'Don't tell me how many you lost on the way, I'm not interested.' I said, 'Thirty, Sir', he said, 'Right.' He slapped me on the back and he said, 'Best of luck, take them ashore.' Now we came ashore and there was a road right opposite us. Our place we had to get to was La Délivrande. Coming to the wall we were confronted by two Germans and these were suitably killed.

Ahead of me was a field, a field covered with gliders and dead cattle and dead personnel. It was a very sorry state. There were posts in the field at ten-foot centres, big posts about twelve inches in diameter. Trees, trees cut down, and it was a sorry sight to see these gliders up-ended. Now I had already given my personnel notification not to tread on grass verges because we had been told they could be mined so we kept basically to the road. We got as far as a farmhouse on the Douvres La Délivrande road and that was the only farmhouse there, all the rest was open country going, looking to Tailleville. Tailleville was about two miles, or a mile and a half to two miles over the back. Over the back there, there were Germans with 88 millimetre guns, firing on to the Douvres La Délivrande road. Any dust they saw coming from the road, they were firing. Whilst we were having a cup of tea, I sent one of my lads to see the woman in the house because he could speak fluent French to see if he could get a pail of hot water so we could have a brew up. Whilst we were in the trench at the side of the road, a Brigadier came up with the Royal Marine Commandos with his driver, and called me over and asked me whether the road ahead was clear. And I said, 'I have no idea Sir, but we have to get there,' and I said, 'If you get your driver, tell him five miles an hour. No more because these 88 millimetres are playing hell with us' (and they will see dust if you go any faster.)...

About eleven o'clock we got to our place in Douvres La Délivrande and cleared the school which was to become the Brigade Headquarters. We had to make sure there were no booby traps or anything left there. We cleared this and on our way out we saw The Royal Marine Commandos. There's a big church in Délivrande and there were some snipers up in the tower, and the Royal Marine Commandos were trying to dislodge these snipers at the top. I asked them if they wanted a hand and so forth and they said, 'Not at the moment, we will deal with those people.' And eventually they dislodged them and killed them. We then went to the blockhouse, which was our next target, to see what could be done there. When we reached the blockhouse at the top of the road, the Royal Marine Commandos were already in position, and told us to 'sling our hook'.

So we got on to Brigade and they told us to go on from there to Hermanville, which is a steady trudge. Now, Hermanville La Brèche is not far from the Orne/Ouistreham Canal, and we got up there and I reported to the Colonel concerned and he could see my men were absolutely bushed. He said, 'Dig yourself a trench in there and get your head down. We will keep guard of the men while you are there.' So we had nothing to do till the following day.

Transcript of tape-recorded recollections.

A home hit by rocket and shell, Bernières-sur-Mer. A Huxley

GEORGES REGNAULD

a nineteen-year-old French citizen of Bernières-sur-Mer

On the fifth of June at first light a formation of heavy bombers, about sixty in number, came to annihilate the famous batteries of Tombette, situated to the south of our village. There were many killed among the Germans and, regrettably, a certain number of civilians who were labour conscripts.

All these bombardments made us realise that a landing in Normandy was imminent for from dusk on June the fifth formations of bombers continued all night long on their way to bomb all the railways and main roads to prevent German reinforcements from reaching the coast.

The whole of the night of the fifth/sixth of June there was nothing but throbbing engines and exploding bombs all along the coast.

I stayed with the Aubrée family where we spent a worrying night not knowing what the dawn had in store for us. As soon as it grew light, we thought we might risk checking to see what could be happening at sea. There was a gate joining the house next door which made this possible.

Goodness to me! An unforgettable sight awaited us! The horizon was covered with ships approaching the shore. We stood there dumbfounded. Then suddenly a fog – an artificial one – hid the whole armada.

Between the sound of two aircraft formations passing overhead we heard the guttural

176

commands of German troops a short distance from our observation post as they prepared themselves for the terrible battle which was about to begin.

We had hardly got back to the Aubrée's house when the German guns began to fire. At once shells flew over our heads and began to land in the direction of the ships. We were about to spend some dreadful hours cowering against each other in our hazardous shelter.

Then suddenly the Navy opened fire with thousands of guns of every calibre.. A hell of fire and steel beat around us and went on for interminable hours.

At last the troops having landed and having advanced into our village, the naval guns increased their range and their shells passed above our heads but the German artillery continued to send a few shells over although most of their guns had been reduced to silence.

We were about two hundred metres from the beach – the range of the machine-guns and sub-machine-guns which were firing towards us. Then a weird noise appeared just by our shelter making the whole place shake as it went past. Several Sherman tanks, still dripping wet, arrived flattening everything in their path. Behind these steel monsters followed the infantry and, in spite of the shells which were still falling, we came out of our shelter to watch.

Then we were astonished to see a tall handsome fellow in khaki coming towards us carrying his sub-machine gun saying to me in French with a sing-song accent 't'es pas un boche', ' et non je ne suis pas un boche' lui répondis-je, 'mais tu parle français', 'on est des Canadiens Français'.

Say, you're not a German', 'No, I'm not a German', I replied, 'but you're speaking French', 'we're Canadian French', he said. I couldn't believe my eyes. At once he offered us cigarettes and chocolate.

These Canadians had landed at the Caline gap and we were the first civilians they had met together with Nicole and the Rault families who lived nearby.

Taking advantage of a calm spell, I was anxious to find my family again. I had left them the previous evening. The roads were strewn with fallen trees, bits of wall blown off by the explosions, timber torn from roofs, gates, windows, shards of glass and of tiles and so on – not to mention the several houses ablaze as well as our brave belfry which, though pierced by a dozen or so shells, still remained tall and proud in spite of the terrible tornado which it had just suffered.

Along the way, I met people who had endured the landing but who, in spite of it all, had kept smiling and were chatting to our brave Canadians. These were the Leseur and Beaudoux families and Madame Duval who gave them cider while others offered calvados etc.

I continued my way among all these people. I met some Canadian stretcher -bearers who were carrying a wounded man. I took the place of one of them as there was another casualty waiting for first aid. Three times I carried the wounded to the Pellequin's house where a room had been fitted out to receive casualties and at last found my family again, still suffering from the shock of what we had just undergone. I made my way back towards the beach.

Every road in the village was crammed with tanks, Bren gun carriers, armoured cars, infantry marching in single file past these steel monsters which were waiting to set off towards Beny... But German 88s still had this single road under their deadly fire. Moreover, there was a mine-field more than a kilometre wide to cross.

At last, once the two 88s had been destroyed, as well as several machine-guns, the whole invading force of troops could start off and scatter among the mine-fields which stretched along the whole coast and establish themselves towards Beny, Basly, La Mare D'Anguerny.

As for me, I set off again along the shore path to have another look at the whole multitude of ships which I had seen at daybreak. It was amazing to see the whole movement and manoeuvering of all these modern machines which we knew nothing about. A great number of landing craft were waiting for the sea to rise so that they could reach the shore again and those which had unfortunately run against mines, causing many casualties whose bodies were dreadfully mutilated, cluttered up the beaches. The wounded were laid out on stretchers waiting to be repatriated on a hospital ship anchored near the shore ready to take its load back to hospitals in England.

The hardest thing was counting the number of victims, civil and military.

Among those who lived in Bernières, there were six hundred dead and wounded. I must mention two families who were grievously stricken that day. These were Madame Quinquemelle who lost her only daughter, fifteen years old, her husband and her brother-in-law, and Madame Loison who lost her parents and was herself terribly mutilated.

Regarding those days there are two views: either time passes and wipes out the memory, or, time passes but the memory remains! As far as I am concerned it's the second view I hold. I remember and don't forget. *Typescript recollections.*

JACQUES MARTIN
a twenty year old French citizen of Bernières-sur-Mer

My father didn't think that a landing could take place at Bernières because of the many rocks which were uncovered at low tide... In spite of his doubts, he had dug a covered trench about ten metres from the house on the seaward side – the sea being some 50 metres away.

Houses damaged by shellfire on the seafront at Courseulles. A Huxley

Citizens of Bernières-sur-Mer listening to an army radio giving out information. P Prior

Each month at full moon he cleaned it up, this consisted mainly of dusting the plank which served as a seat. The reason he did this at every new moon was because he was almost certain that if there was to be a landing at Bernières this would be at full moon when the nights were shorter. His prognostications proved correct: the sixth of June was the date of a full moon...

Three kilometres south of Bernières in a little wood called 'Tombette' the Germans had installed several guns, Austrian 75 and 88 mms directed to fire towards the sea. On the fifth of June at 11 o'clock in the morning some English aircraft came and bombed them. The result was inconclusive – except for some poor French civilian forced labourers working on the embankments. My father's reaction was immediate. 'Something is going to happen soon,' he said. On the evening of the fifth of June we went to bed as usual. At midnight the first bomb fell, so near the house that sand landed in my bedroom through the open window.

My father told us to get dressed, to take a few things with us and go down to the trench where we stayed for a short time until it became calm again. We went back to bed. But not for long for some more bombs or shells compelled us to go down again to the trench in our night things, except for my father who was dressed in his gardening clothes. We expected to be able to go back to our bedrooms again soon like the first time which is why I had left behind my bits and pieces and my savings from working on the farm. During the night when we could stick our noses above the trench we saw a good deal of movement at sea though we didn't know if this was an exercise or if it really was the landing. There was no question of our leaving the trench. Shell splinters were falling everywhere especially at the entrance where my father was sitting in the most dangerous place. At about 6 o'clock my mother and sister began to panic, convinced that we were not going to get out alive. I made them sing Scout songs to keep their morale up – not that mine was all that brilliant.

Soon afterwards things calmed down a bit and my father wanted to go back to the house. I went with him. After crossing the cellar we came to the floor above where everything was already destroyed or in flames. There was nothing that we could do about such a disaster so we went back again to the trench sick at heart.

About half-past 7 we saw the first casualties who had taken refuge in the garden of the house next door to ours. Their friendly gestures encouraged us to wish them good morning.

We saw groups of soldiers demolishing the walls in the street by the sea – our street. Their faces were blackened and they wore shoes with rubber soles. This was sensational. My father bade them welcome but as they had spent many hours at sea they weren't particularly glad to see us. On the way back to our trench we felt the ground vibrating under our feet. This was caused by a tank which had been adapted for blowing up mines. At the front was a drum fitted with lengths of chain which beat the ground violently. As this tank was being driven straight towards our temporary shelter we made desperate signs to the driver who changed direction as soon as he saw us. Phew! Then came another surprise. An English officer addressed us 'Go to the beach!' Twice my father refused, saying he hadn't waited four years for the invasion then to be told to go to the beach where all kinds of shells and all kinds of missiles were still falling. At the third refusal we were taken at point of arms as if we were prisoners to join a group of Germans near the station who had been taken prisoner – certainly less reluctantly than we had. In our weird attire (night dresses for my mother and sister, pyjamas for me) we were lined up in front of the German soldiers, my father pulling a little cart in which were heaped the few things he had rescued from the house. We've still got the cart.

We had been some time at the station when I saw a soldier going past with a badge on his shoulder 'Régiment de Chaudière'. Reacting at once, I asked him if he was French. As soon as I heard his reply in his strong old style French accent I realised he was a Canadian and that he had come to liberate France! When I explained that we were French taken prisoner by an English officer he took us with him to the hotel Grave which was in front of our house. Our liberator was a Canadian Sergeant called Rosaire Gagnon who received an unforgettable welcome from the first inhabitants of Bernières who reached the beach. [He was unfortunately killed later during the Battle for Caen.]

At the Hotel Grave, I made the acquaintance of an English Captain in the Intelligence Service, Peter Prior, and I wanted to explain to him where the principal mine fields were so as to prevent, perhaps, futile deaths. He then showed me a 'top secret' chart showing the position of every mine. This precise information came from a large number of aerial photographs taken in clear weather. The planes flew at high altitude and were unarmed so that they would not be overloaded by the weight of the cameras.

At the Hotel Grave I saw 250 pigeons setting off for England. They were intended to bring the news that the landings had been successful. Only a few ever arrived; the rest were either killed or driven off course by all the disturbances in the air.

Still at the Hotel Grave, my father was the first Frenchman to meet Marcel Ouimé, Radio Canada's first Senior War Correspondent, and was interviewed by him. My father asked him not to mention our name as my brother was still a prisoner in Germany. *Typescript recollections.*

A photograph taken a mile or so from Bernières-sur-Mer immediately following upon D-Day. A relaxed lunch for No 8 Beach Group was disturbed by a sniper's shot. Peter Prior, whose sight was better than that of Captain Brian Carvalho, uses the latter's pistol and his frame to steady his aim as he searches for the marksman. The sniper was in fact to give himself up to other troops.

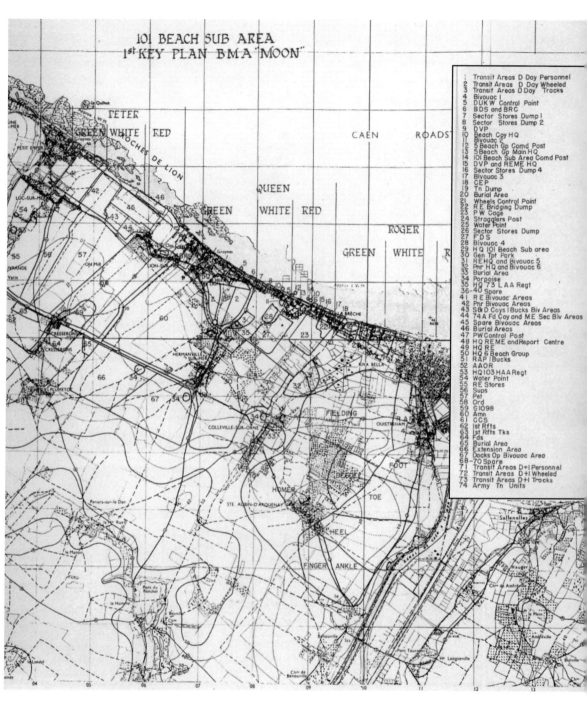

101 BEACH SUB AREA
1st KEY PLAN B.M.A "MOON"

1   Transit Areas D Day Personnel
2   Transit Areas D Day Wheeled
3   Transit Areas D Day Tracks
4   Bivouac 1
5   DUKW Control Point
6   BDS and BRC
7   Sector Stores Dump 1
8   Sector Stores Dump 2
9   DVP
10 Beach Coy HQ
11 Bivouac 2
12 5 Beach Gp Comd Post
13 5 Beach Gp Main HQ
14 101 Beach Sub Area Comd Post
15 DVP and REME HQ
16 Sector Stores Dump 4
17 Bivouac 3
18 CEP
19 Tn Dump
20 Burial Area
21 Wheels Control Point
22 R.E. Bridging Dump
23 P W Cage
24 Stragglers Post
25 Water Point
26 Sector Stores Dump
27 FDS
28 Bivouac 4
29 HQ 101 Beach Sub area
30 Gen Tpt Park
31 REHQ and Bivouac 5
32 Pnr HQ and Bivouac 6
33 Burial Area
34 Porpoise
35 HQ 73 L.A.A Regt
36-40 Spare
41 R.E Bivouac Areas
42 Pnr Bivouac Areas
43 S&D Coys 1 Bucks Biv Areas
44 74 A Fd Coy and ME Sec Blv Areas
45 Spare Bivouac Areas
46 Burial Areas
47 PW Control Post
48 HQ REME and Report Centre
49 HQ RE
50 HQ 6 Beach Group
51 RAP 1 Bucks
52 AAOR
53 HQ 103 HAA Regt
54 Water Point
55 RE Stores
56 Sups
57 Pet
58 Ord
59 G 1098
60 Amn
61 CCS
62 1st Rfts
63 1st Rfts Tks
64 Fds
65 Burial Area
66 Extension Area
67 Docks Op Bivouac Area
68-70 Spare
71 Transit Areas D+1 Personnel
72 Transit Areas D+1 Wheeled
73 Transit Areas D+1 Tracks
74 Army Tn Units

Sword Beach and the area to the rear showing the planned layout of supply dumps, bivouac areas and burial sites etc. after the landings had taken place.

CHAPTER 10

Sword

From St. Aubin-sur-Mer eastwards to the River Orne's outlet to the sea, about seven and a half miles, was designated Sword Beach for the landings. It was a vital left flank in terms of advancing to capture the key objective, Caen, or the heights dominating the city, and securing against German counter-attack knifing through the flank of the inevitably fluid allied advance from the landing beaches. Such a riposte would have presented a real danger of sweeping the attackers into the sea, a defeat of incalculably great consequences.

Here again, offshore, rocks limited approach to the beach, this time on the right flank so that Ouistreham, where the River Orne and the Caen Canal met for their joint (tidal) mile and a half flow north to the sea, would be both a boundary of the Beachhead and an axis for advance on Caen.

Also part of the design for Sword was swiftly to link with the area won by the airborne attack on the bridges over the canal and river. This involved pushing forward from the left too and altogether this necessary emphasis put at some hazard the establishment of a link with troops on the right, that is the adjacent flank of Juno.

The initial landing was made between Lion-sur-Mer and the western outskirts of Ouistreham. It was preceded by a relatively close-range monitor, battleship, cruiser and destroyer bombardment and it should be added an earlier marking of the beach by men from two midget submarines. Amphibious tanks, the Duplex D tanks, launched as close as possible inshore in the choppy waters, and landing craft carried AVREs, were the first to land to give protection and help to the infantry in their landing craft just behind. Most of the Duplex D tanks, the AVREs and the landing craft carrying infantry made it safely to the shore coping with the natural and man-made hazards.

Success so far and then in quickly clearing the beaches was so essential that it is no exaggeration to say that failure at Sword could have been disastrous. German reinforcements lay more readily to hand than for any other beach and in any case the next tasks were fraught with difficulty, the taking of buildings turned into forts, dealing with open areas mined just as the beach was mined and then wired and with concrete flanking emplacements. At one German strongpoint in particular, La Brèche, heavy casualties were incurred and at the 'Hillman' position at Colleville the formidable defences were not overcome until late in the day, a delay still further reducing the chance of taking Caen on the first day of the landing.

As on the other beaches except Omaha, a combination of all arms won what was achieved: foot soldiers, engineers, gunners, tankies (in a range of armoured vehicles), commandos (Army, Royal Marine and French) and naval personnel fulfilling different roles and, to that blanket list, Army and Navy medical personnel must be included.

At Sword, it may be added, a fair proportion of the assaulting force had, until the sand was under their boots, been variably affected by the longer hours they had spent in the open sea, after their rendezvous east of the Solent, distinct from the shorter westerly route for the rest of the armada. Following upon this ordeal, embarkation into the landing craft had still to be managed for the final stage of The Channel crossing and by then the self-control of many in trying to keep down a last meal or drink had been overstrained.

At Sword as elsewhere, the narrowing beach, with the tide racing in, hindered newly-landed armour from moving off. Nonetheless by the time infantry had overcome their immediate objectives and, moving three miles inland, came up against German counter-attack, their tanks had caught up with them and the attack was beaten off. It was however a remnant of this German move which filtered through the gap on the right flank of the advance, reaching the coast, posing a dangerous split of the beachhead between Sword and Juno.

There was more which had not gone as well as had been hoped. Caen had not been taken - perhaps such an objective was too optimistic - but Ouistreham had fallen and the link had been secured to the key tactical gains of the airborne troops. There had been solid achievements at Sword, at a cost, but not at the dreadful price paid at Omaha.

PRIVATE HAROLD A ROWLAND

2nd Battalion, East Yorks

Diary
4 June: Church service on board.
5 June: Cleaned all weapons. Received invasion maps.
6 June, D-Day: Left boat at 6.5am. LCA hit beach at 7.20am. Captured beach. Became a casualty.
7 June: On board LCT converted to hospital ship.
8 June: Docked at Tilbury. Arrived Romford hospital.

PRIVATE ROBERT G MAXWELL
Royal Marine Commandos

I volunteered to help escort two Royal Marine divers who were to check on a French Resistance report that the lock gates at Ouistreham had been mined and ready for demolition. A small boat took us from our LST at about 0230 hours without anyone seeing us, by a pre-planned route we got to the lock gates and the divers found that they were not mined after all! *Transcript of tape-recorded recollections.*

Robert Maxwell in Royal Marine 'Blues' soon after D-Day.

MAJOR ROBIN DUNN
in command, 16th Field Battery, 7th Field Regiment, RA

At first light we started this run-in shoot, which had never been done before. We were in an arrow head. Our regiment was in the centre slightly in front and then the two other regiments were on each side. And we started to come in towards the beach and we opened fire at maximum range, which was about 12,000 yards, and there was a thing called a "Coventry clock" from which you could calculate, based on the speed of the landing craft, how much you drop the range, and the range dropped every three minutes, and we fired three rounds a minute as we came in dropping the range. And at H-Hour we were actually 3,000 yards from the beach and I was on the bridge and I had the most wonderful grandstand view of the actual assault, because we saw these amphibious tanks landing and then the assault infantry in their landing craft running up the beach and then these various, what we called, 'funnies'.

There was a thing called an AVRE, Armoured Vehicle Royal Engineers, which was a Churchill tank with a bombard, and it waddled up to the pillboxes and put the bombard against the pillbox and set it off. There were ships all around us. There was the odd ship on fire. There was a tremendous lot of bombing in the distance. There was the bombarding squadron, which was a battleship and a couple of cruisers, pumping high explosive shells into the beach defences. There were these rocket craft. After we had finished our run-in shoot we then turned away and sailed round in a huge circle, and we actually landed three hours later. *Transcript of tape-recorded recollections.*

Major R H W Dunn, receiving the award of the Military Cross (and an autographed photograph) November 1944.

The run-in to Sword Beach. E Hammill

BOMBARDIER NORMAN G MARSHALL, RA

Driver of a Duplex D tank of 41st Royal Marine Commando
(4th Special Service Brigade)

By now we could clearly make out the houses sprinkled along the shoreline, but the whole shore was one mass of smoke, flashes and explosions as the bombardment from the big ships intensified its accuracy and rate of fire. Adding to the deafening thunder, the rocket ship alongside of us opened up, sending more death and destruction ashore. One thing was certain, we were now chock-block full of confidence. We could not believe that anything or anyone could survive through this bombardment.

Orders came to unshackle the tanks, they had been clamped to the deck with four short tow chains to keep them stable during the crossing. This done, the next order was 'Drivers mount'. I climbed into the driver's compartment, reminding others again to ensure that the water-proofing was good. With the hatch closed, the nine inch circular driver's viewing 'windscreen' battened down and waterproofed, I made a final check of the controls and the wiring for the explosive charge that would release the exhaust extension as soon as we were out of the water. The crews mounted up, tested the radio intercom, ensuring in particular that my set was working one hundred percent. Remember, I would be several feet under water the minute we left the craft and completely blind. I had my two periscopes, glasses one inch by four, but these were in a fixed position, waterproofed and so unmoveable.

'Driver, start up.' I pressed the starter button and my Meteor engines fired and started on the first touch. I had been starting the engine every half hour since midnight to keep it nice and warm, I checked the revs counter, the oil pressure, the temperature, both steering tillers and was satisfied that the vehicle was as perfect as humanly possible. When the ramp was dropped I could for an instant, see the houses about 200 yards away and the beaches 100 yards away.

Then it was 'Driver, advance.' I knew now that I was completely at the mercy of the Sergeant in charge. I was as blind as a bat, and relied on his experience, and his will to live, to guide me to shore. Under his instructions, I got to the end of the ramp, balanced and very, very slowly edged forward. No one knew at what depth of water we were in, it could be only

186

four or five foot deep, on the other hand it could be twelve feet. Over nine or ten feet of water and we would become waterlogged, the engine would be flooded, and apart from the Commander, we would all certainly die. It would be impossible to open the hatches due to the waterproofing. So at the point of balance on the ramp, I had my first taste of terror.

Up to now I had been revelling in the excitement, just like watching the news at the cinema, only actually there, actually taking part in the drama being unfolded.

Over the point of balance and down, down, down, would we ever hit bottom? With a terrific crash we hit the sandy bottom, there was no flood of water in the tank, no panicky screams from the crew and I knew that we were ok for now. All I could see through my periscope was bluey, greenish water with thousands of bubbles rising upwards. Then, in first gear, at maximum revs, I obeyed every command that the Sergeant gave me. Left, left, right, straight on, left and right a hundred times. I was obeying instinctively, my mind was on something else. At some time, maybe at the factory, a tiny bolt had been left out of the side bulkhead, about a foot above my lap on the right hand side, here was a leak, not a serious one I'll admit, but an extremely uncomfortable one. The sea came in at the same speed and volume of a two year old baby boy having a pee, right onto my lap. By the time the water level dropped below my periscope glass outside the tank I was wet through. One thing is certain, it took my mind completely away from the life or death situation that the others were going through.

I didn't know it at the time, but we had been weaving in and out of dozens of tank traps. Angle iron tripods firmly rooted in the sand, these were bad enough, but it was the huge mines attached to the tripods which the Sergeant had been concerned about. From his elevated position, standing on top of the tank, he had been almost directly above the obstacles, so he could see them clearly.

After a few minutes, which at the time seemed like hours, I began to see daylight through my periscopes. I still had about fifty yards to go before we hit dry sand. It appeared to be plain sailing from here on. I got into second gear in a couple of feet of water, and then into third as the water got shallower and shallower. There were only fifty yards or so of flat, virgin beach, and then the sand dunes. I was told to head for the sand dunes and remove the turret extension and the exhaust extension. I drove like mad across the sand, only to be met by heavy machine-gun fire from a pillbox in the dunes. Now, heavy machine-gun fire for an infantry man is deadly, but to a tank it's nothing, just target practice, and that's how the Sergeant treated it. The Gunner, using his power traverse, broke away all the gun's waterproofing and with open sights, blasted it out of existence, along with the Jerry gunners.

Inside the tank, we feared nothing except anti-tank guns, usually the 88mm, and anti-tank mines. A machine-gun is about as much good as a pea-shooter, and is no match ever against armour. In the dunes I inserted the electrical plug into the socket in the dashboard and there was an instant minor explosion at the rear of the tank, as the charges to the exhaust funnel detonated. The next minute the Sergeant had torn away the waterproofing to my hatch, and I was able to get out to release the turret extension and clear away the exhaust funnel, which had got wedged on the engine plates. By now the beach was no longer deserted, men were running forward from the dozens of landing craft disgorging their passengers in one or two feet of water. These men were the strike force, the Army Commandos whose job it was to take the village. They wasted no time, dashing up the beach into the sand dunes and then out of sight. More and more men and machines were being unloaded every minute, and by now the Jerries started to hit back, first with mortar fire, then with infantry. They were dug in a couple of yards from the dunes and were soon wreaking havoc among the incoming Commandos. In the sand dunes there were three tanks about a foot apart and the Army Commandos came through and there was lots and lots of small arms fire. A captain was sheltering between the two tanks and the tank next to mine moved off, slewed round to the right and completely crushed the fellow between the two lots of tracks. A terrible sight. He didn't make a sound, he didn't cry out or anything and he was completely mashed to pieces.

There was a tremendous amount of small arms fire and the shelter he got from a tank was better than any other because he could regroup his men and they could take shelter from the tanks as well. So he was doing his job very efficiently but the driver of the tank next to mine, he had no idea. You just can't see behind a tank. The driver had no idea. He was told to drive forward and turn right and when you turn right with a tank, your back end goes to the left and he was in that wedge between the two.

I saw it all. I was still on the back of my tank removing the exhaust extension which had been wedged in. I was having to kick it. I was possibly within three yards of the tragedy.

Although we had a specific job to do, the Troop Lieutenant gave a troop order for individual rapid fire at our own selected targets. Within five minutes of sustained 95mm HE fire the situation was well under control, and with the advancing Commandos firing from the hip, white flags soon started to flutter.

We had a specific job to do and that was to destroy the post office building in the main street of the village, which was being used as an Army communication centre. So off we went, to the village, up the main street to where the post office should have been. It was not there, it might have been before the Navy blasted it off the face of the map. The job done for us, we were free to render assistance wherever it was needed. Calls for help were coming in thick and fast. We tended to a Commando Officer's request to eliminate a couple of snipers high up in the belfry of a church on the outskirts of town. It appeared that these two snipers had accounted for at least half a dozen dead or wounded in the last ten minutes, and were seriously slowing down the house to house search and clear tactics that the Commandos were doing. Two HE shells from *Hunter* soon solved that, not only removing the snipers but the steeple as well.

We had discarded our sledges back on the dunes, somewhere around a mile away, and whilst not short of ammo, we decided to locate the sleds and top up with shells. Things seemed to be well under control for a while, so off we went back to the sand dunes. On the way down the high street we were met by a six foot, 18 stone gendarme, who stood in the road waving his arms in the air. We stopped to find out what the trouble was, but there was no trouble, he was blind drunk and singing. We stopped to have a bit of light relief, and we were glad we did for he produced a bottle of calvados and insisted we all share with him in his ecstatic happiness of liberation. Never having drunk calvados, we all did the same stupid thing, a big gulp and a couple of swallows. Then, bang, it hit us. The clear watery looking liquid turned to red hot fire in our throats leaving us gasping for breath.

Around lunchtime, *Hunter* was detailed to assist at a strongpoint a couple of miles away. Due to the fact that I had illegally made adjustments to the governor in the rota arm of the distributor, (a court martial offence,) I was able to get fifty miles an hour before the governors came in. Consequently we made very good time to where we were needed. It was right on the coast, a big strongpoint with at least six pillboxes. Their heavy machine-gun fire was playing havoc with the infantry and supplies unloading on that stretch of beach. How or why it had been spared from the Naval bombardment I'll never know, but it had to be eliminated. It cost many lives down on the beach. A Commando captain briefed our skipper.

There was a terrace of houses right on the front, about 100 yards long. All the windows and doors away from the sea had been bricked up and an eight foot wall had been built at either end of the street. In addition to heavy machine-guns they had mortars. The casualties that they were responsible for littered the beach in a field of fire some 200 - 300 yards wide. We were asked to break a hole in one of the walls to allow Commandos to enter the street and eliminate the garrison.

After a couple of dozen shots with the 95, a hole big enough was breached, allowing the Commandos to enter. After a brief fire fight, the Commandos came out with every Jerry a prisoner.

It was now late afternoon, the weather had been brilliant - up in the seventies, and civilians were appearing in the streets. Where they had been during the Naval bombardment and the street fighting, I don't know. Possibly in their cellars, or if they had them, their air raid shelters. Anyway, although we had destroyed half their village, they were ecstatic in their welcome, heaping on us flowers, food, calvados, hugs and kisses. *Typescript memoir and transcript of tape-recorded recollections.*

CAPTAIN J A S NEAVE
Adjt 13th/18th Royal Hussars

Diary
<u>5 June</u>: Sailed for France, shipped about 1.30 p.m. very rough, felt very ill and in no form for the beach fight. Still feels like another exercise. No enemy interference during passage.
<u>6 June</u>: D Day for Operation Overlord - Bigot – Neptune. Landed H + 45 (0830). Fought way inland from Ouistreham to Hermanville. Enemy hedgehogs encountered for most part but reports of tanks in the evening. Reg(imental) cas(ualties) light in pers(onnel): v. heavy in vehicles.

J A S Neave.

PIPER BILL MILLIN
Piper to Lord Lovat, in command of 1st British Special Service Commando Brigade

Then the order came to get ashore, and I was very pleased to get ashore and no one was shouting that they were afraid or shouting that they were going to kill all these Germans. All people wanted really was to get off.

Lord Lovat was in the next ramp. There were two ramps at the front of the landing craft. I was up on one and he was up on this one. He jumped into the water. So I waited till he got in, because he was over six feet tall, to see what depth it was, and someone came up on to his empty ramp. Well, he was immediately shot. A piece of shrapnel or a bullet in the face and he fell and sank. Well, I jumped in pretty smart then. My kilt floated to the surface and the shock of the freezing cold water knocked all feelings of sickness from me and I felt great. I was so relieved at getting off that boat after all night being violently sick. I struck up the Pipes and paddled through the surf playing *'Hieland Laddie'*, and Lovat turned round and looked at me and (gestured approvingly).

When I finished, Lovat asked for another tune. Well, when I looked round – the noise and people lying about shouting and the smoke, the crump of mortars, I said to myself 'Well, you must be joking surely'. He said 'What was that?' and he said 'Would you mind giving us a tune?' 'Well, what tune would you like, Sir?' 'How about *The Road To The Isles*?' 'Now, would you want me to walk up and down, Sir?' 'Yes. That would be nice. Yes, walk up and down.'

Well, there was the water's edge. Just about a few feet up on the beach I walked along that part. I could see people lying face down in the water going back and forwards with the surf. Others to my left were trying to dig in just off the beach. A low wall, and they were trying to dig in there. It was very difficult for them trying to dig in the sand. Yet when they heard the Pipes, some of them stopped what they were doing and waved their arms, cheering. But one came along, he wasn't very pleased, and he called me 'The mad bastard'.

Well, we usually referred to Lovat as a 'mad bastard'. This was the first time I had heard it referred to me.

Well, we moved off in two sections. One attacked the front from the seaside area of Ouistreham. The group I was with attacked the rear of Ouistreham. After the capture of Ouistreham one part of the Brigade went along the towpath of the canal. The part of the Brigade I was with – with Lovat – we went by road towards Bénouville.

We were walking in aircraft formation. That is single file on either side of the road, and I am Piping. After we left the Ouistreham area, I was Piping along the road, and it's a raised road with sloping away towards the canal to the left and then there is the high ground again on the other side of the canal, so we were very vulnerable on this road, but anyway I was Piping along the road. Then we were being attacked by snipers from the other side of the canal and from the cornfields on the right side of the road, and I am Piping along the road and I could see this sniper about a hundred yards or so away ahead of me and I could see the flash when he fired. And I glanced round, stopped playing and they were all down on the road and their faces in the road. Even Lovat was on his knee – one knee. Then the next thing this man comes scrambling down the tree and Lovat and our group dash forward. Of course, I dashed, I had stopped playing by this time, and dashed forward with them and the man's head bobbing about – the sniper's head bobbing about in the cornfield, and Lovat shot at him and he fell down and sent two men into the cornfield to see what had happened, and they brought back the dead body.

Lovat had killed him. Then Lovat said to me, 'Right, Piper, start the Pipes again.' Well, we got to Bénouville. I had to stop again because we were under fire there and we couldn't get down the main street. We were taking shelter behind the low wall to the right of the entrance to the village, and Colonel Mills-Roberts of 6 Commando – he was across the road looking round his side of the wall. So then he came dashing across to me and said, 'Right, Piper, play us down the main street.' So he wanted me to run. I said, 'No, I won't be running. I will just play them as usual.' So I Piped them in, and they all followed behind me and through the village and then stopped.

I was Piping *Blue Bonnets Over The Border* at that time again. Then a shell hit the church on the left and we all stopped, and two Commandos ran into the church to see if it had hit the snipers there. Then I looked round and the Commandos are throwing hand grenades in through the windows of the houses. Then I continued along the road and there was a lot of white dust with the noise and the explosions and everything. So at the end of the village, I stopped there and then Lovat come up to me and he said, 'Well, we are almost at the bridges. About another half a mile. So start your Pipes here and continue along this road and then swing round to your left. Then it's a straight road down to the bridges.' Well, I started Piping, continued along the road, eyes looking this way, looking – no sign of snipers. I had begun to become conscious of snipers by this time. Then turned round left and there is a group of Commandos sitting on the rails outside the Mairie, and I noticed they were the French Commandos so I recognised their faces anyway. Turned round left and then I could see the bridges about 200 yards down the road and a pall of black smoke over the bridges and the sound of mortars bursting. So I kept Piping down the road. Lovat was behind me and when

I came to the bridges, I stopped across the road from a café. A café on the right hand side of the road at the bridge, and I stopped Piping across the road from the café. Lovat passed and he – this Airborne Officer – approached us and Lovat and the Officer shook hands and started to discuss the situation. Then Lovat came to me and said, 'Right, Piper, we are crossing over.' So I start, walking, put the Pipes up. This time we are walking over. We can hear the shrapnel, whatever it was, hitting the sides – metal sides – of the bridge. Well, when we got almost to the other side I started up the Pipes. Coming off the bridge, I stopped again because Lovat put his hand up, the indication was to stop. So I stopped, swung the bagpipes on my shoulder and he said, 'Another 200 yards along this road, Piper, there is another bridge but we won't have the protection that we have here because it's not a metal-sided bridge, it's railings' as he called them, 'and when you get there, no matter what the situation, just continue over. Don't stop.' So I struck up the Pipes and marched along, merrily along the road and he was walking behind me and others strung out behind. I was still playing *Blue Bonnets Over The Border* and we came to the bridge. I could see across the bridge, and there were two Airborne chaps dug in on the other side of the bridge and they were frantically indicating to me and pointing to the sides of the river that it was under fire, sniper fire, and whatever. So I then looked round at Lovat and he indicated to me by his hand, carry on across. So, I kept Piping but it was the longest bridge I ever Piped across, but I got safely over and shook hands with the two Airborne chaps in the slit trench. Then Lovat got across and then at this point an Airborne Officer – a tall Airborne Officer – approached us from across the road, held his hand out to Lovat and said, 'We are very pleased to see you, old boy.' And Lovat said, 'Aye, and we are very pleased to see you, old boy,' and looking at his watch, 'sorry, we are two and a half minutes late.'

We weren't two and a half minutes late. We were just over an hour late, because we should have been there about twelve o'clock and it was now after one.

We set off again. We crossed the road in single file and then we turned down a narrow leafy lane, and walking along there then came to an opening and there were a cluster of French farm type houses with a gathering of French folks. They were poorly dressed French folks and I was walking along here and a little girl with red hair came out in bare feet. Very unkempt looking, and she kept shouting, 'Music, music, music'. And I said, 'Well, she wants a tune.' So I turned to Lovat and I said, 'What do you think?' he said, 'Okay then, give her a tune.' So I started to play a tune called *The Nut Brown Maiden*. It's a famous Scottish tune, and went for a few yards like that then I had to stop because the mortaring had started and the French people scarpered. They all scarpered to every nook and the mortars began to blast. And we came up this road and as we passed, all the hedges were covered with this white dust. We got up the road and we passed on the right hand side a quarry with lots of wounded lying there on stretchers and up to the crossroads and Lovat is stood there directing the attack on the village straight ahead, and so I stayed with him a while. Then I went into the barn to see what was going on there, and that was full of wounded. I looked at Lovat, he just sat on the grass, and I thought 'By ginger, I wouldn't like his job.' And he was thirty-two years of age at that time – very responsible job. But anyway, we moved forward a bit along this hedgerow with the mortars bursting in the field alongside us and I could hear this, we all jumped into a ditch, and we could hear the shrapnel coming through the hedge, and this is the spot where the Pipes were injured. Not seriously, they could still be played.

So the next thing Lovat says, 'Right. We won't go into the village today. We will go up and occupy the farmhouses, the main road and the farmhouses on the edge of the road.' So we stopped there and took over the farmhouse, then attacked the village first thing in the morning. And that was us. Objective taken. *Transcript of tape-recorded recollections*

191

A signed photograph for Arthur Oates with his MC award.

Notification of immediate award of a Military Cross for the distinguished service of Arthur Oates on D-Day.

LIEUTENANT ARTHUR OATES
2nd Battalion, East Yorks Regiment

Contemporary Notes

Lowering and pull away was done well with a heavy swell running – men stood up and this prevented recliners. 10 accepted tablets and quite a few were sick.

During 'run – in' we kept long distance and closed up twice. Were extraordinarily close to LCTs – they gave us V's.

Four miles out dished tea out to those who wanted it – only 7 accepted.

Beaching – 3 Lewis's fired continuously – cover was good. We changed course 6 times and at least 30 points at each. I observed for port and – Sgt for starboard. Touched one tetrahedral and lift of wave carried free board to within 3′. Beached and door down in 18″ – covered in oil – not under fire. Lewis's still in action.

Drake (?) and self first out with life lines – excellent – though oil between poles to LWM – first mortars 50 yards ahead slightly left – 'flail' static and smoking from turret. Churchill near and in action against A/TK gun, latter firing from 100 yds left at 'Flail'.

Cleared water and made for our Flail – more mortars and MG 5 yds left – deployed and engaged. Silenced after 5 minutes. Flail burning fast and exploding – centre section near it – told them to move away – mortars hit them – self hit in R arm – approx 7 others out of action.

Moved with Barker up to wire, placed Bangalore across trapeze – Bangalore blown on left – looked like minefield beyond so called up mortar & cortex. Could not blow Bangalore because troops on left. Beach group bunching badly and having casualties.

Blew cortex – 2 AP mines up – jumped wire and went forward to buildings near track. Saw Banger.

Moved near Wilson up on L, Jobling R – HQ rear. RE had not appeared – waited for Reid to come up on L.

Banger said advance – more mortars dropping both sides but chiefly on beach – kept 50 yds from it and astride track. MG found us and hit houses all round us – removed further up.

Carrier hit near us – Kilby reported MG post 200 yds ahead. 3 boche with white flag 20 yds ahead – could not move for MG on revolving tower – firing on beach.

Banger got a tank to fire and silenced MG. Kilby went to fetch in prisoners – would not stop so I got Jobling to cover him – James I/C prisoners moved up to RV with S Lancs took 15 prisoners killed three – Found MG post and mortar position, mortar still intact – met RE of Beach Group in house – shelled & mortared – moved back to HQ trenches – met S. Lancs FOO and sent him through.

R/T Good – Banger said rejoin on PIKE to COD wood. Recovered down to road. Saw ?'s Platoon hit badly, kept in dead ground. Waist deep in swamp but got through.

Wilson, Coverdale, Everett, Jobling & self hit ? 9' ditch for 25 minutes – observed & had to crawl 150 yds. Robinson very good with ? all time.

Shells 5 away all sides – Moved back on road to join Banger – took over Coy – Banger back in action – my arm starting to swell – bleeding from top wound.

Moved behind D Coy to rear of Daimler – Scholes and Smith killed – C.O. hit. I felt very weak. Met Reid near Daimler as barrage went down – decided to flank from R.

Went into Ouistreham patrolled the town & left some money in church – tanks in village – flags – dead commando – bombs from 3 x 217's – set fire to Boche billet.

Had wound bandaged & ate sandwiches (Later evacuated).

PRIVATE LEN BROWN
1st Battalion, South Lancashire Regiment

We had a strong feeling that it was going to be a success and at least we were going to see the end of it all because the training for it was very difficult. And the landing itself was a lot easier than the training we had done...

We had instructions to follow in the tank tracks. Let the tank go forward and the track it makes, if you run in that you can't run on a mine. And that was the way we got off the beach. But we did get people getting killed with snipers on the beach and they were shelling us from Caen at the time, but eventually we did get off the beach and ...

As soon as the ramp went down we started. Fire was hitting the ramp before we put it down – Snipers. And, of course, when it went down you were to dash looking for the tank tracks to run off the beach. A couple of them missed it and were blown up, but eventually we got off the beach, but we must have left an awful lot behind.

I was a Battalion Medical Orderly, or stretcher bearer, carrying two first aid kits on my back and no weapons at the time. We were non-combat, and we treated what men we could on the beach.

I remember one chap had a very bad leg wound. I think it was almost hanging off. I cut the trousers off him and I put a bandage on it and I put a tourniquet on, and when we put a tourniquet on in them days we had to put a 'T' on the forehead marked in puce lead and went on to the next man.

We had received orders not to stay with the wounded too long. To keep up with the men who were going forward to get off the beach. That these would suffer the most heavy casualties and need the most treatment. And as soon as we got off the beach we did come under fire, funnily enough from a church. Now this was funny this because they were coming from high up in a church and we could do nothing about that. But a tank I had passed on the beach, I went back and told him, and he came up with a tank and the barrel pointing up and the white flags came out and the rifleman went in and brought five women out. Women in the belfry. One had shot herself in the church and he brought the other five out, and we don't know whether these women had married the Germans because they had been there four years, you know, or what. Don't even know if they were French.

We have to start moving forward. Our ambition was to reach Caen in twenty-four hours, which we couldn't do, and the company runner came past and said that there was snipers at the crossroads further on, and the Sergeant went forward with two men to recce. And the Sergeant came back. He said, 'The two men have been killed at the crossroads'. So we bypassed this and went round the fields and came in and we saw the two men lying on the road, but we couldn't bring them in because the same snipers were pinning us down. We knew where it was coming from. It was an old barn to the left and there was a tank in the next field. So we brought the tank over. We had a system, what we used in training, if we were in trouble we used to put our fist on top of our head, bring it down and point to where the trouble was. The Tank Commander standing up in the turret saw this and he came down and said 'What is it?' I said, 'There is a sniper in this building stopping us from bringing us two men in.' The next thing I heard a word of command and one heck of a bang and the barn had gone, and we never had any trouble after this. We brought the two men in and buried them. But this is what we had to put up with, the snipers. You never knew where they were.

Transcript of tape-recorded recollections.

SIGNALMAN ALAN WHITING, RN
Beach party Signalman, Sword Beach

At 0605 hours, in LCA 146, we roared away from the ship (*Glenearn*), engine throttled wide open towards the beach and the row of houses at the back of it growing steadily nearer. Clearly carried over the air to us the sound of shells bursting ashore, when each man distinctly felt the thudding detonations deep inside himself and his stomach muscles ached with the tension and felt as though, if you relaxed them even momentarily, your stomach would BURST!

All the trivial talk and 'small nervous jokes' ceased and I offered up a small prayer to The Almighty. Men deliberately took up their rifles and machine-guns, while there was a distinctly audible 'clattering' of bolts being drawn back and rammed home firmly, with a fresh clip in position.

Then, with twin engines slowing down, the

Alan Whiting (left) in Devonport, 1943.

wallowing motion of the LCA eased as we drifted into shallower water up to waist high. Further along, an assault craft was disgorging its troops in deeper water, perhaps to avoid uncleared underwater obstacles, or just too plain scared to 'touch down' with the ramp on the beach, and some poor sod who couldn't swim, his boots leaded under 90 lbs of kit, sank out of sight immediately where he fell as they all desperately jumped wide to reach the shore!

Ahead of us, heavy, dense smoke drifted across the 200 yards deep and 2 mile wide beach, while beyond the row of fiercely burning, damaged houses, with their black-eyed windows, were the black plumes of incessant explosions, each with a cherry-red flicker at its heart, while the dry grass clumps along the sand dunes on the beach were fitfully smouldering. The village of Graye-sur-Mer being 3 miles east of La Rivière and the fishing port of Courseulles and St. Aubin-sur-Mer and Bernières were all in view.

The landing craft gently nosed ashore to a standstill through a mass of floating debris and I thought, this is it 'Operation Overlord' was a reality!!

The ramp dropped with a loud thud and we all piled out, running as fast as possible up the soft, sandy beach towards the row of houses and almost reaching them before running into heavy fire from enemy Spandau. Diving for the nearest cover, my chief worry the battery acid might leak or the aldis get damaged and thought: 'A revolver's a fat lot of good against machine-guns, must keep up with the nearest bunch of troops, some already into the houses with hand grenades, and where's my two marines got to?' There are many casualties (dead ones at that) so quickly re-holster the .45, borrowing a Sten gun and relieving its very dead owner of the magazines, feeling immediately much better and firing at anyone firing in my direction. More men go by from the beachhead, the sten overheats and jams, with constant firing they get red hot being all metal, seize up and blister your hands. I threw it away in disgust, can't wait for it to cool down. Not so much opposition now.

I find a tommy gun with full clip, then more spare clips, which I knew more about from Home Guard days, edge up warily through what have been bits of garden and locate my bodyguards a few yards in front of me. The 'third wave' are catching it heavily from streams of automatic gunfire and a deluge of mortar and one of our LCAs has received a direct hit from a shell.

As more and more support troops poured ashore, the enemy began to fall back to prepared positions and our forward troops to advance, after having flushed out the battered shells of the beach houses, and so I began to roam in search of the Beach Master (a full RN Commander), with whom I had to work, this being my real job and merely routine signalling.

I remained signalling on the beach for the situation reports, progress reports and additional requirements with the odd request for particular information, until relieved later in the morning by my 'oppo' Joe.

He and I then doubled up watch-about until early in the evening when we were both recalled, by which time both RT and WT had become firmly established.

Typescript recollections.

LIEUTENANT E L K A CARR

in command of 'B' Troop (Heavy Weapons Troop) No. 4 Commando

My landing craft gently grounded on the sand, the ramp went down, and we advanced up the beach as fast as our loaded 70 lb Bergen rucksacks would allow us. In addition to the rations, weapons and ammunition we were carrying we each had to carry a 10lb mortar bomb for the 3 inch mortars. Shell and mortar bombs threw up great spurts of sand. Ahead of me was a strong point with gun barrels sticking out, and I made for this. As I moved across the beach I was hit three times, twice on my hand and wrist by small splinters and once on my rucksack, but not seriously. As I came up to the strong point a German soldier behind it threw two stick grenades into the air which exploded harmlessly behind me. He was immediately shot, and the strong point was captured. We advanced to the road and reached the assembly area where we dumped our rucksacks and I set up the two mortars ready to give supporting fire to the assault troops as they went through the town. There were no German soldiers in the main part of the town as, apart from the beach defences, they were concentrated in the coastal gun battery position at the eastern end near the mouth of the River Orne.

No 4 Commando captured and cleared the German coastal gun battery and the assaulting troops made their way back to our original assembly area. Here I found a two wheeled horse-drawn cart, unfortunately without the horse! We loaded all the three inch mortar bombs and the two mortars onto it and with relays of six men pulling it we set off across country on the road leading to the only road bridge over the Caen Canal and the River Orne just east of the village of Bénouville. The rest of No 1 SS Brigade, consisting of Nos 3,6 and 45 Commandos had landed to the west of Ouistreham and pressed inland to join up with the units of 6th Airborne Division. Parachutists of the Division had been dropped over a wide area immediately to the East of the River Orne with the aim of securing the high ground overlooking the whole of the landing area.

Our route to the bridges in bright sunshine through cornfields and orchards went past the villages of Colleville-sur-Orne, St. Aubin-d'Arquenay and Bénouville which had already been cleared of any German patrols or snipers. At Bénouville we arrived at the bridge over the Caen Canal and to our relief we were greeted by Paratroops. The bridge was under intermittent sniper fire so I arranged for a quick smoke screen from one of my mortars to be

Casemate for anti-tank gun at Ouistreham. A Huxley

Another neutralised casemate; west of Ouistreham. A Huxley

put down on the bridge and we managed to get our cart and ourselves across it without any casualties. We then crossed the bridge over the River Orne without any opposition and finally arrived in the evening at the little village of Hauger after a journey of about eight miles. It was a beautiful evening and except for the distant sound of gunfire and occasional sniper fire there was little enemy opposition. The last part of our advance from the bridge had been across a flat open plain and it was here that the gliders of the Air Landing Brigade of 6th Airborne Division had landed their soldiers to secure the bridgehead over the river as a prelude to the Allied advance eastwards and south through Germany. It was an incredible sight. Scores of now empty gliders lay all over the flat ground, many with smashed noses and some with one wing tilted aloft.

At Hauger we were quickly allotted our areas of defence because we knew that a German Infantry Division was in the area and would soon attack us. Using our little individual methylated spirits stoves we had a quick 'brew up' of tea and ate some of our 24 rations in their little cardboard boxes. Looking out to sea we could see the whole of the landing area, a vast array of ships of all types and sizes, the blue sea criss-crossed with white as the small assault landing craft ferried troops ashore not only in the British sector but further West to Omaha Beach where the Americans were having a hard time fighting to get up the cliffs and inland.

At Hauger I chose a small open meadow with part of a shallow dry ditch across it and we at once started to dig pits for the mortars and slit trenches for ourselves. Of necessity, to allow clearance for the flight of our mortar bombs, there were only trees round the edges. The majority of the Commando troops had to be in the wooded areas. Initially they suffered casualties from shell and mortar bombs bursting when they hit the branches of the trees and throwing their splinters like shrapnel downwards. As quickly as we could we built overhead cover for our slit trenches. In the late evening we 'stood to', a standard practice for troops in defence, for often the enemy would launch an attack just before dark, but that night, a beautiful warm night, no serious attack came. About midnight all of us not on watch collapsed into our slit trenches and fell asleep after twenty hours of continuous intense activity and danger. *Typescript recollections.*

LIEUTENANT *(Temporary Captain)* WILLIAM C S CARRUTHERS, RE
in command of a Troop of Tanks

Citation for Military Cross

At H Hour on 6 June 1944, Captain Carruthers led his troop of tanks in the assault upon the Beaches of Normandy with rare courage and skill.

Later, he and his men worked, dismounted, under heavy shelling and fire from snipers, who killed two of his tank commanders before his task was completed. His personal bravery was a fine example to the men working with him.

Captain Carruthers was wounded early in the operation, yet he stuck to his task beyond the stage where his gap was clear for tracked vehicles. He refused to stop work until his gap had been improved under his direction for the certain passage of wheeled vehicles from the high water mark to the first inland lateral road. Captain Carruthers courage and devotion to duty were responsible for this task being completed successfully.

PRIVATE RICHARD J HARRIS
1st Battalion, Suffolk Regiment (eighteen years old)

W C S Carruthers and local pri[a]
in the local press on Merseyside.

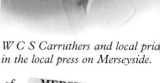

I was determined to present myself for the minimum time as a target at the top of the ramp and being one of the first off I had a clear run. On the order to go I leapt up, bounded down the ramp, jumped and landed in about four feet of cold seawater. I managed to retain my balance and holding my rifle clear of the water waded as quickly as I was able to the shallows and the beach. My impression of the scene there was of a complete shambles. Had the whole thing failed? Was it a gigantic cock-up? Against a backdrop of smoke, gutted blazing buildings were several burning, knocked out DD tanks and strewn about from the water's edge up to the sea wall were sodden khaki bundles staining red the sand where they lay... I remember hearing cries of 'Stretcher bearers', and one plaintive youthful voice repeatedly calling, 'Help me, boys,' and then breaking off into shuddering sobs. This plea for aid was one of my most poignant memories of the beach. *Typescript recollections.*

Richard Harris.

MERSEYSIDE M.C.
BRAVERY IN INVASION ASSAULT

In the new list of Army awards for gallantry and distinguished services in Normandy is Captain William Charles Sinclair Carruthers, R.E., of Waterloo, who receives the M.C.

Captain Carruthers, who is aged 24, and is the son of Mr. and Mrs. W. T. Carruthers, Stoneleigh, Park Road, Waterloo Park, is cited for personal bravery in the assault on the beaches on D-Day. He was wounded in the operation, but carried on with the vital task to the point where an important success was obtained. Born at Llandudno, he came as a boy with his family to Merseyside and was educated at Bootle Secondary School. Upon leaving school he became a research chemist, but at the outbreak of war volunteered for service in the Royal Engineers.

CAPTAIN W. C. S. CARRUTHERS.

CORPORAL PAT HENNESSEY
13th/18th Royal Hussars, in command of a Sherman DD tank

There was to be a 24 hour delay, so we were condemned to spend another day incarcerated in the LCT.

We were assembled for our final briefing where we were issued with maps which showed that we were headed for the coast of Normandy, to land at the small resort of Lion-sur-Mer. We formed the left flank of the assault with the Americans far over to our right. We each received a copy of an Order of the Day signed by General Eisenhower, and at nineteen years of age I was caught up in the universal feeling of excitement and pride. It crossed my mind that 'Gentlemen in England, now a-bed, must feel themselves accursed they were not here'. I, certainly, would not have wished to be anywhere else.

That night we shipped our anchor and felt the increased throb of the ship's engines as we headed out to sea. At last we were on our way. There must have been a mixture of feelings amongst the troops on board. For those of my generation, who were young and keen for excitement, it was all a great adventure, we had no responsibilities and our morale was high. There were others, though, who had wives and children at home, who had been taken from their civilian careers and had a more mature appreciation of what was involved. Looking back, it must have been much harder for them, but we youngsters did not give thought to that at the time.

We were roused long before dawn on the morning of the 6th June. The sea was still rough and there was a strong wind blowing. We heard and watched the Airborne Force pass over us,

Patrick Hennessey, 1942.

hosts of gliders following their tugs, preceded by the aircraft carrying the parachutists and the busy fighter escorts above them. As daylight slowly appeared we could see ships of every description stretching away to the horizon on both sides of us and to the rear. It was a stupendous sight which must remain in the memory of all who saw it. We marvelled that such a gigantic force could assemble over a period of five days and move across the English Channel, undetected.

At last the order came to board the tanks. We climbed on, stowed away bedding rolls and made sure that everything was in its place and we took post to inflate the screen. The air bottle was turned on and the screen began to rise. We took particular care, this time, to make sure that the struts were secure because we could feel the effect those large waves were having on the LCT, and we were under no illusions as to what they would do to a puny DD tank once we got into the water.

The bombardment started with a tremendous roar of gunfire. On our left we heard a terrifying 'whooshing' noise and saw a veritable fire-work display as the rocket firing ship, (LCR), went into action. The burning projectiles carved an arc through the sky as they sped towards the shore. Beyond her stood HMS *Warspite* adding a loud contribution from her large guns. We had been warned that it would be very noisy, but this still took us by surprise.

We heard the order over the ship's tannoy, 'Down door, No 1' and we knew this was our cue. The ramp on the bow of our LCT was lowered into the sea, the ship hove to, tank engines started, and Sgt Rattle's tank moved forward down the ramp and nosed into the waves. We followed, and as we righted in the water I could just see the shoreline some 5000 yards away; it seemed a very long distance and in a DD tank, in that sea, it certainly was.

Slowly, we began to make headway. The crew were all on deck apart from Harry Bone who was crouched in the driving compartment, intent on keeping the engine running because, as we all knew, if that stopped we stood no chance of survival. The noise seemed to increase and the sea appeared even rougher from this low point of view, with only a flimsy canvas screen between us and the waves. We shipped a certain amount of water over the top of the screen from time to time, so Trooper Joe Gallagher, the co-driver, whose task it was to man the bilge pump, was kept hard at work.

Each side of us other DD tanks were launching. To my right and behind me I saw Captain Noel Denny's tank as it came down the ramp and into the sea. It straightened up and began to make way, but behind it I could see the large bulk of its LCT creeping forward. The distance between them closed, and in a very few minutes the inevitable happened. The bows of the LCT struck the DD tank and forced it under the water. The tank disappeared beneath the LCT and was never seen again. Capt Denny managed to escape and was picked up, but the tank was sunk and the rest of the crew was lost. There was nothing anybody could do, it was our first casualty.

We battled on towards the shore through the rough sea. We were buffeted about unmercifully, plunging into the troughs of the waves and somehow wallowing up again to the crests. The wind, fortunately, was behind us, and this helped a little. The noise continued and by now the shells and rockets were passing over our heads, also, we were aware that we were under fire from the shore. The Germans had woken up to the fact that they were under attack and had brought their own guns into action. It was a struggle to keep the tank on course, but gradually the shoreline became more distinct and before long we could see the line of houses which were our targets. Sea sickness was now forgotten. It took over an hour of hard work to reach the beach and it was a miracle that most of us did. As we approached, we felt the tracks meet the shelving sand of the shore, and slowly we began to rise out of the water. We took post to deflate the screen, one man standing to each strut. When the base of the screen was clear of the water, the struts were broken, the air released and the screen collapsed. We leapt into the tank and were ready for action.

'75 HE , Action – Traverse right, steady, on. 300 – white fronted house – first floor window, centre.'

'On.'

'Fire!'

Within a minute of dropping our screen we had fired our first shot in anger. There was a puff of smoke and brick dust from the house we had aimed at, and we continued to engage our targets. Other DD tanks were coming in on both sides of us and by now we were under enemy fire from several positions which we identified and to which we replied with 75mm and Browning machine-gun fire.

The beach, which had been practically deserted when we had arrived, was beginning to fill up fast. The infantry were wading through the surf and advancing against a hail of small arms fire and mortar bombs. We gave covering fire wherever we could, and all the time the build-up of men and vehicles continued.

Harry Bone's voice came over the intercom, 'Let's move up the beach a bit – I'm getting bloody wet down here!' We had landed on a fast incoming tide, so the longer we stood still the deeper the water became. As we had dropped our screen, the sea was beginning to come in over the top of the driver's hatch and by now he was sitting in a pool of water. The problem was that the promised mine clearance had not yet taken place, so we had to decide whether to press on through a known mine field, or wait until a path had been cleared and marked.

Suddenly, the problem was solved for us. One particularly large wave broke over the stern of the tank and swamped the engine which spluttered to a halt. Now, with the power gone, we could not move, even if we wanted to. Harry Bone and Joe Gallagher emerged from the driving compartment, soaking wet and swearing.

More infantry were coming ashore, their small landing craft driving past us and up to the edge of the beach. There was quite a heavy fire fight in progress so we kept our guns going for as long as possible, but the water in the tank was getting deeper and we were becoming flooded. At last, we had to give up. We took out the Browning machine-guns and several cases of .3 inch belted ammunition, inflated the rubber dinghy and, using the map boards as paddles, began to make our way to the beach. We had not gone far when a burst of machine-gun fire hit us. Gallagher received a bullet in the ankle, the dinghy collapsed and turned over, and we were all tumbled into the sea, losing our guns and ammunition. The water was quite deep and flecked with bullets all around us. We caught hold of Gallagher, who must have been in some pain from his wound, because he was swearing like a trooper, and we set out to swim and splash our way on to the beach. About halfway there, I grabbed hold of an iron stake which was jutting out of the water to stop for a minute to take a breather. Glancing up I saw the menacing flat shape of a Teller mine attached to it; I rapidly swam on and urged the others to do so too.

Somehow, we managed to drag Gallagher and ourselves ashore. We got clear of the water and collapsed onto the sand, soaking wet and shivering. A DD tank drove up and stopped beside us with Sergeant Hepper grinning at us out of the turret. 'Can't stop!' he said, and threw us a tin can. It was a self-heating can of soup, one of the emergency rations with which we had been issued. One pulled a ring on top of the tin, and miraculously it started to heat itself up. We were very grateful for this, and as we lay there on the sand, in the middle of the battle taking turns to swig down the hot soup, we were approached by an irate Captain of Royal Engineers who said to me; 'Get up, Corporal – that is no way to win the second front!'

He was absolutely right, of course. Rather shamefacedly we got up, moved further up the beach and found some medical orderlies into whose care we delivered Joe Gallagher who cheered up considerably when someone told him he would be returning to Blighty as a wounded 'D Day Hero'. We left him at the Field Dressing Station and moved on. We had only our pistols with us, but we found a discarded Sten gun and some magazines. Attaching ourselves to a section of the South Lancashires, we made our way inland. The beach, by now, was a very unhealthy place to be, it was under intensive small arms and mortar fire, mines were exploding and being detonated by our own mine clearance services, and all the time the build-up of troops and vehicles continued, making it a very crowded area. Clearly, we were not of much use to the infantry in our unarmed state, so I found the Royal Navy Beach Master and reported our presence to him. He was a very busy man at the time, and advised me to: 'Get off my bloody beach!' We made our way to the road which ran parallel to the sea, some four or five hundred yards inland, and there we met up with some other un-horsed tank crews.

I could not help feeling a bit unwanted at that stage. There was plenty of action taking place, but there was not a lot that we could do to influence the course of the battle and nobody seemed keen to invite us to join in. Of course, we had already played our part, and we could look back with some satisfaction. We had done what most people thought was impossible, we had swum a 32 ton tank through 5000 yards of savagely rough sea and had given that vital support to the infantry to enable them now to have the chance to do their job of clearing the beach. On reflection, I had learned a valuable lesson from the events of that morning. Sgt. Hepper, for instance, had clearly not been deterred by the prospect of mines on the beach and had driven his tank ashore, accepting the risk. If I had used initiative and done the same, our tank would not now be standing submerged some 150 yards out in the sea. The RE Captain too, had the right idea of 'Press on, regardless'. In the heat of battle it really does not pay to sit back and weigh up the pros and cons of a situation, it is quick decision and immediate action which brings results. I mentioned these thoughts to Harry Bone, whose only comment was: 'Bugger that! – If we had hit a mine, I would have been sitting right on top of it'.

The beach was still a scene of frantic activity. Landing craft were coming in, depositing their loads of men and vehicles, then backing out to sea again. The area was swept by machine-gun and mortar fire and snipers were busy from the windows of the houses, shells and mortars were kicking up clouds of sand, the noise level remained very high, and the infantry were taking a lot of casualties. I saw death for the first time that day, and also for the first time I came face to face with the German Army, about two dozen prisoners were being marched down the beach, hands held aloft, some were wounded, all looked shocked and frightened. They were a scruffy crowd, not at all the 'Supermen' we had been led to believe were opposing us. Most professed to be Russians or Poles, but there were a few who were arrogantly German. Eventually, we were found by Major Wormald who directed us to make our way to the village of Hermanville. We were delighted to see him and to know that he had survived the landings. As he drove off in his tank, we felt a return of confidence as we started the three mile trek to Hermanville.

At Hermanville we settled into a barn and some farm buildings, and eventually what was left of 'A' Squadron came together. We had not suffered a great number of casualties in terms of men, but we had only 5 serviceable tanks remaining from the 21 which had launched that morning. *Privately published memoir.*

LIEUTENANT ROLF FLECKENSTEIN
111 Battalion, 736 Regiment, 716 Infantry Division, 7th Army, *Wehrmacht*
Stützpunktkommandant Ostufer der Orne

First there was a report about the paratroop landing east of the Orne in the area occupied by 711 *Nachbardivision.* We just had to wait. Around 2 o'clock 7th Army was alerted. Towards dawn, at about 5 o'clock I saw through the telescope the massive fleet on the horizon. It was clear enough, this was the invasion.

At about 6 the guns from the ships opened up with the beach west of the Orne their target. At the same time bombers came in, bombing the beach over which thick, black clouds of smoke formed. Shortly after noon there was a telephone report that the position held by Colonel Krug and his regiment had been occupied.

Between 3 and 4 in the afternoon, gliders moving inland overflew the Orne. Between 8 and 9 in the evening German stragglers from the fighting in the hinterland came up to our support point. My own position did not come under fire from the sea nor was it bombed and the telephone communication between our battalion and 711 division was maintained throughout the day. *Typescript recollections in a letter to Peter Liddle, December 2003.*

Rolf Fleckenstein.

Rolf Fleckenstein and anti-aircraft defence.

Rolf Fleckenstein and Atlantic Wall defence.

GEFREITER HERBERT MEIER

Wireless Operator, *Panzer Lehr* Division Communications, *Wehrmacht*

On 6 June we heard the news way too late. We belonged to *OKW* reserves, one of three divisions. We could be engaged only by the Führer's orders. Our division lay the furthest away, being near Le Mans so we had the furthest march to make. It was sometime the next morning that the *Führer* allowed us to be used which was, of course, far too late. We were attacked constantly by the *jabos* [fighter bombers] during our march – ceaselessly, taking cover and having vehicles blown up even though we were not even close to the front. *Typescript recollections. The Eisenhower Center for American Studies at the University of New Orleans and the National D-day Museum, New Orleans, USA.*

GEFREITER ALFRED MERTENS

716 Regiment, *Wehrmacht*

I was perhaps lucky to be in Normandy. I had stolen some cream from a farmer in France and was caught. While I was serving my military punishment my unit was sent to the Eastern Front and I was then sent to join a unit remaining in France. My new unit was moved to Ryes between Bayeux and Arromanches. Our Company Commander lived with his men in a bunker we'd dug in a hill outside Ryes. Our principle task was to construct foreshore obstacles at Arromanches. Here we set out stakes of various lengths in the sand.

About a fortnight before the landing we had received new machine-guns. We tried them out and adjusted them at the steep slopes of the coast near the port but with bad results. Four wouldn't shoot at all and a number of them would only produce single shot fire. A few days after the adjustment to the guns I was close to the anti-aircraft guns in their position near our bunker and on anti-aircraft watch. All at once twelve fighter-bombers flew over us towards the radar at Arromanches and came back for a second sweep.

I ran to the anti-aircraft gun and was able to aim and fire but to my great disappointment only a single round could be fired. We counted the empty cartridges and we'd got off 42 rounds.

Around midnight 5/6 June we received a telephone call raising security to level 2. The deafening noise of aircraft engines confirmed that the invasion had begun.

As our company assembled our area was carpet-bombed. I was on my way to an assignment and so I was on the edge of the attack. Five soldiers of my company were buried in their foxholes and killed.

Then the order came to counter-attack. We marched in a column to the right of the Ryes Arromanches road for this. It wasn't long before we met machine-gun fire from in front of us. We now moved forward in a ditch or trench that ran along the side of the road. All at once I got a blow on the right side of my head. I dived to the left hand side to take cover shouting, 'Sniper to the right.'

I took off my helmet and saw on the edge a deep indentation which was causing a massive swelling to my right temple. My Captain, who was near me, sent me straight away with a comrade, slightly wounded in the neck and an English prisoner, to the main first aid post.

We ran like hares – fighter bombers above us and naval shelling endangering us too. The shells seemed to fall first on one side and then on the next. We reached the aid post but as we were only slightly wounded we were sent up for treatment to the next unit engaging the enemy.

My comrade and I got past the outskirts of Bayeux to reach a farm near Juaye Mondaye. It was late in the evening. We broke into a barn and fell asleep in the hay. (We were captured the next morning.) *Typescript recollections.*

CHAPTER 11

Air Support

It is important to have a broader vision of RAF and USAAF responsibility in the immediate preparation for D-Day and for the day itself than the deception role already referred to, the airborne assault by paratroops and glider-borne forces and the bombing of key targets, because British and American aircraft had been conducting supply-dropping operations for the French Resistance facilitating their sabotage work on railway lines and roads which so seriously affected the speed with which the Germans could get reinforcements to their coastal defence. However there is no doubt that superiority in the air over the Normandy beaches was almost assured well before the landings. The Luftwaffe was over-stretched by the Eastern Front, German homeland and occupied territories to the West commitment. Additionally their fighter organisation may not have deployed scarce resources most effectively. Compounding these problems were the allied raids on synthetic oil plants, aircraft production and coastal radar installations.

One after another, contemporary personal accounts of allied air, sea and land service on D-Day express or imply the refrain 'Where is the Luftwaffe?'. This book is not entering the lists on controversial issues, but there is some irony in that a D-Day victory won before the day itself, was achieved despite high level bitter inter-allied, inter-command, inter-personnel battling by some of those appointed to work together or in a position where they faced the challenge of working together. Aware, or more likely not, of such high-level jousting, air crews and ground crews fulfilled their tasks of the day as a matter of course.

FLYING OFFICER RICHARD H ROHMER
of 430 Squadron, Royal Canadian Air Force, 39 Recce Wing,
flying Mustangs on tactical reconnaissance from RAF Odiham, Hampshire

All our aircraft were painted at wing-roots and at the fuselage just ahead of the tail with broad black and white stripes, a further safeguard that the troops on the ground and the crews of ships would recognise us as friendly.

I was assigned with Flying Officer Jack Taylor to do a tactical reconnaissance over the beachhead area south to Caen and for a short distance along the roads leading into that town from the south and south east. Our take off was to be 06:00 hours (there were to be sections of two ahead of us).

All six of us were quietly wakened in our tents at 03:00. We dressed quickly, and without taking time to wash or shave, hurried to the mess tent. Our fabulous chef, Stradiotti, personally appeared to produce eggs, bacon and coffee for us. After breakfast it was over to the Wing Operations tent to be briefed on our operations.

We were airborne at 06:00 just before sun up. In the semi-darkness we did a stream rather than formation take off. As soon as I was airborne, I began to turn to the left in order to place my aircraft inside of Taylor's banking to port about half a mile ahead of me. That

Richard Rohmer, January 1944, at Gatwick beside his Mustang Mark I.

way I could catch up with him quickly as our paths crossed. He was already in a gentle arc in the same direction toward a course that would take us south to exit the coast just to the east of Portsmouth. As I caught up with him, crossed under and moved out to my comfortable battle formation position 200 yards to his right and just slightly behind, the darkness was fast disappearing. But that day the sun was invisible, obliterated by a solid blanket of high, gray cloud that looked to me to be sitting above us perhaps at 10,000 feet. We knew the wind was strong, close to 20 mph from the west. It wouldn't affect us but it would undoubtedly play havoc with the men crossing The Channel in ships big and small.

As we approached the crossing-out point on the south coast the sight that lay before us was awesome. As far as the eye could see the sea was covered with ships in a vast miles-wide unending column reaching south to the horizon, plowing through white-capped waves toward the Normandy shore. Ships coming in from ports to the east or west of Portsmouth converged on the column about ten miles south of the coast. Even I could judge that we were flying over the largest armada that had ever sailed on any water.

While I was constantly checking the sky for enemy aircraft and occasionally catching glimpses of Allied fighter squadrons in the distance, it was impossible to keep my eyes off the amazing sight below us. The water was thick with ships rolling in the heavy seas, some of them towing protective barrage balloons to stave off low-level enemy aircraft attacks. From my vantage point everything appeared shaded by the diffused light filtering through the heavy overcast above us. Even the whitecaps had turned gray. The bobbing ships painted in their myriad patterns of dark, blending colors gave off a common grayness only slightly contrasted against the uninviting blackness of the wind-whipped channel waters carrying them.

Then we could see the outline of the Normandy coast dead ahead. Sitting over it was something we had not anticipated. It was a high, towering wall of broken cloud that had built up over the entire sector of Normandy beaches to be assaulted. That unexpected cloud barrier would make it next to impossible for the heavy and medium American daylight bombers to work effectively against the targets they had to be able to see. Our fighter squadrons would have great difficulty in catching any marauding enemy aircraft because they could quickly take cover in the clouds. Allied fighter bombers and rocket aircraft would be similarly impeded, for, as we soon discovered, the uneven base of the cloud was only 500 feet above the ground. Anybody flying under it would be highly vulnerable to flak and for that matter, fire from machine-guns and rifles. Furthermore, defending enemy fighters could use the low scud cloud as they maneuvered into firing position on one's vulnerable tail.

Heading straight south for the beach just to the west of Ouistreham and by Lion-sur-Mer off my right wingtip, we dove down below the unwelcome cloud bank to cross the still vacant beach. Our speed was well over 400 miles an hour. Our eyes were completely peeled and our heads on swivels. It was Taylor's job to lead. He had to do the map reading and the reconnaissance. He would note the location of tanks, moving vehicles, and gun emplacements, and whether there was artillery or flak to be seen. If possible, he would photograph with his 14 inch port oblique camera the important items he observed.

Within two minutes we were over Caen where the wall of cloud that sat over the beachhead had dissipated. We were able to climb rapidly to 6,000 feet, a far safer altitude at which to operate. During the less than two minutes it had taken to fly at low level from the coast to Caen we had swept by fields littered with huge Horsa troop and vehicle carrying gliders. They had gone in in the darkness in the early hours of the morning to attempt to seize the bridges over the Caen Canal and the Orne River. Some of the gliders were still whole, others had wings ripped off or had crashed, totally torn apart.

As Taylor and I made our first run over Caen we could see brilliantly burning light anti-aircraft tracer shells slowly arcing towards us, behind and on into the clouds above. Those first welcoming barrages were coming in fairly close but there was nothing to worry about. I always had a feeling of detachment and they'll-never-hit-me attitude to the apparently slow-moving flak I could see on its way. It was no different that morning when I felt particularly fearless and invincible.

Thirty minutes were spent checking all the roads leading into Caen. Taylor saw some motor vehicles moving toward Caen on the main highway about five miles south-east of the city. Beyond that little movement was seen.

Then we turned back for the beaches, again diving down to low level to get under that wall of cloud. Arriving at the coast just to the west of Ouistreham, we swung west to follow the beach line about half a mile inland.

It was H-Hour. Below us the terrain was crater-pocked from the thousands of bombs that had rained down during the night. New craters were being made before our eyes as shell after shell from the battleships, cruisers, and destroyers standing offshore smashed down under us. The devastating barrage was now lifting from the shore working inland in an attempt to destroy any enemy forces that might impede the imminent beaching of the first landing craft.

Out to sea we could see them coming, the first lines of landing craft filled with men, tanks, rockets, flak vehicles. Landing craft designed to explode any minefields were in the vanguard, the swimming Sherman Duplex Drive tanks wallowing behind like rectangular rhinoceros in the surf. They were almost there, almost at the point where bottoms and tracks would touch the sands of Normandy. They bobbed and plowed through the heavy waves about a hundred yards offshore, their gray white wakes marking the growing distance between their sterns and the naval force that had escorted or carried them across The Channel during the stormy night. That mighty armada was now standing about three miles offshore with all its guns trained and firing at the beachhead and us.

From my cockpit I looked out onto a horizon filled with the thick cordite smoke from the constant firing of huge naval guns. So heavy was the blanket of smoke that it almost totally obscured the massive fleet. Through the heavy black pall, but made more visible and pronounced by it, I could see the flashes of the countless guns, like a long unending line of Christmas lights winking on a dark, foggy night. That they were firing directly at us never crossed my mind.

At Arromanches we turned around and headed back towards Ouistreham, arriving there just as the first landing craft and Duplex Drive tanks hit the beach under heavy fire from German machine guns and 88's. We could see the landing craft disgorging tanks and men into what was rapidly becoming a shambles as enemy fire concentrated on the beaches.

As we turned back once again toward the west the same scenario was developing where the 3rd Canadian Division was coming in on Juno beach at Courseulles. Beyond them and to the west of Arromanches, 30 Corps of the 2nd British Army was beginning its assault.

Back and forth Taylor and I ranged over this incredible, lethal theater of death and destruction. So entranced and enthralled was I by the enormity of the scene that I failed to monitor my instrument panel regularly. When finally I did drop my eyes for a split second to run over my engine instruments, temperatures, pressures, and the fuel, I was shocked. The fuel contents gauge on the floor to the right of my seat registered on the empty mark! And there I was sitting over the Normandy beaches, at least 100 miles from the coast of England. Time to get the hell home. *Drawn from Major General Richard H Rohmer's autobiography, 'Patton's Gap: Mustangs over Normandy'.*

Major Ian Neilson in St James's Park, London, January 1945. He has just been invested by HM King George VI with the Distinguished Flying Cross.

MAJOR I G NEILSON

Air Observation Post

Because there was no aircraft carrier available for 6 June in spite of all our intensive shooting practice with both the Navy and Royal Artillery during the previous three years, we were unable to direct fire on D-Day and had to wait until an Advanced Landing Ground (ALG) was established ashore in the eastern corner of the bridgehead on D plus 1. That was in fact to be my task – with a small ground party of six – to reconnoitre, find and prepare an ALG – clearing any obstructions. As soon as this was achieved a message would be sent via HQRA 3 (British) Division back to 652 Squadron at Old Sarum and the first few aircraft would fly over, escorted by a Fleet Air Arm Walrus Amphibian, to avoid Naval anti-aircraft fire – notoriously trigger-happy.

Major Ian Neilson was searching for a small landing ground for this 'spotting' aircraft, an Auster.

So my ground party and I went to Normandy on a Landing Craft (Tank). The party consisted of Captain A W Keen and five other ranks, both RA and RAF. Our waterproofed 3-tonner was heavily laden with explosives, small arms, aircraft spares and some fuel and a small motorcycle for my use. Another Officer of my B Flight 652 Squadron, Captain R E Linton, accompanied by two RA signallers and a No 11 Set on a trolley came ashore at Gold Beach at midday on D-Day on the top of the tanks of the Queen's Westminster Dragoons. They made their way to HQRA 3 Div, awaiting a report from me that all was ready for the aircraft to come over, and also that Linton could now rejoin the Flight. My first contact with him was by radio about midnight on D-Day.

Having got very wet coming ashore on the early evening of D-Day - it should of course have been at midday – I collected my ground party and our vehicles and soon found a relatively quiet and sheltered spot beside a disused tennis court about a mile from the shore at Gold Beach. Leaving the ground party there, I set out on my James 125cc two-stroke motorcycle in the usual cloud of blue smoke to reconnoitre the three possible ALG's which we had selected in advance from the vertical air photographic cover. I went up the road to the south through St Aubin D'Arquenay and found the first area – off to the east of the road leading down to the River Orne and the 'Pegasus' Bridge. It was littered with wrecked gliders, parachutes and anti-landing poles. It soon became obvious that even if we cleared suitable lanes for our aircraft, the whole place was in full view of the opposition to the east across the Orne valley. There was also very little tree cover and that was on the west side near St Aubin.

So, somewhat encumbered by a khaki parachute, I went off in a north – westerly direction towards field No 2. There was now some difficulty as a Company of the East Yorks Regiment were preparing to advance in a south – westerly direction towards Perier and Douvres la Délivrande against some quite lively opposition. This inspired some caution in the 'Lone Wanderer' and I had to take cover for a short period until the Company had advanced. I then called in on the ground party, reported briefly and left them, and the parachute, to await my return. The moral of this episode is that one should always follow the line of advance and not cut directly across it. It was interesting to see at close quarters how the Infantry functioned.

The second field was alongside and to the north of the lateral road running eastwards from Douvres. In addition to a number of large trees on its eastern side, it also turned out to be a minefield. Having rapidly decided that this was not acceptable, I went south-westwards towards Perier and the village and farm of Plumetot. Our third choice was a large area – in fact, three fields to the east of the farm and its orchards, with large trees on the south. Apart from various obstacles such as anti-landing poles, electric pylons, a large concrete water tank and quite a lot of wire fences, it seemed acceptable. The surface was smooth and there were no dead animals. There was good cover for many vehicles.

Having returned to collect the ground party, it now being past breakfast time on D plus 1, we demolished all that (needed it) at Plumetot and that evening were 'operational'. *Typescript recollections*

Roland Beamont (on the right), Manston 1943. He is talking with Sir Archibald Sinclair, the Air Minister. Bernard Sheen, the Station Commander, is to the left.

WING COMMANDER ROLAND BEAMONT
in command of 150 Wing flying Tempests from RAF Newchurch, Kent

Log book

6 June: Patrol Invasion forces moving up from Dungeness.
6 June: Scramble at 10.20 to patrol British beachhead at Ouistreham. Weather and light bad. Beaches active. No joy. Returned Ford and orbited until midnight for other (?) Wings to land.

SERGEANT DES CURTIS
Navigator 248 Squadron Coastal Command, RAF Portreath, Cornwall, attacking German U-boats off the coast of North West France with 'Tsetse' Mosquitos – that is Mosquitos equipped with a 57mm field gun. U-boats and E-boats presented a potentially serious threat to The Channel crossing on 6 June and the subsequent supply of the beachhead.

We had three aircraft and five crews and we were put on a one hour's notice, twenty four hours a day, to be ready to fly. There were only six mine-swept channels leading from the Bay of Biscay onto the French coast and we knew the positions of each. So our briefing was simply to be at the seaward end of one of those channels which were designated A, B, C, etc at a specific time, to the minute of course, because, using Ultra intelligence, the Royal Navy was aware of the likely times when German U-boats would have to surface to run at speed through the mine-swept channels to get to their pens. Our task was to meet them as they surfaced and to make sure they didn't get into their pens. We had the fifty seven millimetre six pound gun. We carried twenty four rounds of ammunition which were fired singly by the pilot. Automatically reloaded, it made a hell of a bang when it went off and initially the flame from the explosion shot out 130 feet in front of the aircraft.

When you consider that you had a wooden aircraft and this twelve foot long piece of artillery was bolted on to the main spar of the aircraft, slightly off centre in a longtitudinal sense you can imagine the recoil effect. There was a recoil chamber, but we proved on one occasion by firing all twenty shots, flying in formation, that we had momentarily stopped each time we fired, because we gradually moved further back in the formation as we fired. There was a tremendous noise because the cartridge case was some two foot long. We couldn't drop the spent cartridge cases from the aircraft because that would have damaged the tail unit so there was a steel box underneath the breech of the gun. So after the gun was fired the breech was opened, this heavy cartridge case fell into the steel box with a clatter. The next round came down from the carriage, into the breech and then the breech was hammered home ready to fire again. So there was this succession of very loud bangs, but you know, one got used to it.

We had one success with a Canadian pilot who found a U-boat and attacked it. He was on his own – found the U-boat and attacked it and severely damaged it. About twenty days later two of us were (on patrol), Doug Turner and myself leading – I was the leading navigator – we had four Mosquito fighters as escort to us. We made our rendezvous at the appropriate entrance to the mine-swept channel at about 9 o'clock in the morning and as we lifted up from sea level we saw this small convoy, in the centre of which was a U-boat which was weaving very firmly and he was escorted by four armed minesweepers. So the four escort Mosquitos turned off and started to attack the minesweepers. We had to go and climb up into the sun because our firing technique was to climb up to 1,500 feet, and as soon as the target disappeared out of sight below our nose we put the aircraft into a thirty degree dive. The speed would then move from 240 miles an hour up to 360 miles an hour and during that brief dive the most number of shots that you could achieve would be five. The pilot aimed and fired and his target was the water near the conning tower but aiming to hit the water rather than the U-boat because when the solid shell hit the water its path changed and it ran parallel to the surface. The impact of the water pressure. It entered through the ballast tanks and being solid it would then ricochet within the U-boat hoping to hit the engine casing amongst other things and possibly exit elsewhere. So one would make two holes if possible. So you had the chance of making ten holes if every round was successful. We attacked this U 976, got at least four shells in exactly the right position. Hillard, our number two, came in and attacked behind us. I then saw some brown oil starting to spread on the surface which I realised was diesel oil. The weaving motion of the U-boat had stopped and it almost came to a halt and we realised then that it was severely damaged. We were being fired at by the coastal batteries because we were so close inshore there and the coastal batteries had been trained in an event such as ours to drop their heavy coastal shells into the sea just ahead of us. So rather than try to hit us they made enormous splashes and if you hit one of those splashes, you were doomed. So we had to be very careful watching what the shore batteries were doing, but we later learned that the U-boat sank within twenty minutes.

Two days later with six escorts we went back and almost at the same time and at the same position, 9 o'clock in the morning roughly, we found two U-boats with two German merchant ships which had had most of their superstructure removed and replaced by anti-aircraft fire guns. They were very lethal ships, and a number of destroyers and others. The Germans had realised that something new was attacking them. We decided to attack the second of the U-boats. We attacked it and damaged it but the concentrated anti-aircraft fire was so great that we knew if we went round three or four times we certainly would not survive, and our task was to survive and fight another day. So within two days we had put one U-boat to the bottom and had severely damaged the other one. We went on using this weapon very successfully right through D-Day and, once it became known to the Germans, we were then free to use it for surface vessels. *Transcript of tape-recorded recollections.*

SERGEANT FRED P J L DANCKWARDT

463 Squadron Royal Australian Air Force,
Rear Gunner in a Lancaster bomber,
RAF Waddington, Lincolnshire

<u>5/6 June</u>: Our target was the gun position at St. Pierre-du-Mont. Only two positions were clear of cloud so most bombing was on Oboe (radar beam). Our route was to Weymouth, then skirting the Cherbourg Peninsula to the target and then across the Peninsula to Weymouth and home. We were in the last force to bomb and on the approach to the target saw three aircraft shot down, so there were some fighters in the area. We came down below cloud on the way home and as we neared Alderney a considerable anti-aircraft defence opened up on a Lancaster ahead of us, fortunately without success. A few minutes later the invasion fleet came into sight and it was obvious to us that this was D-Day. When we landed at about 7 o'clock in the morning we were told to get some sleep as we would be flying again that day.

<u>6/7 June</u>: Our target was the railway system at Argentan (cloud affected operations that night) but reconnaissance showed that considerable damage was done to the railway yards. This was the last trip of our tour and when we landed one could almost hear the sighs of relief all round. *Typescript recollections.*

Sergeant Fred Danckwardt, aged 19, RAF Stormy Down in 1943.

A photograph taken from Fred Danckwardt's Lancaster in the night attack on Argentan. It was taken at 0235 hrs on 7.6.1944 and 'it would appear that an ammunition train was hit. Flak is exploding dead ahead of us. We are at 6,500 feet'.

Number 463 Squadron RAF at briefing before a raid on Juvisy in France, in April 1944. The crew of the Lancaster in which Ron Fairburn was flying is around the table in the foreground. He is on the right without a cap but with a smile. [see page 214]

Gliders at Ranville. I G Neilson

SERGEANT RON FAIRBURN

Flight Engineer, 463 Squadron Royal Australian Air Force,
Flight Engineer in a Lancaster bomber, RAF Waddington, Lincolnshire

Logbook:
5/6 June: D-Day attack on a battery of artillery at dawn, prior to Allied landings on French coast (near Cherbourg) St Pierre-du-Mont
6/7 June: Moonlight attack on road and rail junction at Argentan.

SERGEANT LES FOSTER

443 Squadron (F) Royal Canadian Air Force, RAF Ford, Sussex,
flying Spitfires Mark IX's

Diary:
4 June 1944: Dive bomb radar installation at Cap D'Amtifer – wizard prang. Intense accurate flak.
6 June 1944: D-Day second front opens in France. I flew #2 on the Wing Commander, while we patrolled the eastern flank of the beachhead. No action at all.
6 June 1944: Patrol eastern flank of Omaha Beach. No nothing. PO Bentley hit by 20mm flak.

Leslie B Foster, No 443 (F) Squadron, Royal Canadian Air Force.

| Aircraft | | Pilot, or 1st Pilot | 2nd Pilot, Pupil or Passenger | DUTY (Including Results and Remarks) | Single-Engine Aircraft | | | | Multi-Engine Aircraft | | | | | | Pass-enger | Instr./Cloud Flying [incl. in cols. (1) to (10)] | | Link Trainer |
Type	No.				Day Dual	Pilot	Night Dual	Pilot	Day Dual	1st Pilot	2nd Pilot	Night Dual	1st Pilot	2nd Pilot		Dual	Pilot	
				TOTALS BROUGHT FORWARD	150:20	462:10	11:50	18:00					4:30	25:20	4:00			81:00
TYPHOON	882	SELF	-	SQDN FORMATION		30												
TYPHOON	682	SELF	-	RAMROD		1:20			Bombing Cap D'Antifer Delay Bombs									
TYPHOON	491	SELF	-	NEEDS OAR to TANGMERE		:15												
TYPHOON	491	SELF	-	TANGMERE to NEEDS OAR		:15												
TYPHOON	682	SELF	-	AIR TEST		:10												
TYPHOON	682	SELF	-	RAMROD		1:25			Bombing Ault - Le Treport Area. Lost S/Ldr Ross									
TYPHOON	682	SELF	-	TANGMERE to NEEDS OAR		:15			Very Thick & Accurate - Light & Heavy Flak. (Hit)									
TYPHOON	682 JP. SELF OV-X		-	RAMROD BAYEUX AREA		1:10			D-DAY Low Level Bombing of a GHQ AT ZERO HOUR. CHANNEL A MARVELLOUS SIGHT									
TYPHOON	682	SELF	-	ARMED RECCO DIEPPE AREA		1:25			ATTACKED & DESTROYED GERMAN STAFF CAR WITH BOMBS + CANNONS STRAFED DUMP & CAMP									
TYPHOON	682	SELF	-	ARMED RECCO SOUTH BAYEUX-CAEN		1:35			BOMBED & STRAFED ENEMY TANKS & M.T.									
TYPHOON	549	SELF	-	FORMATION		:40			behind ENEMY LINES. CARRIED 1 LONG RANGE TANK									
TYPHOON	682	SELF	-	ARMED RECCO CAEN-FALAISE AREA		1:50			Bombed & Strafed Gun Positions In Dense Flak (Hit)									
TYPHOON	682	SELF	-	ARMED RECCO CAEN - FALAISE ARGENTAN AREA		1:35			Strafed M/T Truck at Argentan Many Strikes									
TYPHOON	629	SELF	-	RAMROD		1:30			Bombed & Strafed Trucks. 1 Flamer + 1 Smoker									
TYPHOON	682	SELF	-	RAMROD		1:10			Close Support to the Army near CAEN									
TYPHOON	682	SELF	-	RAMROD		1:05			Close Support S. of Bayeux Bags of Flak.									
TYPHOON	688	SELF	-	RAMROD		:40			Bombed & Strafed Bridge South of Cabourg									
TYPHOON	688	SELF	-	RAMROD		1:30			RETURNED Mid-Channel. Weather u/s F/c Baker.									
TYPHOON	752	SELF	-	RAMROD		:55			Bombed Bridge Thury Harcourt. Lost Watson									
TYPHOON	881	SELF	-	RAMROD		:16			RETURNED French Coast.									
									RETURNED Weather u/s.									
		GRAND TOTAL [Cols. (1) to (10)] 611 Hrs. 30 Mins.		TOTALS CARRIED FORWARD	100:00	491:40	11:50	18:00					4:30	25:20	4:00			81:00

James Kyle's logbook entry for D-Day.

FLIGHT SERGEANT JAMES KYLE

197 Squadron, RAF, from Need's Oar Point, Hampshire, flying Typhoons

We were up at half past three in the morning, and had a general briefing. We took off at about quarter past six. Twenty four Typhoons, and our target was the German Headquarters in Bayeux. We crossed over the coast of Normandy at about 500 feet because the weather factor wasn't all that good. We found the Chateau and bombed it and strafed it and left it in ruins and came out within about twenty minutes. We came out at about 1500 feet because of the vagaries of the weather. The cloud base had lifted and so I crossed back looking at the hundreds of ships sailing towards France, wondering what was going to happen in the future.
Transcript of tape-recorded recollections.

James Kyle's logbook records:
D-Day low level bombing of a GHQ at zero hour. Channel a marvellous sight.

Amongst James Kyle's papers is a document recommending him for an immediate award for meritorious service dated 6.6.44 and it states 'This pilot is tough and aggressive at all times with a great contempt for flak defending targets he is detailed to attack. Strongly recommended.' [He was to be awarded the Distinguished Flying Medal.]

Typhoon being bombed up during the fighting in Normandy. Taylor Library

Typhoon being loaded with bombs and rockets.
Taylor Library

Winston Churchill visits Typhoon squadrons now based in Normandy. J Kyle

Typhoon pilots with a moment to relax, East Grinstead, 1944. James Kyle, now a Flight Lieutenant, with French, Polish and New Zealand pilots, WAAF and film stars Clark Gable and Elizabeth Allen and celebrated surgeon, Sir Archibald McIndoe.

FLIGHT ENGINEER MALCOLM MITCHELL
No. 190 Squadron RAF Transport Command, Fairford, Gloucester,
flying Stirling Mark 4's towing gliders

The whole squadron seemed to be out there and the gliders and the men standing around, engines roaring and so on, and then it became our turn to be on the runway when we were hooked up to a glider.

We took off with the glider, got ourselves into the stream, and the stream didn't go towards Normandy. It went about halfway around east England to pick up the other streams of aircraft and then we finally made our way as a stream. You could see aircraft behind you as far as you could look and aircraft in front of you with gliders as far as you could see. And we went over a big town, which I assume was Portsmouth, and then it looked as though you could walk across the Channel by stepping from one ship to another. There were so many of them. An incredible sight I shall never forget. What with that and the stream of aircraft above it was astounding.

The weather was very good. It had been bad in previous days, but the sun was shining. We made our way to Caen where we dropped our glider, or at least the glider pulled away from us, and then we circled. Of course, there was a bit of flak there, especially over Caen, but once we were back over the sea it was calm again, and we were part of the stream returning to base over ships still going to France. *Typescript recollections.*

Malcolm Mitchell.

FLIGHT LIEUTENANT BERNARD MARTIN
Engineer Officer, 514 Squadron, RAF
flying Lancaster bombers, RAF Waterbeach, Cambridge

I was told of D-Day on its eve and instructed to meet the incoming aircraft. I was up early and ready by half past seven. We reckoned that the first aircraft should be back by that time and sure enough they were.

Within five minutes the first aircraft were touching down and some of them were badly shot up. There was one with a great big hole in the leading edge. When I'd got hold of the Flight Sergeant I said 'You better have a look and see what you can do with this, Flight', and so he said, 'Okay, Sir.' Well, they couldn't do much with that aircraft, and there were two or three others which were in a similar condition. We had been told that the next op was going to be at midday. So having landed at half past seven, they had to be off again at midday. Well, you can't do much by way of repair in, you know, hours. So it was a question of again deciding which aircraft to concentrate on, get them repaired or not, and it fell to me to say yes or no, and so they took off again – those which were flyable or could be repaired or were not sufficiently badly damaged – that is the other way of doing it, and so they took off and landed again about

Flight Lieutenant Bernard W Martin,
Daily Servicing Engineer Officer, RAF
Waterbeach, Cambridge.

three hours later, because it was a short trip you see. It was only across The Channel and some more were damaged then, and then we were told there would be a third trip that same day. You know take off about six or seven I think.

And so the third and final trip was laid on for about seven, I think, and they took off and came back about ten or eleven. Well, by this time everybody was absolutely flaked out. You know we just couldn't take any more, and so I said to Hurd, I said 'Look, you put your 'I and R' people at my disposal to get these aircraft ready for tomorrow as possible.' And that is how we carried on. We slowly coped on an emergency basis that was the way it was. *Transcript of tape-recorded recollections.*

SERGEANT A B FRIEND
'A' Flight, 512 Squadron RAF Transport Command,
operating Dakota III aircraft from Broadwell, Oxon

From his logbook:
June 5, 2325 (hrs): F Sgt Perry (pilot) Jump Master. Op 'D'Day minus
One: Drop paratroops six miles NE of Caen whose objective was coastal battery. Drop further supplies nearer Caen. LAA opposition. 3 (hrs) 40 (mins).
June 6, 2230 (hrs): F Sgt Perry (pilot) Op re-supply with panniers and containers: 'D' Day Navy prevent sortie from being carried out. Our aircraft damaged, others in 'vic' destroyed. 3 (hrs) 25 (mins).

JUNE 1944					WITH 512 SQDN., BROADWELL	Time carried forward :— 881.50	54.35	
Date	Hour	Aircraft Type and No.	Pilot	Duty	REMARKS (including results of bombing, gunnery, exercises, etc.)	Flying Times		
						Day	Night	
JUNE '44 B.D.S.T.		DAKOTA III			"A" FLIGHT.			
" 5ᵗʰ "	23 25	KG324 "A"	F/SGT. PERRY	W.OP. - JUMP MASTER	OP : "D" DAY MINUS ONE : DROP PARATROOPS SIX MILES			
					N.E. OF CAEN WHOSE OBJECTIVE WAS COASTAL BATTERY			
					DROP FURTHER SUPPLIES NEARER CAEN. L.A.A. OPPOSITION		3 40	
" 6ᵗʰ "	22 30	KG324 "A"	F/SGT. PERRY	W. OP.	OP: RE-SUPPLY WITH PANNIERS & CONTAINERS: "D" DAY			
					NAVY PREVENT SORTIE FROM BEING CARRIED OUT			
					OUR AIRCRAFT DAMAGED, OTHERS IN 'VIC' DESTROYED.		3 25	

The D-Day logbook entry of Wireless Operator, Jumpmaster, Sergeant A B Friend in a Dakota III.

A Dakota (KG598), the aircraft type crewed by Sergeant A B Friend on D-Day.

FLIGHT ENGINEER ALFRED BARNES

75 (New Zealand) Squadron RAF,
flying Lancaster bombers from Mildenhall, Suffolk

We were going to a place called Ouistreham at the eastern end of the Arromanches beaches and were loaded up with 250lb bombs. The smallest we ever carried, and lots of them. We were also told to be aware of a great deal of activity on the sea below us if anyone had cause to jettison the bomb load in case of engine difficulties or whatever.

We were very excited as we knew this was the big one. We didn't take off until three o'clock on the morning of the Sixth and this time we were in daylight by the time we reached the Channel and the sky was full of planes, both us and the USAAF. We seemed to be spread as far as the eye could see left and right with our fighter escort flying above us. It must have been a terrifying sight for anyone on the other side of the Channel. The sea below was full of ships of all sizes. The most awe inspiring were the battleships and cruisers that were already firing big guns at the coast. We could see the flashes and smoke as they fired and the explosions just beyond the beaches. The huge troop carriers were a bit behind all the other RN ships waiting for the go after we had been in.

To be a part of this gave me a great deal of pride. *Typescript recollections.*

Alfred Barnes (extreme left) with the crew of his Lancaster bomber.

Number 130 Squadron Spitfire pilots at RAF Horne, one of the three squadrons in John Checketts's Wing.

WING COMMANDER JOHN M CHECKETTS

flying with 130 Squadron RAF (Spitfire VB)
from Horne, Sussex

It was interesting working from the area because we were accommodated under canvas and did the normal flying and escorting bomber and fighter sweeps from there. It was quite obvious that the invasion was not far away and we did a lot of interdiction work against bridges, German traffic and escorting bombers to isolate the area. We had no idea where the landing would take place but all the paraphernalia for the invasion was being assembled at Selsey Bill, huge concrete cassions and material for landing on a foreign shore were towed there ready to be dispatched over to France. It was an exciting period and we were

Wing Commander John M Checketts at RAF Horne.

very busy and the build-up of the invasion unfolded before our eyes. Strangely we did not encounter much opposition from the Luftwaffe but I think this may have been in part brought about because of the long-range fighter escorts done by the United States Air Force into Germany which caused the Luftwaffe to be dispersed back into the home territory at the expense actually of covering France. There were German fighters there but not in the numbers there had been previously and those we did strike did not seem to be so aggressive as the earlier models.

We missed flying the Spitfire 9 aircraft which were comparable to the German types and found that we did not have the performance we would have liked in escorting bombers at altitudes in excess of 10,000 feet. However the Spitfire 9 Wings from the Second Tactical Air Force were always flying above us. We did not see any German aircraft of consequence during this period. It was tremendously exciting to be called to the briefing by the Air Marshals for the Invasion on that June morning.

I flew out before daylight with 130 Squadron to cover the first part of our patrol over the beachhead and was astonished to see the size of the Fleet of Ships approaching the Normandy shore. The reaction of the Germans in Coastal Defence as far as anti-aircraft fire was concerned was secondary only to the stupidity of the Royal Navy who shot many of our aircraft down. Their attitude to aircraft was one of hostility and it annoyed us intensely. In fact, we had to do our patrols in many instances behind the German lines because of attacks by our own guns. However, I did manage to get a damaged Focke-Wulf 190 on the second morning, in fact I think I shot him down but by that time I was so short of fuel I could not stay to see what had happened. It was a long way back across The Channel, a hundred miles of water.

I lost some pilots and it grieved me to lose these men because they had become good friends. I liked the Polish and Canadian boys very much and 130 Squadron with its mixture of nationalities was unique. I was fortunate enough to command such a conglomerate of lovely people and it was really a very competent Wing. *Typescript recollections.*

FLYING OFFICER WILLIAM RODNEY (RCAF)
78 Squadron RAF, Four Group, Bomber Command, Breighton, Yorkshire, flying Halifax bombers

Two broad horizontal white stripes were painted with non-permanent pigments on the fins and rudders of all our Squadron's aircraft a day or two before 6 June signifying that what we were expecting was in the immediate offing. We soon discovered that the stripes were the distinguishing markings applied to aircraft destined to take part in D-Day operations and were intended to aid formation assembly during subsequent daylight missions.

It was no surprise when shortly after midnight, 5/6 June, at our briefing, Group Captain Brookes and senior officers stressed that the strike we were about to carry out at first light was undoubtedly the most important task ever assigned to 78 Squadron.

The moment was further dramatised by Group Captain Brookes performance for he stammered and usually limited his send-off remarks to a brief sentence or two. His performance that early morning exceeded all expectations for its eloquence and length.

Our task was to attack the German gun emplacements at Mont Fleury, about a mile inland of what we later learned was designated as Gold Beach.

In the early dawn light the camouflaged Mont Fleury battery was hard to see. The weather over the target was terrible; low cloud with only occasional breaks, compounded by poor visibility. Late arrival, inaccurate marking and back up by the Pathfinder Force, together with the proximity of numerous aircraft streaming into the target, exacerbated the situation. Since the Mont Fleury gun battery was only a mile or so from the beaches the short distance from the shoreline made a timed run to the site virtually impossible. Given the specified time on target and the number of aircraft involved in the operation, there was little opportunity to carry out navigation or bombing run-up adjustments.

We attacked from comparatively low altitude, jettisoning our load of five one thousand pound and 10 five hundred pound bombs from 5,000 feet according to instructions and encountered no ground fire or attacks by the Luftwaffe. Over or near the objective I saw an aircraft, a Halifax, going down. Since we encountered no opposition the loss was probably the result of a mid-air collision or a bomb falling from one of the attacking force flying at a higher altitude striking the aircraft. Weather conditions, the need for careful flying, together with the vigilance that springs from a heightened sense of self-preservation inhibited me from noting whether any of the aircrew managed to get out of the plane.

The results of the Squadron's effort were, at best, indifferent, and I thought at the time that the operation was a failure, a view that I still hold. Coming out of the target area, and as the dawn lightened and visibility improved, we caught glimpses of the great fleet of naval vessels, transports, and tank landing craft advancing towards the invasion area, a magnificent and unforgettable sight. Together with views of great numbers of aircraft of every type heading towards or leaving the beach areas the scenes that morning were dramatic and striking. They are lodged in my memory, reflecting moments, conditions and times that have never been forgotten.

We landed after a flight of over five hours and were dispatched again that same night, 6 June, to St Lô in connection with the Omaha Beach landing. *Typescript recollections.*

CHAPTER 12

Support, Supply, Medical Provision

After the assault waves and with adequate control of the landing beaches secured, more armour, guns, ammunition, vehicles of all description and troops were landed during the morning and later in the day. Where it was possible quickly to move off the beaches into more advanced positions this was immediately attempted, designated roles to be fulfilled after months of training.

The Beachmasters had a critical rôle managing inflow, exit, semi-static then changing circumstance in a way which demanded a rare combination of authority, grasp of opportunities, management of difficulties and dealing appropriately with officers and men working under the stress of battle.

Relatedly those establishing medical aid posts and dressing stations had a challenging task with no areas safe from shelling and few routes certainly cleared of mines, to say nothing of finding cover in buildings suitable for taking and treating casualties.

Throughout the day stores had to be landed from various types of landing craft and the celebrated Rhinos, huge powered platforms which had taken their cargo from a range of landing craft and merchant ships (Liberty Ships and coasters for example). Of course, the troops landing in the assault 'faced the music' first but the second waves and those remaining on the beaches saw and had to stay working among the human and material wreckage of the initial landings, and this sometimes under continued enemy shelling.

SERGEANT D SMITHSON
The Glider Pilot Regiment, No. 10 Flight, 'G' Squadron,
operating from Fairford in Gloucestershire, Second Pilot with a Horsa glider

In the morning we loaded our glider with three Airborne Gunners along with their Jeep and trailer filled with stores and ammunition. We were now ready for take-off late in the afternoon. All went well and we lifted off easily and flew in a large square touching the edge of Birmingham before heading towards the south coast. This was to allow all the gliders to get airborne. At a height of 1000 feet we crossed the coast near Bognor Regis and headed towards the Normandy coast. Here we changed from high tow to low tow position. This meant we were now flying lower than the Stirling. It also meant that flying became much more difficult. This was because we were following so many aircraft, the airstreams from the other planes plus part of our own threw us all over the sky almost like a paper aeroplane on the end of a string. It also meant that we were flying the Horsa together and not taking turns and thus became more tired. However we soon saw the coast of France and the great number of landing craft and small boats going back and forth to the beaches from the larger

224

ships off shore. No noise from below as our own sizzle through the air was too loud even though we had no engines. The slip stream noise at 160mph airspeed is loud. We had now to keep our eyes open as to where we were, relative to the ground. There was little time before we needed to cast off. We were over the coast and could see the River Orne beneath us. A right turn by the tug, a loss of height and there below us our LZ with some gliders already on the ground. We cast off, put the nose down and with full flap were soon heading steeply for the ground. Poles and wires could now be seen. Spinner picked a path between the poles. A slight shudder as our wheels took the wire and we were down, brakes on and we bumped to a stop. The glider was a little lop-sided as one wheel was in a hole but no damage. The main wheels could have been dropped over The Channel but our decision to leave them on was right as they clearly took the wire first and slowed us down quickly.

I told the gunners to get out and start unloading. They were not to tell twice. We soon had the tail off and the runners in place. We all helped push the jeep and trailer out, connect them together, load them with the gunner's personal kit and they were ready to join their unit. The Lance Corporal thanked us for a good trip and a safe landing. Then with best wishes they were far away. I thought at the time, that it had not been a good trip for us as, over The Channel, it had been very rough. The fact of being safely down on the ground again probably influenced their views.

We looked around and shouted to other pilots nearby. We then re-entered the glider and took out our own kit, had a look at the map, not really necessary as pilots from other gliders were making their way to a small orchard alongside some farm buildings. Here we started to dig slit trenches for ourselves. It was easy going in the French soil. We could hear a few sounds of fighting in the far distance but nothing near us. Many of our own fighters were flying around us, far different from Dunkirk when it was the other way about. Then they were mainly German.

Three Junkers 88s did fly over us at about 2000 feet and watching them I got ready to take cover at any sign of bombs dropping. Not a chance, within seconds they were attacked by our fighters and made off for their own lines. We carried on digging and soon Spinner and myself were sitting in our slit trench looking at each other. This was the first trench Spinner had dug. We spent the night there. *Typescript recollections.*

SERGEANT LEN WRIGHT
The Glider Pilot Regiment, 'C' Squadron, 6 Flight, Tarrant Rushton, Dorset
First Pilot of a Hamilcar glider

D-Day was June 6. We went just after tea and we took Locust tanks. The Hamilcar was heavier but still flyable.

The Locust was shackled and we would tell the tank driver that we were pulled up and ready for landing. We had to tell him to start his engine. Now the idea was that when he started his engine he was ready for coming out. When we landed we could jump down from the top. We were high up, we had to jump down and let the oil out of the legs or shoot the tyres off. That was one of the things and that dropped it. He would unshackle it, put it into reverse just slightly, to drop the shackle, then in forward and he came out and the door opened at the same time as he was coming out. I don't know exactly how it was done but that is what happened.

The only thing that happened to us was that when we had to get our tank away, we had to defend the field where we landed in case there was another do coming in the following

Sergeant Len Wright (bottom row, far right) and men of the Glider Pilot Regiment.

day and we just found our rendezvous spot when one of my mates well, he came in and landed with me actually. We landed together and his Second Pilot came dashing up to say that they couldn't get Robbie out of the plane. The plane was on fire. So we dashed across to him and we lifted him out of the cockpit and found out that he had been hit by an 88 before he could get out and he was very badly wounded. We couldn't do anything for him. He was one of the lads who had been on the tours of North Africa, Robinson. He was a Manchester lad, and we lifted him out but we had to leave him, we left him with his Second Pilot who waited for the Medics to come, you see, but he died that night. He was absolutely riddled with shrapnel and stuff I think.

We didn't get on fire, we had no problems. They hit him when he landed. These people were in hedges. He was on the ground when he was hit.

We just guarded the landing zone the first night and we marched into Ouistreham and got a lift back. *Transcript of tape-recorded recollections.*

CORPORAL JOHN HODGSON, RAMC
9th Field Ambulance
attached to 2nd Battalion Lincolnshire Regiment

As soon as we reached dry land (soon after mid-day) we moved to our muster point, with some Lincolnshire Regiment soldiers. We were told to move off as soon as possible and in single file walked up the main street of Hermanville-sur-Mer. After about a kilometre, the person leading the column turned right towards Lion-sur-Mer. A hundred yards before the first building of Lion our Section was told to 'set up' near the gates of an orchard where a small stone building would give some shelter to any wounded. The swishing sound of shells going to and from the beach area was a constant reminder that we were in a battle zone. There was a constant stream of various vehicles coming off the beach. We prepared to receive any wounded. After an hour a young soldier with a wound on his forearm walked to our Post. It was 1300 hours, his name was Private C Harmer, he was the first casualty of the Lincolns on D-Day. Shortly afterwards a young German was brought to us, he was wounded in the foot and was carried on a stretcher, after treatment, to the beach area. The third casualty, another Lincoln was dead. We buried him under one of the apple trees. 2100hrs saw dozens of aircraft and gliders bringing airborne reinforcements. Firework-like displays over the nearby beaches as our Anti-Aircraft Guns fired tracer shells into the night sky to ward off any enemy aircraft. The sound of overhead shelling continued throughout the hours of darkness. *Typescript recollections.*

John Hodgson, 1946.

2ND LIEUTENANT KEN DAVENPORT
5th Battalion, The King's Liverpool Regiment

Diary

<u>6 June</u>: Landed OUISTREHAM 13.45. Saw gliders. Beach a shambles. Bodies everywhere. Proceeded inland to HERMANVILLE on SHERMAN. Sniped coming through streets, up all night - bombing and shelling. Phil killed.

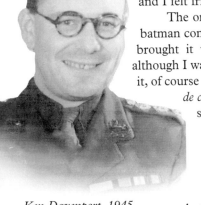

It was only when we got on to the landing craft, the ship carrying us out before we landed on the LCT, that I realised that there was trouble ahead and I felt frightened. To be perfectly frank, I was quite frightened.

The one thing I do remember on that short trip in the LCT was my batman coming from the galley with a cake. He hadn't made it but he had brought it with him. That, more than anything made me realise that although I was frightened, as everyone was of course, (and you didn't admit it, of course you didn't), but the very fact that he could land with such *esprit de corps* and produce a cake on the moment of landing was quite a stimulant. And then we landed.

When I had landed and got to the top of the beach, I remember seeing a tank making its way into the town. It couldn't get through a narrow passageway and it gouged the sides of two houses to get through.

We found an orchard and dug a trench, or at least my batman did. A good job we did because no sooner had we got in,

Ken Davenport, 1945.

The 5th Battalion King's Liverpool Regiment 'Beach Group', June 1944. J K Davenport

than a German fighter came over and strafed us. Hit our ammunition truck and up it went, blowing to pieces two of my men who were inside it.

I also lost a friend, Philip Scarfe, a Second Lieutenant about the same age as I was. Landed on D-Day and I learnt later that there was a gun position - the Germans had positioned pillboxes (very menacing) to oncoming LC assault craft, and Philip and his men attacked it. He was shot as he ran up the beach firing his revolver. He was wounded, but he carried on and was shot at again and was killed. We buried him above the high watermark. His wife sent her wedding veil to put in his grave which was rather touching. I was the Godfather to the unborn son she had later. Later he was disinterred and put in Bayeux cemetery, the military cemetery there. *Transcript of tape-recorded recollections.*

SERGEANT GEORGE WHEATLEY
16th Field Battery, 7th Field Regiment, Royal Artillery

Our job as a recce party of four was to follow the advancing infantry and establish a gun position a couple of miles inland ready for the battery to come into action when they arrived later.

As we sailed into shore we were on the right hand craft and came under machine-gun fire from a building to our right but couldn't fire back because they were out of range of our Sten guns. BSM Lacey and I were perched precariously on a pile of shells and beginning to think that perhaps our part in the invasion was over when a naval rating opened up on the machine-gun post with, I think, an Oerlikon and silenced it. I gave him the thumbs up and shouted to him, 'Thanks, mate' to which he replied, 'That's OK, anytime,' with a big grin on his face.

All this time there were shells dropping in the sea all around the LCT and, as we went down the ramp, one landed in the middle of the deck that we had just left.

When we hit the shore we scrambled off the vehicle, met up with the other two and hiked up the beach to an alleyway between the buildings, which was obviously the way out.

On the way we passed a tiny field gun pointing out to sea with a dead German lying between the trail and I remember wondering whether he was a very brave man facing the armada with that small gun or whether he was a fool doing a King Canute. We got through without incident, past a couple of bodies, ours and theirs and arrived at the main road of Lion-sur-Mer.

Turning left, we pushed on to the first crossroads where we turned right and proceeded

228

inland. All the time there was the sound of heavy gunfire and shells passing overhead, in both directions, I supposed.

As we were approaching the outskirts of the village, we caught up with a number of infantrymen who, with fixed bayonets, were searching the houses. We had a quick confab and came to the conclusion that they were in the second wave making sure that there were no enemy about and pressed on accordingly into open country.

We marched a couple of miles inland without seeing a soul and came eventually to a T-junction on the outskirts of Hermanville-sur-Mer, where we halted while Lieutenant Ferguson looked at his map and had a quick look around.

While we were waiting, we were surprised to see a priest walking towards us from the direction of the village with a huge smile on his face.

I was standing slightly apart from the others and he came straight to me, put his hands on my shoulders, kissed me on both cheeks and said, 'Welcome, liberators'. BSM Lacey said, 'Watch him George, I think he fancies you'. The priest spoke perfect English (much better than my Yorkshire dialect) and having told us we were the first British troops he had seen, he said, when asked where the Bosches were, 'Oh, they've gone, they are a couple of hundred metres up the road.' He pointed towards the village, and there we were having mistakenly believed there was at least a battalion of infantry between Jerry and us.

We turned left at the T-junction and the CPO chose a field a few yards further on for our gun position. I could do nothing until my line-laying truck arrived and was walking round the field with Tom Page deciding the route for the telephone cable when we were machine-gunned, went to ground and fortunately didn't get a scratch.

When the vehicle arrived with a couple of signallers, we commenced to lay the telephone line between Command Posts (Troop and BHQ) ready for the guns arriving and within a couple of minutes we were under heavy shell fire but were able to lay the line without mishap.

The guns arrived shortly afterwards, having been led into position by BSM Lacey, who had gone to Hermanville Beach to meet them and while they were in action and firing away, our tanks came across country at great speed from the direction of the sea and went roaring through our position towards the enemy. *Typescript recollections*

MAJOR DAVID PATON, RAMC
223 Field Ambulance

Unit War Diary:
6 June: By 1200 hrs HQ Coy transport are assembled and advance to Hermanville-sur-Mer, North of Caen where an ADS (Advanced Dressing Station) is established & the evacuation of casualties begun. This ADS is sited in the avenue of a chateau and is under canvas utilising two very large pits dug by the enemy which provide excellent cover.

Forward of this, Nos 1,2 & 3 sections are draining the casualties of their respective battalions. The local population afford us quite a good friendly, if rather reserved reception.

Since it is impractical to move the ADS further forward evacuation is carried out largely direct from CCP to 21 & 22 FDS's which are only 1/2 a mile behind the ADS. Despite this the casualties passing through the ADS on this day numbered 35.

* * * *

I got ashore almost with dry boots would you believe at half past nine. We were told 'just get off the road, don't muck about, get off the road' and we stayed off the road because some of the chaps had stuff in the big packs on their backs and we had to get that out. We had nowhere to put it. We had no cover. We had nowhere to go and there wasn't room for us. We found a farm. We were not dealing with wounds really. We were putting dressings on them,

A Landing Ship Tank disgorging her cargo at Courseulles during the afternoon of D-Day. Bob Pykett

Bob Pykett (third from right) in Germany with the Bedford lorry, the Counter Battery's 'office', and the staff.

Labelling them – I did the labelling and moving them back – Gunshot wound leg – GSW leg – that's all the War Office needed. Our business was to move men not to treat them but on D-Day evacuation of the wounded took a long time. You were too tired. We were stood down at 6pm because the chaps couldn't carry any more. I was getting men off the road to come and help carry stretchers. *Transcript of tape-recorded recollections*

GUNNER J B PYKETT, RA
Driver and Radio Operator with Counter Battery 1st Corps

All Assault Drivers had waterproofed their vehicles using newly-developed compounds and materials to seal the entire ignition system and converting the carburettor intake to a 'chimney' of hose beside the windscreen. In rehearsal exercises I had come through a run of successful 'wades' and as I watched the sea breaking over our Rhino I wondered anxiously whether under the law of averages I was due to experience a stall in sea water. We landed about 5 in the afternoon on Juno. First down the ramp went a bulldozer for the Beach Engineers holding on its raised blade three motorbikes of the Military Police. Next it was us. The waterproofing did not let us down and the four wheel drive Humber staff car, after chicaning through the taped track on the beach, carried the Counter Battery CO, his Staff Sergeant, Radio Operator and Driver up through Courseulles sur Mer to 1st Corps assembly area. *Manuscript recollections.*

This Mercantile Marine vessel was, in June 1944, the Blue Funnel Line's Empire Capulet, *Ray Buck's ship.*

ABLE SEAMAN RAY BUCK

Mercantile Marine, *The Empire Capulet*

Having just got into Avonmouth and expecting leave, I was told that the 'V' on my card required my going to London. It seems I must have volunteered for something and this was it. My new ship was in The Victoria and Albert Dock. She was *The Empire Capulet* and her Chinese crew had prudently disappeared.

    The Empire Capulet was laden with tanks, munitions, and God knows what and we went across to Sword Beach, I think it was. We were attacked by German aircraft as we were discharging our cargo onto a Rhino alongside us, a huge pontoon with four engines at each

Ray Buck's Merchant Marine Certificate of Discharge, showing the entry for his D-Day service.

corner. A bomb went down Number Two hold but it didn't explode and a cannon shell set fire to the Rhino. There was a huge volume of flame and it was quite serious for the ship. Some brave Pioneer Lieutenant, I think he was – went down in Number Two hold and retrieved the unexploded bomb and this Irish Able Seaman, I only knew him as Mick, cut the wires or ropes (linking us) and it drifted away and it had a lot of men on board, wounded men, and it drifted away to the beaches. *Transcript of tape-recorded recollections.*

LIEUTENANT COLONEL NAPIER CROOKENDEN
5th Parachute Brigade, 6th Airborne Division

In the original plan 3rd Parachute Brigade would drop at ten minutes to one on D-Day morning and our Brigade would land by glider at the same time. There were not enough aircraft to carry the whole Division in that first lift and the 5th Parachute Brigade would therefore follow in a second lift on D-Day evening. Then on April 17 – and I remember it all too clearly – the usual, daily batch of RAF air photographs came in showing a mass of white dots all over our chosen landing zones. For a moment we thought that the Germans knew we were coming, until our expert photo interpreters confirmed, that these dots covered every open field along the whole Belgian and French coastline and were in fact holes being dug for the erection of anti-glider landing poles. General Gale changed the order of landing, so that we were to land at 9pm on D-Day, a bitter blow to our pride. As it turned out, those poles would have made little or no difference to the success of our actual landing.

I had to wait at Moor Park, the HQ of The Airborne Corps, for the success signal and then to give the order for take off to the units of the Brigade, waiting beside their loaded gliders at eight airfields in Oxfordshire and Berkshire.

By midnight on June 5 I was sitting in the operations room at Moor Park, listening to the rear link radios from the Division in Normandy. Since the Parachute Brigades were due to land at ten minutes to one, we expected the first messages soon after one and we sat there in growing disquiet as nothing came in. Only at 1130 am did an RAF reconnaissance aircraft radio back that there were ground to air signal strips laid out on the lawn of the small chateau which General Gale had chosen as his HQ. The staff officer who received it, could not make out what it meant until I turned the signal book in his hand and we could read 'All objectives taken'.

I at once telephoned all our take-off airfields with the message 'GO' and the time of take-off 1800 hours and set off in a staff car for RAF Brize Norton to rejoin Brigade Headquarters. As we drove through Slough I saw a paper boy, standing on the corner with the banner headline 'SKYMEN LAND IN EUROPE' and, buying his whole stock, I was able to distribute copies of the paper to my friends in the Parachute Brigades that same evening.

At Brize Norton our Headquarters people were sitting in the sun beside their gliders. By 3pm I was eating bacon and eggs at the Officers Mess, when Bill Collingwood limped in. He was the Brigade Major of the 3rd Parachute Brigade and should have jumped early that morning. He was still covered in camouflage cream and looked pale and dishevelled. He at once asked me if he could hitch a ride in our gliders for himself and the men of his stick. I allotted him one of our spare gliders and they were all back with their Brigade by 10pm that evening.

Jumping at 10 minutes to one that morning, his static line had wrapped itself round his leg and he had hung there beneath the aircraft for some minutes while the rest of his stick struggled to pull him in. By the time they had succeeded it was too late to go round again and their aircraft returned to England.

At half past five we were all emplaned. In my glider were two jeeps and trailers, carrying the Brigade Command and Rear Link radio sets. Driving one of the jeeps was Val Kinch, Hugh's batman, and with us too were three Brigade signallers and Major John Darlington, a staff officer from Division. At 6 o'clock we took off and the whole mass of tugs and gliders from all the Brigade airfields – 258 combinations – began to form up into a long procession of 'loose pairs'. One of our signals gliders at Brize Norton began to swing on the take-off run and finally crashed into a hangar killing all on board. *Typescript recollections.*

ROYAL MARINE CORPORAL JACK BEST
Gunner's mate aboard a Block Ship to be sunk to make,
with such other ships, a breakwater within which stores unloading
and troop reinforcement disembarkation could more easily take place.

About four miles out, we had picked the Naval Officer up and everything was set, or so we thought. Whilst we had been on the guns, the Merchant Seamen had quietly lowered the boat and left. They had got the ship in position but there was no one to drop the anchors and so the ship had drifted nearly 90 degrees out of position. I think the Naval Officer panicked because there was a loud explosion and the ship stopped. Whether we hit a mine or an obstacle, I don't know, all I know was that the ship was sinking and we had nowhere to go. The ship started to roll to port and some of the lads were on the ship's side. I had told them what the engineer had said, that it would roll on its side, but of course it was a case of panic stations. Suddenly there was a great rumble down in

Jack Best and his father, Gilbert. Gilbert, of the 4/7 Royal Dragoon Guards, had landed on D-Day in the first assault. He returned to the beach for spares, meeting the second wave of his regiment, to be told by the Regimental Sergeant Major that his son, Jack, had 'swum to their landing craft'. Jack's account shows that things had not been quite so straightforward, but at least the father knew his son was safe.

the engine room and the ship started to roll to starboard, the lads were trying to scramble back up (some made it I reckon) but George and I waited and then jumped and swam like hell to get away before the ship could land on top of us.

Despite the engineer's boast, he had been left behind along with the Captain and the Naval Officer, but I never saw any of them again so I don't know what happened to them. When the ship had settled down (on its side) George and I went back and found a hammock each to float on. We had taken all our gear on deck earlier ready for getting away but we hadn't time to look for it. In any case it was hopeless, there was wreckage, oil and everything you can imagine floating around so we dog paddled away together. We intended to try and stay together but it was too difficult, the water was very cold and after a while the hammock became waterlogged and sank so I had to find something else to float on. I managed to climb onto a hatch cover and there I lay frozen to death. I was so cold I couldn't think straight and all I had left was trousers and shirt. The tide was going out and we were going with it, I really thought I'd finally bought it. After what seemed like days, suddenly there was a ship slowing down and I hadn't even seen it, it was a huge LST manned by Americans. They dropped a scrambling net over the side but we couldn't make it, so a big bloke climbed down and hoisted me up whilst another bloke got George. We later realised it had been nearly twelve hours since the ship had gone down. The crew couldn't do enough for us, hot showers and wonderful food soon brought us back to the land of the living, but I was never to feel the same after that experience. *Typescript recollections.*

LIEUTENANT *(Acting Lieutenant Commander)* E F GUERITZ, RN
Principal Beach Master, Queen Red Sector, Sword Beach

I was conveyed to Normandy with Commander Currie (HQ Operations), the Brigade Commander of the tanks and the Beach Group Commander. By 7. 30 we could see this fantastic vista of craft stretched across the horizon, ships and craft. We had seen the horizon erupting from the bombardment from the air and from the sea. Then Commander Currie said, 'Well, I suppose it's about time we went ashore', and so off we set. We hailed a landing. We seemed to get into quite deep water and had to pull a Roman Catholic Chaplain of the Beach Group from out of water too deep for him.

We landed on Queen Red Beach and the point was the obstacles were the biggest determining factor as to how you landed because you have got to get between these obstacles without exploding the mines or the bombs they had on them. Then after craft had attempted to drive firmly up the beach, they had difficulty getting off again, slewing round or entangling kedge-anchor wires with their neighbours on the beach. Adding to the confusion, armoured vehicles were blowing off the heavy metal exhaust trunks fitted to help them 'wade' in. I could see men struggling down the hen-house gangplank from the Infantry Landing Craft struggling with bicycles built for long life not lightness. Beach exits were jammed with vehicles, impeded by soft sand and mine explosions. Our task was to bring some order into this chaos. The RN Commando had to reconnoitre the beaches and set up signs to mark the beach limits, approach channels and navigational hazards. Landing craft obstruction clearance units co-operated with Royal Engineers to clear the beach obstacles, explode mines and booby traps and mark potholes and quicksands. Landing craft recovery units with waterproofed or amphibious vehicles brought help to damaged or stranded craft. Specialised units got to work marking and clearing the beach exits. There were particular difficulties on Queen Sector.

Reinforcement arrives. A H Barnes

My biggest anxiety had been weeks and weeks before, that I would not be there on the day, because I had been preparing for this for years in different capacities. I had been involved with landing craft for three years, and this is what we were due to do. And when I got ashore it seemed to be much as I expected. It was not as bad as I had expected, and I knew some people found it, obviously because somehow or other they were not mentally adapted. But a lot of people were taking it in their stride because training had been pretty elaborate, and I did see people who were terrified (reduced to incapacity). My immediate boss had gone ashore. He had no right to go ashore early and he was wounded straight away. And then my Army opposite number was killed just after we had landed. I had stopped to talk to my immediate boss who, as I say, shouldn't have been there anyway, and Colonel Maude walked on and we didn't see him again until that night when we found his body with his escort just up the beach. And there was mortar fire, there was sniper fire and there was artillery fire. But the mortar and the sniper fire obviously were diminishing factors because we were pushing our way forwards. However when foul-smelling smoke was released to screen the beach this provided a great impediment to our own forces with people stumbling around choking and with streaming eyes. *Typescript recollections and transcript from tape-recorded recollections.*

CHAPTER 13

Women and D-Day

There were women officially 'in the know' on D-Day, in the various establishments of Supreme Headquarters Allied Expeditionary Force (SHAEF), in Royal Navy and Royal Air Force HQ establishments too, and there were women in the services and as civilians – wives, girl-friends, mothers – who knew unofficially of the immediate imminence of what was of course generally known, the launching somewhere, presumably in France, of the long-awaited Second Front.

The evidence today, of this knowledge then, is in a sense more predictable than the range of reaction of men at the sharp end of *Operation Overlord*. There is the excitement, the tension and loyalty of Wrens, the professionalism and forethought behind planning about to be tested, the competence of respected seniors for whom they had such anxious pride now being examined and, beyond the Senior Service, the war effort of Britain and her allies 'on the line' as it were. Confidence, yes, but just a little undermined by fear of one of a thousand things which could go wrong and of course the inevitable cost however fortune were to cast her favour. For many of these women there were likely to be friends or family members who would be crossing The Channel and so they will not have been free from the additional stress of a loved one sailing into danger.

For the women who knew unofficially and probably by a degree of infraction of the intense security wrapped round those on the starting blocks, prayers and hopes will have been first for the safety of their soldier or sailor loved one and then for the wider success of what was being attempted. The extent to which pride at having one's man going to the battlefront on what might be a day to turn the war round for the Western Allies, fought a losing battle against the desperate anxiety that he would come back safe and sound, would be variably answered in the expressed emotions of those women. When one considers too that from workplace or home these thoughts were not necessarily limited to the destinies of two because there could be children involved, one may judge that being 'in the know' was a two-sided privilege.

PETTY OFFICER WREN HILDA CRAVEN
Operational Signals (Teleprinter) Plymouth

I remember sending messages about evacuating all the villages and farms in the Slapton Lee area. Everyone and everything, animals, fodder, furniture, schools were all evacuated to make way for the US Army training in preparation for D-Day. The US Navy arrived in large numbers bringing all kinds of landing craft with them. There was a gradual build-up of vessels in every creek and estuary in Devon and Cornwall and by Spring of 1944 our daily chart of vessels in the Command was absolutely full. At this time the South and South West coastlines and land for some ten miles or so inland was a closed area. No-one was allowed

Hilda Craven's D-Day diary entry. ND is Night Duty, ASD is Admiral Superintendent of Devonport Dockyard, Devon.

Hilda Craven, on the left, and Peggy Allen, December 1943, WRNS quarters, Plymouth, Devon.

out or in without a special permit. We saw in our signals and charts everything building up and felt the push must come soon.

We were on the evening watch on 5th June and for several days our traffic had steadily slowed down and that evening most of the machines were strangely silent. Next morning the night watch girls woke us all up when they came back to the house and said 'they've gone'. We scrambled out on to our balcony from where we could see part of the Sound some two miles away. There wasn't a ship in sight. When we got to work in the afternoon our port chart was blank except for six ships in for repairs – everything had gone in the dark hours. *Manuscript recollections.*

COMMISSIONED WREN CHARLOTTLE DYER

(later Pippard) at Chatham

Diary: Tuesday 6 June 1944.

It has got so busy during the last few days that two extra people have to come on during the afternoon and evening watches. The work has, of course, been extremely interesting, until the climax last night. We were told, by S.S.O. when we went on duty, that the landings were timed for 0745, and that there would be 6 hours preliminary bombardment, by the ships. We were busy but nobody wanted to go to bed, during the night we each went up to the top of the tunnel, and watched hundreds of bombers going over. Apparently, at about 5.30 this morning, a bomber and fighter collided over Gillingham. The fighter blew up, and the bomber crashed, on six houses in a street in Gillingham. Apparently we only lost 17 fighters, and one bomber during the night's work, so that must have been the bomber in question. The crew of the bomber jumped out, but their parachutes did not open, presumably they were too low. The sentries at the mouth of the tunnel saw them jump, and said they saw them dropping like stones. Considering the immense numbers of planes in the air, I think it was

Charlotte Dyer, on the right, with a sister Wren and the dog, Max, in the garden of the WRNS quarters in Rochester, Kent.

wonderful that there were not more accidents. Of course there may have been more, which we did not hear about, but I hope not. It seems such terrible waste of several good lives, before they'd even been over and attacked the enemy.

The main landings have been in the bay of the Seine, and by the evening troops were fighting around Caen. Tanks have been landing, and losses are very much lighter than was expected. The only major war vessel sunk, so far as I know is *HMS Wrestler*. One LCT was mined 17 miles off Beachy Head, but, as tugs were going to her assistance she must have been still afloat. Really we don't know very much yet, except that we have got ashore the other side, and that "everything is proceeding according to plan" which means exactly nothing. The King is speaking tonight, but I'm afraid we shall be on duty, and unable to listen. Still, we shall probably get full reports on what he says, by those who do hear.

It was rather funny at breakfast this morning, as somebody had heard on the German News, that landings had already taken place, and the quarters officers and admin. people were discussing it. We were all very growly, and tired, on purpose, as we couldn't very well say anything. Still the news came out very soon after, a good many people stayed up to hear the news, at ten, but I was so dead tired, having done an extra night watch the night before, I went straight to bed, and Roma told me about it when she came up. I suppose they were bound to release the news almost immediately as the German radio was certain to say something about it. It was given out that 4,000 craft took part in the landing apart from hundreds of small craft. Thousands of aircraft took part in the bombardment, and we have 11,000 front line aircraft, which means we must also have an immense reserve. German opposition seems to have been very slight, but I expect it will stiffen up, as they bring up their reserves. The obstacles on the beaches themselves were much less formidable than had been expected.

Quite a lot of people here have relations, or boyfriends going over, it must be terrible for them – I/0 Austen, who is now in charge of the Cypher Office, has her husband in *H.M.S. Scylla*, who is the flagship of Force S, I think. Mrs Miller's son, Barry, was in a landing craft, in the spearhead of the attack, and Sybil Sutton's two brothers have gone over, with tanks. One in charge of a squadron of them. I'm terribly glad Tony (her brother) isn't in it, although I daresay he would like to have a finger in it. We are not in the thick of it, at the Nore, as we would be at Portsmouth, but nevertheless we've got plenty to do, as we are guard on one of the two invasion W/T broadcasts. I think most of the stuff we shall be dealing with will be convoys of supplies, from the Thames warehouses.

PETTY OFFICER JEAN WATSON (later Gadsden)
WRNS Communications, Southampton area

It is difficult to describe the atmosphere during that period. The sheer size of the invasion force was mind-boggling. The assembly areas around the New Forest, Portsmouth and Southampton were saturated with allied troops, tanks, guns and armaments of all shapes and sizes, trucks large and small, for mile after mile in and around the New Forest. Naval ships of all types and sizes crammed into the coastal waters and Solent and we in our signals office sending, receiving and distributing signals to bases, ships and flotilla skippers, while countless naval 'exercises' were being held as dress rehearsals for the real thing. Our watch-keeping duties were long and intense and as things became more hectic the tension mounted. For a week all shore leave was cancelled; no-one was allowed in or out of the Base without special permission; we were not allowed to speak to civilians and no mail was sent or received.

Signals Office Team, 1944/45 HMS Mastodon. Jean Watson, centre, middle row.

Jean Watson (later Gadsden), 1945.

I was on duty when the first signal confirming that D-Day was to be the 5th of June came through and all troops were to assemble on their respective craft. The weather was foul and a further signal came through stating that sailing was to be postponed for 24 hours. The atmosphere was electric, people spoke in whispers, the troops were battened down in the landing craft, there was an eerie 'calm before the storm' feeling everywhere and no-one spoke of what was to happen.

I was again on watch when the final signal ordering all ships to sail came through to our office. I can't remember who gave the signal to me, but he just said 'This is it; you'd better get it out straightaway'. I also remember someone saying 'Let's hope we win this time, because if we don't this country is finished'.

Just before going off watch in the morning, my friend and I were given permission to go down to the river to see the last landing craft sail away and I remember thinking 'I'm watching history being made and I am part of it'. I remember too, the awful deathly silence that pervaded the Base as we walked back to our quarters. Where there had been thousands of troops, armaments and incessant noise, there was nothing. The tents, the troops, the guns, the ships – all were gone. *Transcript of tape-recorded recollections.*

Three WAAF at Eastbourne in June 1944. Joan Parker (left) Marjorie Hann (middle) and Bess Richardson (right). Soon after this, battle dress uniform was issued.

LACW Joan M Parker.

LEADING AIRCRAFTWOMAN JOAN M PARKER

Radar Operator, RAF Beachy Head, Sussex

On 5 June I went on duty at 6pm and when our crew took over there was little activity. We were surprised therefore to be told we were only to plot within a limited area on our screens. We all looked at one another and there were various exclamations, the basic theme being, 'It's tonight'.

We were given copies of General Eisenhower's message to the Allied Expeditionary Force and we signed our names on the backs.

Then came the questions as we waited and waited. Where would the crossing take place, is that something in the Straits of Dover? (which was outside our area.) Almost too soon it was 11pm and the end of our watch. We would have given anything to have stayed on duty.

I was not on duty again till 1pm on 7 June. Eastbourne's streets were now empty of Army trucks and the service personnel reduced considerably. Very many friendships came to an abrupt end on D-Day and I often wondered what had happened to the Norwegian I had been expecting to meet on 6 June – my day off.

SADIE GREAVES (later Hall)

Women's Land Army (Rat trapping in Devon)

Diary:

6 June: The invasion of Europe. Now we know why we were awake all through the night with troops on the move, and why the sky was full of Dakota planes and gliders. Why we were banned from working as usual at the airport and why crowds of British airborne troops passed through – not to mention tanks and landing barges. While out walking one day we were even given a shout and waved at by some Americans who knew us from Tavistock. That was a week or so ago and we didn't realise exactly what was about to happen.

Sadie Greaves (later Hall), second from the right with other Women's Land Army girls at Honiton, Devon.

SHEILA BODLE (later Hoblyn)
a secretary at Benn Brothers
in Fleet Street
producing 'Newspaper World'

Sheelagh was a Corporal in the Girls Training Corps (preparing young girls for a range of war work when they were older). She had a boyfriend who, she knew, was to be involved in the Second Front. They had an understanding that they would get married but he was not to survive.

Diary:
6 June: D-Day 6am. Hectic day in Fleet Street. Most of afternoon at Ministry (of Information). Girls Training Corps in evening. Talk by ATS Officer and PT. Then dance at Fire Station.

The D-Day diary entry for Sheelagh Bodle (later Hoblyn), working in Fleet Street.

Ivy Dean (later Ryalls) with her fiancé.

The D-Day diary entry of Mrs Jean Dunbar.

IVY DEAN (later Ryalls)

in Engineering war work,
her fiancé in the Royal Navy though not in Home Waters

The day held its own foreboding right from the beginning. All around was a quivering awareness. A kind of helpless, sad gut feeling. No announcement had been made that it was going to take place. We just knew. It was a time of great urgency, great effort, a time to just keep going and trying not to think of what might be happening to all of our men. *Typescript recollections.*

MRS JEAN DUNBAR

an Australian girl married to an English Army Officer

Mrs Dunbar was living in London

Diary, 6 June:

Probably one of the most eventful days in history. The long awaited invasion of Europe started in the early hours of this morning, almost four years to the day after Dunkirk. The news to date reports that all is going according to plan and that obstacles and losses are less than expected. Of course the testing time will come later when the Germans can gather forces for a counter attack.

The King spoke tonight, calling the Nation to prayer.

London has gone about its business in a normal fashion on this most momentous of days.

244

Mrs Betty Elliot and her baby son near RAF Dunkeswell, post D-Day and after her husband Harry had left for the war in the Pacific. The picture was taken by a US Navy photographer trying to capture a modern parallel to the celebrated US Civil War painting 'The Empty Chair'.

CHAPTER 14

At the End of the Day

Perhaps it is with the knowledge of the overwhelming allied need for clear-cut success on D-Day and the decades of debate on the conduct of the operation and the campaign which followed, that hindsight almost inexorably draws one to consider what had not been secured by the end of 6 June 1944. It has to be recognised that the Normandy campaign was not swiftly won. The nature of the ground, determined soldiering by German reinforced defenders, perhaps over-ambition in the planning, perhaps flaws in top and senior command and even unit under-performance, in combination, explain why Northern France was not liberated more quickly. Clearly the failure to take Caen immediately and Cherbourg in fairly short order brought heavy consequence, certainly as far as Caen was concerned. However, along the whole line of coast assaulted, the Allies were ashore with at least a measure of security and with key inland objectives attacked from the air, won and linked to the shore landing. The following days in June would ensure against any danger of the Americans, Canadians, British and other allied forces being swept into the sea and no concentration upon 'what might have been' should detract from what was clearly a momentous achievement marking incontrovertibly a stage towards victory in the Second World War.

LIEUTENANT ALASTAIR BANNERMAN
2nd Battalion, Royal Warwickshire Regiment

7 June

D-Day is over. It was a day which I can never forget. What pictures, what sounds! An accumulation of extraordinary emotions when one fantastic adventure followed another. When we came in close we could see that the beach was completely choc-a-bloc with vehicles. We had to steer over to the east and to look round for a bit. There was very little beach because it was high tide. Occasionally, a mortar exploded in the sea but otherwise there was very little going on. We at last touched ground, France! Down with the landing ramp and when, after long last, the SP gun was off I got my two guns out. The waves were running high, but our waterproofed carriers made it safely. There were no ready-made beach exits anywhere but finally I got hold of a bulldozer which brought our gun and carrier up a dune and then we had to wait and actually queue up to move inland. The houses along the coast were only shells and it was a terrible experience when I saw for the first time dead bodies, first a German soldier and afterwards quite a few of our own soldiers. I can never forget all this or somehow forgive. Finally, we could move on and arrived at the end of a lane at a cross road where I met the CO. He looked pale and a little shaken but was sitting quite cold-bloodedly upon a bicycle. He told me that the battalion would be moving up there and would join me. This time I had only one gun, all the rest were stuck at the beach, two without tracks. I brought my gun into action in a garden after I had tried my French out on an old lady who complimented me, darling! Finally I hurried off behind Toon Poynton on his motorbike to find out how the battalion was faring. On our way we got fired at, but accelerated madly and found the battalion at last much handicapped by White Russian snipers. Of all things to meet here! Dicky Pratt got a shot in the knee here and also one through the leg. A good ticket to go home! The CO passed on his bike and the Divisional Commander in a jeep. At last the battalion came through. George's company had arrived and in the meantime also my guns. I was very happy to see them all again. The Frenchmen were quite genial in Hermanville but not too reliable. Nice old houses with red poppies. A few Junkers 88 bombed the village but I haven't noticed any damage and they were driven away. Soon we marched on. I just had time to get a sandwich from Sgt Millman and a cup of tea. Then we had to stop in St. Aubin d'Auvergnes. This meant that our original plan had gone awry. I believe that in spite of the fact that the Eighth Brigade has fought remarkably well, we have met more resistance than we expected. There is no hope of reaching Caen tonight. We took up positions around the village but soon had to go forward again. Two Messerschmits flew over us firing at our vehicles. This village was a complete heap of ruins with the exception of a white church. Two very scared girls lived in a dug-out near one of my guns. The streets were still congested with rubble. At last we moved off and then we suddenly saw one of the most amazing sights. A whole regiment of Airborne troops were arriving. One swarm after the other of these aeroplanes and gliders came over from England, the gliders turning and swooping down onto the ground and crashing through the anti-gliding poles. They really looked magnificent landing all around us and soon men, guns and jeeps were unloaded and they dashed off. We followed the battalion which was attacking a village. Occasionally, snipers shot towards us. One house was burning, covered in smoke, and a little further down a tank. Now the night came on and we were again annoyed by snipers and a single machine-gun which caused some losses in Kent's platoon. The CO ordered a stop and we dug ourselves in by the streets of Bénouville. A cold night, I put out my guns and then Toon Poynton and I tried to warm each other by huddling together under his gas cape in a ditch, but without success. Only a terrible cramp in the bottom. *A notebook in the form of a diary/letter written during and immediately after the events. Privately published by Alastair Bannerman who was captured, escaped and re-captured, 7 June 1944.*

SUB LIEUTENANT JOHN G H GRITTEN RNVR (Sp)
Official Naval Reporter who had been aboard LCT 903

A report written in the Admiralty on Gritten's return from Normandy. Note the cut made by censorship. The report printed here incorporated corrections made for the Editor of *Lloyd's Gazette.*

D DAY (TUESDAY EVENING) OFF La RIVIÈRE.
(ON COAST DUE NORTH WEST OF CAEN)

Tonight, I have seen the embarkation of the first 500 German prisoners on this particular sector of the invasion coast. Most of them had come along the road from Caen.

Lined up on the shingle about seven deep, they looked as dejected as their comrades we have seen in Russian newsreels. A high breeze was blowing off the sea, which apparently, penetrated their grey-green top-coats. Many had bare feet and were huddled together for warmth. One of them must have been caught napping, for he was trouserless. With only a short uniform coat barely covering his pants, he sought shelter from the wind in the midst of his fellow prisoners as they scrambled aboard the landing raft – known to Combined Operations as a 'Rhino' – which was to take them to a ship laying off-shore. They were guarded by Royal Marines.

Through binoculars I could see another batch of prisoners coming back down a road, which, in the morning, I had seen almost blocked with our tanks going inland towards Caen.

It was at 9.15am, that our flotilla of Landing Craft tanks (LCTs) began to make their

HEADQUARTERS EUROPEAN THEATER
United States Army
Office of the Commanding General

ADVANCE COMMAND POST

13 June 1944.

A week after D-Day and the Commanding General's congratulations to all concerned.
Ian Sayer Collection

TO: General Montgomery
Admiral Ramsay
Air Chief Marshal Leigh-Mallory
Air Chief Marshal Harris
Lieutenant General Spaatz

and to

Soldiers, Airmen, Sailors and Merchant Seaman, and
All Others of the Allied Expeditionary Forces:

One week ago this morning there was established through your coordinated efforts, our first foot-hold in Northwestern Europe. High as was my pre-invasion confidence in your courage, skill and effectiveness in working together as a unit, your accomplishments in the first seven days of this Campaign have exceeded my brightest hopes.

You are a truly great Allied Team; a Team in which each part gains its greatest satisfaction in rendering maximum assistance to the entire body and in which each individual member is justifiably confident in all others.

No matter how prolonged or bitter the struggle that lies ahead you will do your full part toward the restoration of a free France, the liberation of all European nations under Axis domination, and the destruction of the Nazi military machine.

I truly congratulate you upon a brilliantly successful beginning to this great undertaking. Liberty-loving people, everywhere, would today like to join me in saying to you "I am proud of you".

DWIGHT D. EISENHOWER.

Air Chief Marshal Sir Trafford Leigh-Mallory, K.C.B., D.S.O.
Air Commander-in-Chief
Supreme Headquarters, AEF.

run inshore from the waiting position about one and a half miles out.

A little before this, we had passed within a stone's throw of two British cruisers which were belching orange flames as their 8″ guns pounded the batteries on the coast. About a mile further inshore, we passed through a screen of destroyers, including two Frenchmen and a Pole, pumping broadside after broadside of 4.7″ projectiles into the fortified buildings and emplacements.

To the left of us were the remains of the little village of La Rivière, its lighthouse still erect, but with a gaping hole torn in its side. About half a mile inland on a slope was the village of Mont Fleury, also in ruins.

But resistance hadn't been entirely quelled. As our flotilla turned inshore, four shells burst close on the starboard quarter of the leading craft, fired from a light battery holding out in La Rivière. More shells followed, some falling short of us, others whining harmlessly overhead and bursting in the sea on our port quarter. The shrapnel spat against the steel frame of the bridge.

'My first birthday presents,' commented the Commanding Officer (Sub Lieutenant LG Metcalfe RNVR of Richmond, Surrey, a former bank clerk,) who was celebrating his 21st birthday.

One of our flotilla was holed by a shell forar'd of her bridge, but she managed to make the beach and disgorge her precious cargo of 17-pounder field guns.

I saw another LCT bump into one of the forest of half-submerged stakes to which mines were attached, and, with a dark red flash, a hole was torn in her side, and another under her ramp-door. But, she, too, beached and disembarked her cargo of vehicles and soldiers, all intact.

The immediate problem, was not the shell-fire (which soon drew the attention of our destroyers) but was to find a vacant spot of beach on which to land.

Although only about an hour and three quarters after the first assault, the beaches were packed with craft, with very little space between them. By scraping the paint off one of our sister craft, we managed to wedge ourselves in between two of them, and drop our ramp door into two feet of water.

It was high tide, and only a narrow strip of shingle separated the water's edge from a path bordered by a fenced mine-field. A notice at the edge of the field warned, 'Achtung! Minen.' This narrow strip was jammed with slowly-moving vehicles and men, winding their way up the road on the left which ran inland, up the slope past Mont Fleury.

One by one, the second a space occurred on the path, our lorries, ambulances, and Bren-gun carriers, and six-pounder anti-tank guns, revved up, trundled down the ramp off our craft, into the water and ploughed up the narrow, sloping, beach on to the path. A bull-dozer came and, with three sweeps, cleared away the shingle and sand making a level causeway from the water's edge to the path, to expedite the disembarkation.

Admiralty censor officer cut a slice out of the original here!

Meanwhile, destroyers were keeping up a continual barrage, which had now lifted to the other side of the line of hills behind Mont Fleury, about a mile inland, as the crow flies. Several of the tanks added their fire to the barrage as soon as they had trundled off the LCTs on to the beach. Commands rang out between the salvoes, as the guns laid their shells forward of the slowly-moving procession of tanks winding their way out of sight over the brow of the hill. This was an example of the perfect co-operation between the two Services.

The tide began to turn, and the water receded swiftly. Those craft that were able to do so, moved out to sea as soon as the soldiers, tanks and vehicles had been landed. Except for an occasional submerged Jeep or tank, casualties were very slight. Not a single enemy plane had penetrated the air cover, and all the shore batteries were silenced by this time.

Many of the craft, however, were unable to re-float in the shallow water, and remained beached until the next tide.

Our craft got clear, but, when well-off-shore, began to take in water rapidly. Her bottom had been ripped by one or more of the thousands of beach obstacles. With the water rising well over her engine room plates, and her engine out of action, the Commanding Officer decided to beach her. At low-tide it would be possible to patch her up and make the passage back to her home-port and carry on with the 'shuttle-service'.

The tide receded a long way, to reveal an amazing sight on the beaches. Thousands of rusted iron-girders, bolted together in threes like stacked rifles, had been driven into the clay and sand. Their jagged edges at high tide either barely protruded above the water, or, more often, were just submerged. How so few craft had sustained really serious damage, was a miracle. That there was not a single landing craft bigger than the smallest assault craft (and these were very few) actually sunk, throughout our sector, was a tribute to those who designed and built them, as well as to the seamanship of the crews.

Between them, wooden stakes were driven into the beach to which shells, mines, and other under-water booby-traps, had been attached.

At low-tide Naval beach parties co-operated with Army sappers to remove as many of these obstacles as possible, before the next wave of craft came in. All afternoon, there were shattering explosions and shrapnel hummed through the air and clattered against the craft left high and dry on the beaches, as the parties touched off the mines. Bulldozers and mobile cranes, under the direction of Petty Officers, worked ceaselessly, tearing away the iron-girders and stakes. Large spaces had been cleared by the evening when the next wave of craft brought in men and material to support the Army that had already penetrated, in places, as far as 10 miles inland.

Meanwhile, Naval repair parties, including electric-welders, went aboard the craft that had been holed, and worked against time and tide cementing up the rents or welding on new plates, so that they could get under way when the water lifted them again.

Not till after dark, did the Luftwaffe put in an appearance. Then, a few planes, operating singly, passed over the fleet waiting off-shore, and were met by a terrific barrage. Red, green and yellow tracers cascaded into the sky, and vivid orange flashes stabbed the darkness. The Navy let loose everything it had in the way of ack-ack, and not a ship was hit.

ANDREW HUXLEY
Civilian Scientist attached to the Admiralty
to report on the effectiveness of Naval Shelling on D-Day

I was given really very little training in recognising what kind of shells a particular fragment came from so I wasn't confident whether a particular fragment came from a heavy or medium gun and I don't believe I had detailed information about which ship bombarded which target. I was impressed by what I saw and photographed four days later but I wasn't able confidently to say what damage had been done by Naval shelling and what damage had been done by bombing so I think I was only a moderate amount of use on that particular occasion. *Transcript of tape-recorded recollections.*

Lieutenant Andrew Huxley, RNR.

CAPTAIN G M WILSON
7th Battalion, The Green Howards

And that was D-Day. Looking back at it afterwards, I have little hesitation in saying it was just about the easiest day we had in contact with the enemy in the whole six months stay in Europe. How the casualties in the Battalion were kept so low – about 20 – it is impossible to say but the deaths and injuries from the dreaded network of mines which we knew existed was NIL.

Come what may, we at least had a foothold.

From an unpublished account written soon after the end of the war. The Green Howards Museum, Richmond, North Yorkshire

British troops utilising for communications a captured German strong-point. A Huxley

Major T.S. Bigland receives an American Commendation for his liaison work during which he 'gained the complete confidence of my staff' as reported by General Omar Bradley.

A signed photograph of Field Marshal B.L. Montgomery presented to Major T.S. Bigland.

B.L. Montgomery
Field-Marshal.

Long after D-Day but regimental bond made the stronger by this veteran's distinguished participation on an historic day. Brigadier S J L Hill's signature, much more than a token souvenir.

SERGEANT JOHN GREEN

No. 50 Field Security Section
attached to GHQ 21 Army Group

Diary

June 6 1944 Invasion of Europe began this morning. SHAEF communiqué 8 am News – North France. Gliders and paratroops and seaborne force. Great excitement in some quarters. Weather just good enough for landings. Newspapers report surprising calm all over the country on receipt of news. Services held in churches all over England. Surprising lack of dislocation of railway or road traffic. Wireless sets listened to throughout the day with great eagerness. 3 British Div landed with few casualties. Beaches etc definitely held. Fighting reported in the town of Caen. Much air activity over Southwick throughout the day. Press conference in village school at 3pm. 4pm Address to Press by Monty. 6pm Address in open air to whole of GHQ by Chief of Staff.

MAJOR T S BIGLAND RA

one of General Montgomery's Liaison Officers
with General Bradley's US Army Group

Diary

6 June, D-Day: Off Portland at dawn and astonishing sail all morning through thousands of ships. Off beaches lunchtime and move into the shore in evening. Information not very good but all one can expect on D-Day.

No diaries or letters of D-Day from these men, no memories of their own, no years following upon their youth – but, a service for which their families, comrades, friends and their nations can remain proud without diminution of an unrelenting sense of loss.
The Commonwealth War Graves Commission

Recommended Reading

Cawthorne, N, *Fighting them on the Beaches: The D-Day Landings, June 6 1944* (Chartwell, 2003).

Copp, Terry, *Field of Fire. The Canadians in Normandy.* (University of Toronto Press, Toronto 2003).

Ellis, Major L F, *History of the Second World War - Victory in the West. Volume 1. The Battle of Normandy* (HMSO, 1962).

Hastings, M, *Overlord. D-Day and the Battle for Normandy* (Michael Joseph, 1984).

Howarth, David, *Dawn of D-Day - These Men Were There, 6 June 1944.* (re-issued by Greenhill Books, 2004).

Kershaw, R J, *D-Day. Piercing the Atlantic Wall* (Ian Allan Publishing, 1993).

Miller, R, *Nothing Less Than Victory. The Oral History of D-Day* (Michael Joseph, 1993).

Neillands, R, *The Battle of Normandy 1944* (Cassell, 2002).

Neillands, R and D Normann R, *D-Day 1944 Voices from Normandy* (Weidenfeld and Nicolson, 1993).

Ramsey, W G (Ed) *D-Day. Then and Now* (2 Volumes in the *After the Battle* series. Publisher: Battle of Britain Prints Int Ltd, 1995).

Van der Vat, D, *D-Day. The Greatest Invasion. A People's History* (Raincoast/Madison Press, 2003).

For reference

Chandler, David G and Collins, James Lawton Jr, (ed.) *The D-Day Encyclopedia* (Helicon Publishing Ltd, 1995).

Index

Akridge, First Lieutenant Harold (US), 43, 95-6

Allen, Rifleman Douglas V, 69

Anderson, Private G M (US), 120-121

Bache, Lieutenant R M, RNR, 174

Bannerman, Lieutenant Alistair J M, 83-85, 246-247

Barnes, Flight Engineer Alfred, RAF, 220

Barnes, Captain A H, 46-48, 236

Beamont, Wing Commander Roland, RAF, 210

Best, Corporal Jack (RM), 234-235

Bigland, Major T S, 32-33, 44, 47, 251-252

Blakey, Private Thomas J (US), 63-64

Blaylock, Private Joseph S (US), 102-103

Bodle, Sheelagh, later Mrs Hoblyn, 243

Bond, Ensign Calhoun, US Navy, 133

Bright, Corporal John, 172

Brown, Corporal J, 154

Brown, Private Len (W L), 193-194

Buck, Able Seaman Ray, Mercantile Marine, 232-233

Campbell, Captain I D, 46, 89-90, 171

Carr, Lieutenant E L K A, 196-197

Carruthers, Lieutenant W C S, 198

Checketts, Wing Commander John M, RAF, 221-222

Clark, Rifleman H W, 66-68

Craven, Petty Officer Hilda, WRNS, 237-238

Crookenden, Lieutenant-Colonel Napier, 233-234

Curtis, Sergeant Des, RAF, 210-211

Dahlia, Private First Class Joseph A (US), 59

Danckwardt, Sergeant Fred P J L, RAAF, 212

Davenport, 2nd Lieutenant J K B (Ken), 12-13, 227-228

Dean, Ivy, later Mrs Ryalls, 244

Dougherty, Private Joseph (US), 122-123

Dragoo, Private Ralph (US), 98-99

Dunbar, Mrs Jean, 244

Dunn, Major Robin, 49, 93, 185

Dyer, Charlotte, later Lady Pippard, Commissioned Officer, WRNS, 239-240

Eikner, First Lieutenant J W (US), 119-120

Elliot, Flight Lieutenant Henry, RAF, 24, 245

Fairburn, Sergeant Ron, RAF, 213-214

Farrell, Lieutenant Charles, 154

Feinberg, Captain Bernard S (US), 121-122

Fleckenstein, Leutnant Rolf (German), 202

Floyd, Petty Officer Hilton M, US, Merchant Marine, 34

Ford, Lieutenant Robert, 24-26

Foster, Sergeant Les, RCAF, 214-215

Francis, Lieutenant D G, RNZNVR, 23

Freeman, Lieutenant R, RN, 85-86

Friend, Sergeant A B, RAF, 23, 78, 219

Gockel, Gefreiter Frans (German), 52, 125-130

Greaves, Sadie (later Mrs Hall), Women's Land Army, 34, 105, 242

Green, Sergeant J H G W (John), 20, 252

Gritten, Sub Lieutenant J G H, RNVR (Sp), 150-153, 247-250

Gueritz, Lieutenant E F, RN, 235-236

Hair, Captain W P (Canadian), 161-162

Hammerton, Captain Ian, 168-170

Hammill, Corporal Eric, 29-30, 186

Harris, Private Richard J, 198

Hennessy, Corporal Pat, 198-202

Hill, Brigadier S J L, 30-31, 76-78, 252

Hodgson, Corporal Jack, 227

255

Holdsworth, D C, 49-51
Hollis, Company Sergeant Major Stanley E, VC, 138-142
Hoskot, Lieutenant-Colonel Nathaniel J (US), 44, 64-66
Howard, Major R J, 71, 73-74
Hudson, Captain R H E, 144-145
Huxley, Lieutenant Andrew, RNR, 250

Irwin, Lieutenant H Michael, RNR, 135-138
Isaacs, Lieutenant Jack (US), 60-63
Jones, Gunner W T (Canadian), 160-161

Kiln, Captain Robert J, 143-144
King, Gunner William L (US), 107-109
Kitching, Lieutenant Colin, RN, 86-88
Kite, Sergeant J, 173, 175
Kyle, Flight Sergeant James, RAF, 215-217

Lawrence, Lieutenant Peter, RNVR, 107-109
Liebich, Gefreiter Gotthard (German), 131

Macleod, Colonel Rory, 35-38
MacPhee, Private John H (US), 130-131
Mann, Private First Class Ray A (US), 99-100, 102
Marshall, Bombadier N G, 186-189
Martin, Captain Peter L de C, 49, 147-148
Martin, Flight Lieutenant Bernard, RAF, 218-219
Martin, Jacques (French), 178-180
Maxwell, Private Robert G, RM, 185
McLean, Lieutenant John D (Canadian), 157-159
Meier, Wireless Operator H (German), 203
Mertens, Gefreiter Alfred (German), 203
Miller, Staff Sergeant Victor (US),114-116
Millin, Piper Bill, 91, 189-191
Milton, Second Lieutenant John, 145-147
Mitchell, Flight Engineer Malcolm, RAF, 218
Munro, Ross, Press (Canadian), 162, 164

Neave, Captain Julius A S, 27-28, 42-43, 189
Neilson, Major I G, 208-209, 213

Oates, Lieutenant Arthur H, 43, 192-193
O'Brien, Lieutenant William, RN, 88, 90-91
Otway, Lieutenant-Colonel Terence, 74-75

Paisley, Sergeant Jim (Canadian), 165-166

Pankey, Private H (US), 133
Parker, LAC Joan (later Mrs Dinnage) WAAF, 53, 242
Parker, Private William E (US), 123
Parker, Signalman H H, 41
Paton, Major David, 229, 231
Pease, R S, 38-40
Peck, Corporal Sidney, 79-80
Plews, Private Les, 149
Prideaux, Lieutenant-Colonel Humphrey, 20-21
Prior, Lieutenant Peter, 22-23, 92, 163-164, 166-168, 180-181
Prosser, Lieutenant Austin, RNR, 124-125
Pykett, Gunner J B, 230-231
Raaen, Lieutenant John C Jr (US), 116-119
Read, Signaller Harry, 80-81
Regnauld, Georges (French), 176-178
Rhodes, John C, US Navy, 109
Rodney, Flying Officer William, RCAF (Canadian), 222-223
Rohmer, Flying Officer Richard, RAF (Canadian), 204-207
Rowland, Private Harold A, 184
Russell, Lieutenant Hector (Canadian), 159-160

Scott-Boden, Major Logan, 14-20, 112-114
Seelye, Rifleman I 'Turk' (US), 56-59
Smithson, Sergeant D, 224-225
Sorensen, Private Clifford R (US), 44, 96-98
Steer, Corporal Geoff, 52, 149
Struthers, Lieutenant D G (Canadian), 165

Todd, Captain Richard, 78

Upson, Sergeant Bernard E, 170-171

Wallace, Sergeant H E G, 92-93
Walter, Private George L (US), 106
Watson, Petty Officer Jean (later Mrs Gadsden) WRNS, 240-241
Wheatley, Sergeant George W, 228-229
Whiting, Signalman Alan, RN, 31-32, 194-195
Wilson, Captain G M, 143, 250
Winters, Second Lieutenant William R (US), 104, 106
Wood, Lieutenant D J, 69-74
Wright, Sergeant Len, 225-226